# RAJ & NORAH

# RAJ & NORAH

*A True Story of Love Lost and Found in World War II*

PETER R. KOHLI &
SHAINA KOHLI RUSSO

HarperCollins *Publishers* India

First published in India by
HarperCollins *Publishers* 2021
A-75, Sector 57, Noida, Uttar Pradesh 201301, India
www.harpercollins.co.in

2 4 6 8 10 9 7 5 3 1



P-ISBN: 978-93-5422-304-4
E-ISBN: 978-93-5422-305-1

The views and opinions expressed in this book are the authors' own and the facts are as reported by them, and the publishers are not in any way liable for the same.



Typeset in 11.5/14.7 Adobe Caslon Pro at
Manipal Technologies Limited, Manipal

Printed and bound at
Thomson Press (India) Ltd

MIX
Paper
FSC FSC™ C010615

This book is produced from independently certified FSC™ paper to ensure responsible forest management.

God moves in a mysterious way,
His wonders to perform;
He plants his footsteps in the sea,
And rides upon the storm.

– WILLIAM COWPER

To Raj and Norah, may this book honour them well.
To the Indian men who lost their lives in WW II, you have not and will not be forgotten.

To my wife, Susan, and my four children, Joshua, Daniel, Maraina and Shaina, without whose help this book would have remained an incomplete project.

— PETER R. KOHLI

To my husband, Matt, who was a well of encouragement and strength while writing.

— SHAINA KOHLI RUSSO

# PROLOGUE

## *Mussoorie, 2019*

On the way up to Mussoorie from the village of Barlowganj – a hill station made famous by the British during the Raj, nestled in the foothills of the Himalayas at 6,000 feet – are scattered numerous houses, made of the same cold concrete walls and floors, and only distinguishable by the names given to them by their present and past occupants. There is Whitfield Cottage, Tammany Hall, Orchard Cottage, and one Florence Cottage, with its pale yellow outer walls and various plants, both wild and cultivated, climbing aimlessly up them. The front garden is barren – grass doesn't grow at that altitude – but for a smattering of ancient rose bushes that still bloom to this day. The screened-in veranda had long ago been enclosed because of the mistaken belief that nothing of importance existed outside those gates. It is on this veranda, while seated on a steel trunk made bearable only by a blanket and moth-eaten cushions, that Florence Cottage's sole resident conducts his daily business with the help, though he prefers to call them 'domestics'.

Florence Cottage was built at the turn of the last century, as evidenced by the numerous cracks in the concrete floors and walls, bandaged with plywood and other handy materials. It has been home to Raj Kohli since his retirement from the Indian Army in 1967. Visitors to the house have been known to exclaim that the place is more like a museum than a home, whilst another proclaimed it needed to be torn down. But while these observations have been made often enough, Raj has no interest in moving. To him, life beyond the front gate of Florence Cottage does not exist. He is very content living there with his memories and photographs.

Each morning, whether the sun peers through the skylights or not, Raj awakens between 3.30 a.m. and 4 a.m. to begin his day. This routine has not changed in decades, nor is it likely to. Raj locates his walker and swings his legs on to the cold floor before grabbing the bars and pulling himself up. The first order of business is to put on his dressing gown and slippers, without which he cannot face the world. He begins his steady journey one step at a time and eventually reaches the doors leading to the TV room. He reaches for the wall switch and turns on the light. The room is not large. A threadbare Persian rug, which at some point was valuable, lies in the centre. The rug is not large enough to cover the entire floor, but manages to make a nuisance of itself, especially when it comes to Raj manoeuvring himself around. Invariably, it gets caught up in the legs of his walker and requires some manual dexterity to smooth down again.

The concrete walls of the TV room are dull yellow from age and are adorned with a few paintings. A portrait of Raj's father, Mohan Singh Kohli, hangs over the fireplace, which hasn't been used in decades. On an adjacent wall, above the door that leads to a bedroom, hangs a painting of Raj and his wife in their late sixties, both wearing matching colours. On the other walls hang a curious assortment of miniature reproductions by old masters, and framed postcards sent over the years by friends.

A wheeled table had been set up the night before by one of his domestics, Manju, with all he would need to make himself a pot of tea. Raj bends forward, turns on the electric kettle and walks to a chair, settling down with a sigh as he waits for the kettle to boil.

'Good morning, darling! You fill my life with heaven and joy!' he says loudly and waits for a reply. 'Yes, thank you,' he continues, 'I slept very well last night. The tea kettle is on, and I'm sitting in my favourite chair waiting for it to boil.' He pauses for a moment before he begins again. 'Yesterday, before I went to bed, I was watching the television and on came a programme about Italy, and I immediately thought of the first time we met.' Raj lets out a slight laugh as his mind wanders back to those days. 'I'm sure you remember it as well. Anyway, I thought I should recite a poem for you today, something that reminds us of those days.' He pauses for a moment as a smile grows. 'Yes, quite right, "Ode on a Grecian Urn".'

Just as Raj is about to begin the day's recitation, the kettle begins to whistle. 'We have to stop for a moment, darling,' Raj says. 'The kettle is boiling and making an awful racket.'

He pulls himself up with difficulty, wondering why he ever sits down to wait, and slowly makes his way across the annoying carpet. The kettle, furious at his delay, screams louder and louder.

'All right, all right, all right,' he says, as if the kettle can hear him.

Finally, he reaches the switch and turns it off, putting the kettle out of its misery. He fills the teapot with the boiling water and expertly pulls the cart backwards with him until he reaches his chair. He sits back down heavily and begins the countdown to when he can finally pour his cup of liquid gold. Five minutes. That was a time fixed, perhaps by the Viceroy of India, during the days of the British Empire. Obviously, a random number which someone decided would be optimum before the tea was fit for consumption. For Raj, though, it was a matter of guesswork as the only clock in the room, sitting on the mantelpiece, had last worked before World War I.

While Raj waits for his first cup, he returns to where he left off reciting the poem. By his expert judgement, he feels that once he completes the recitation his tea will be ready.

'Now, where was I?' A question he asks himself every morning, the answer to which he already knows. 'Ah, yes!' And with that, he begins again.

The words of the poem envelope him, his mind drifting back some eighty years, to when he first embarked on his journey across the seas to university in England.

# *Part One*

# CHAPTER ONE

## *Mussoorie, 1937*

Raj's father had always wanted his son to receive 'the highest of higher education', and that would be an education at the most prestigious institution in the world, Cambridge.

Mohan Singh Kohli was the chief of police in Mussoorie and had never attended university – a decision he had come to regret. He was a brilliant mathematician and an extremely accomplished poet. The latter was a passion he was encouraged to pursue, but had decided not to, given his insecurities, though he would lament the lost opportunity. This regret then fuelled his decision when it came to Raj. He did not want his son to be like him, to look back later in life and wish he had done things differently. It was April, and Raj was in his last year at Bishop Cotton School, a boarding school in Shimla, the summer capital of the British. He would be graduating soon, in June to be exact, and was hoping to go to university in India. Cambridge wasn't his idea.

'... as nonpolar molecules are hydrophobic...'

Raj was trying to concentrate on his chemistry tutor as he explained molecular composition, but it was proving to be quite the task as the sounds of a heated discussion arose from the next room.

Raj stared at the door. Did this conversation have to transpire now and right outside this room?

'Sir,' he said, rubbing his forehead and sighing, 'I'm having difficulty following along.'

'Not to worry. What would you like me to explain further?' His chemistry tutor peered over his glasses and flipped a few pages backward in the textbook, looking for a good place to start once again.

Raj wondered how his tutor could possibly stay on task through the shouting and the pounding of angry fists, although he could have sworn he saw the man flinch a couple of times.

He watched the glow of yellow light spill across the floor and dance under his door as it mimicked the gestures of those occupying the adjacent room.

Raj put down his pen. 'Sir, I'm sorry, but I don't think it's possible for me to concentrate.'

His tutor opened his mouth to protest, but he was interrupted by the dining room's occupants once again.

'You're wasting your money,' he heard his uncle Teja Singh Soorma, his mother's brother, say with a clink of his teacup on its saucer. 'Send Raj to the Government College in Lahore. There's no need to send him to England.'

A guttural sigh from his uncle Sohan Singh. 'But an education at Cambridge counts for a lot more than one from the Government College,' he scoffed, coming to the defence of his half-brother, Mohan Singh. 'You can't tell me that when you go for a job interview, they won't be impressed by a degree from Cambridge!'

A thud as a shadow flickered, interrupting the light under the door, which Raj could only interpret as Sohan Singh pounding the table to emphasize his point.

'They may be impressed, but that doesn't mean he would get the job.'

'Why? Why do you say that?' Sohan Singh's pitch rose with bewilderment at Teja Singh's opinion. 'After all, a British university education is the envy of the world.'

'Because even though Rajendra may get a degree from a British university, he is first and foremost an Indian!' Teja Singh spat out the last few words, the teacup clanking louder against its porcelain mate. 'He will be treated like a second-class citizen in England and will be despised by Indians and the British alike when he returns.'

'Preposterous!' A sharp and quick screech of a chair as it slid across the concrete floor, and in sync, another shadow pierced the light.

'Arre yaar, can't you see beyond your nose? The British rule India. We are their servants. They will never treat us as equals.'

Raj's heart beat in time with what could only be Sohan Singh's pacing footsteps.

His eyebrows drew together, and he licked his lips in anticipation as an unnerving pause drew on.

'Brothers, please, sit. Finish your tea.' Raj's father sounded calm.

A thud of a chair being put back into place was followed by the creak of wood as weight pressed upon it. Sohan Singh reluctantly sat down. 'Bhai, do you hear what Teja Singh is saying? Do you not have any words for him?'

'Maybe he knows what I am saying is right,' said an irate Teja Singh.

'But you're not going to pay for university – he is,' insisted Sohan Singh.

'That's true, I am only speaking so he doesn't waste his money. Especially by sending Rajendra to a British university.'

'Ah, I see why you are saying this now' – a creak indicated that Sohan Singh had leaned back in his chair – 'you don't want Raj to go to a British university because of what happened to you, bhai.'

Raj then remembered one particularly rainy afternoon when his mother, Kundun, had rambled on about Teja Singh's misfortunes to the woman who lived next door.

Teja Singh Soorma had been a very accomplished civil engineer. After his studies at an Indian university, he had left for Canada, where he was one of the lead engineers on the Canadian Pacific Railway. Because of his success there, he was in much demand and next went to Singapore, where he designed the causeway linking the island to the mainland of Malaya. From there, he travelled far and wide, designing projects and living like a prince. Money was of no consequence, until suddenly, it came to a halt.

'He went and spent all his money. Can you believe it?' His mother announced as she scooped several spoonsful of sugar into her tea.

Upon his return to India, Teja Singh looked for employment and answered an advertisement for a senior engineering position with a British firm located in India. When he went for the interview, it became obvious that one of the men on the panel was exceptionally racist, holding the belief that Indians were inferior to the British. To the man, Teja Singh's accomplishments and experience were meaningless. Teja Singh came away from the interview with an unwavering conviction that, regardless of which university you attended, whether it be the top school in the world or the lowest-ranked governmental school one could possibly imagine, being Indian was an impediment, always.

'Regardless of me experiencing it first-hand, it is a fact true for all Indians. The British will always choose their race over ours any day. They believe they are superior, and that's all there is to it.'

'I understand that was your case, bhai,' Raj's father's voice was low, aiming to de-escalate the tension that encompassed the whole house, 'but it will be different for Raj.'

Startling Raj was his mother, who burst through the side door of his room. She hurriedly scampered across his room to glue her ear to the dining-room door, eager to not miss a word.

'Madam?' the confused tutor stopped his instruction upon her arrival.

'Shh!' Kundun urged, emphatically waving at him to be quiet. 'I am trying to hear.'

'Not unless he can change the fact that he is Indian,' Teja Singh continued in his debate.

Kundun's eyebrows furrowed, trying to understand why that would be of any relevance.

'I tell you, it won't matter for him. We will make sure he impresses everyone he meets.'

Kundun shifted her ear on the door, anxious for Teja Singh's reply.

'But to get into Cambridge he must have applied a year ago. When did he apply, tell me?'

'He hasn't yet.'

'He hasn't yet?' Teja Singh's roaring laugh caused Raj's mother to detach from the door with wide eyes. But it wasn't too long until she pressed her ear to it once again.

'Let me try and understand. You're going to send Raj on a boat to a country he has never been to, have him show up at a university's doorstep and hope they will break their rules and accept him?' Teja Singh's voice soared in pitch. 'You're crazier than I thought!'

'Why shouldn't they break their rules for Raj?' Sohan Singh piped up.

Raj's tutor shifted in his chair, unsure if he should be listening.

'I know Raj is going to pass with the highest marks ever given to a student, and I know he came fourth in the entire British Empire in religious studies, but these universities,' Teja Singh's speech was slow with careful diction, a last-ditch effort, 'they will not break their rules. They are set in stone, they do not deviate, they haven't for five hundred years, and especially for an Indian.'

The silence that followed made it seem as though Teja Singh's impassioned speech had changed his father's mind. Breaking the silence was a clink of the teapot and the pouring of tea into a cup.

Once it was filled, Raj's father cleared his throat. 'Raj, come here one moment.'

Raj looked to his tutor and mother as if they could advise him on the situation. Kundun moved out of the way and Raj pushed the door open. The door closed behind him, his mother no doubt still eavesdropping.

'Yes, Father.' Raj bowed, his hands shaking slightly. His eyes darted around to take in the room. Teja Singh sat staring out the window while Sohan Singh eagerly waited with his arms crossed.

'I want to inform you of something,' his father began, stirring sugar into his tea, 'you're going to go to Cambridge in England to university, do you understand?'

'Yes, Father,' he replied dutifully.

Teja Singh stood as he looked at Raj's father before lowering his gaze. He knew there wasn't more that could be done. He nodded to Raj, and without another word, left the house.

Kundun opened the door to the dining room and walked in. She angrily clenched her jaw as she held back tears.

Sohan Singh, feeling tension threaten his sister-in-law's composure, drank the last bit of his tea before he too stood up. 'You will make a fine scholar and be the pride of your family, Raj,' he said with a smile, shaking Raj's hand. He made a quick nod to Kundun, who did not reciprocate, and left.

Once the door shut, Mohan Singh shifted in his seat, readying himself for what was to come.

'You can't do this!' Kundun's tears fell freely, her sobs punctuating her protest. 'My son!' Sob, sniffle. 'My only son!' Sob, sniffle.

'Arre yaar! Can't a man make a decision in his own home?' Mohan Singh tugged at Kundun's elbow. 'I've already bought Raj's ticket. He's leaving in August.'

Kundun let out a shrill shriek as she collapsed to the floor.

Mohan Singh continued, speaking louder, competing with Kundun's screams. 'Raj, you will study chemistry.'

Raj's only choice was to answer in the affirmative. 'Yes, Father.'

'And you will be leaving in three months.'

Even though it seemed impossible, Kundun's sobbing grew exponentially.

'Yes, Father,' Raj replied again.

His mother looked on in horror, utterly helpless.

'Why not let him go to Government College in Lahore?' she asked in all sincerity. 'Then we can see him all the time. But if he goes to England, who knows when we will see him again.'

Mohan Singh poured another cup of tea, weighing the decision of whether he should answer his wife or not.

'Mohan, answer me, please,' she took the seat that Teja Singh had occupied.

He sighed and set his cup down. 'If someone were to ask you where Raj was in university, and you told them he was at Government College in Lahore, what would they say?'

Kundun, even though she had never had any formal education, was far from stupid and knew exactly what her husband was attempting to do.

'They would say, "That's wonderful, I always knew that Raj was very bright and has a great future ahead of him."'

Mohan Singh didn't give his wife much credit when it came to intelligence and hadn't caught on to her line of answering. 'But,' he continued, 'if you were to tell them that Raj was at Cambridge, then what would they say?'

Kundun already had her answer ready and shot back, 'They would say, "Why did you send your son, your only child, to England when there are colleges here in India just as good?"'

Mohan Singh had not anticipated that answer and just shook his head. 'Clearly you've been talking with the wrong people.' Noticing that she was wasn't going to persuade him otherwise, Kundun waved off her husband's comments with a flick of her hand. She knew she wouldn't have any say, but there was one thing she was in control of in this house.

Determined, Kundun turned to Mohan Singh and pointed past Raj. 'You tell that professor–'

'He's a tutor.' Mohan Singh pinched the bridge of his nose.

'Whatever he is. Tell him he can leave now. Seeing that I will no longer see my son in three months, I'd like as much time with him as I can get.' She huffed, grabbed Raj by the hand and led him into the kitchen to be fed.

The education of her son may have been the purview of her husband, but when it came to feeding him the best a Punjabi mother could offer, well, that fell to her.

As they reached the kitchen, Kundun forced Raj to sit on a nearby stool and cupped his face in her hands. She smiled warmly.

'Puttar, you are my miracle. No one can take you away from me.' She pulled up her sleeves as she turned to the stove, every once in a while taking time to look back at Raj in between stirring the pot. 'You know, when you were born, we were told you were too sick. That you would only live for six days.'

Raj did know. He had the story memorized. His mother reminded him, and the whole village, of it as often as she could. No matter the subject of the conversation, she somehow found a way to bring up the story of Raj and the miracle of the hakim.

When Raj was born – on Tuesday, 26 August 1919 – in Benares, the doctor at the hospital had told his mother he would only live for about six days.

'We were devastated.' His mother covered her eyes with her hands.

They took him home, resigned to that eventuality. A hakim happened to pass by the house and asked to see the baby.

He then gave his mother a medicinal mixture he had prepared using betel leaf.

'He told me, "Memsahib, you take this medicine and give it to your baby."'

She did as she was told, and Raj suddenly began to make a miraculous recovery.

'The hakim left and was never seen again.' She threw up her hands and caressed Raj's face once more. 'My puttar, my miracle baby.'

His mother miserably counted down the days until Raj was to leave, causing great annoyance to his father. Conversations between the two had become infrequent. Raj had even noticed his mother duck out of a room once his father walked in.

Raj, on the other hand, was growing increasingly excited, especially since he would be visiting London, though at first it would only be briefly, and then on to Cambridge. He had not given any thought as to how he was going to go about obtaining admission to the venerable institution. His father's hope was that Raj would carry with him numerous letters of recommendation from an array of masters and, most importantly, from his headmaster, and a copy of his marks from his final exams. His marks were exceptional and would be considered as such at any university. In his father's mind, that was all that was needed. The procedure, and where he should present himself, would have to be figured out by Raj alone when he got there.

As the days of his departure grew nearer, Kundun's cooking became more elaborate. Maybe it was her attempt to persuade Raj to stay. But it was not to be. The day Kundun dreaded arrived, and with it her explosion of tears, which streamed down her face and inadvertently Raj's as she hugged him close.

'Here's food for you, puttar.' His mother handed him a sack, aromas of home floating out of it. 'I don't know what sort of food they will give you on board the ship.'

'Thank you, Mummy.' Raj looked to the car waiting outside the front gate.

'My son, I love you so much. It's not too late to change your mind, if you want to,' she whispered in his ear.

Raj hugged her tighter. 'Father is only doing what is best for me,' he said, trying to convince himself as well. 'I will be back in the summer.'

'Come along now, Raj.' Mohan Singh tapped the car door as he waited for Raj to get in.

Peeling himself from his mother, he squeezed her hand. Mohan Singh opened the car door for Raj and gestured for him to get in. Sohan Singh was already in the car, which would transport the three of them to the Dehradun train station.

There they caught the fast mail train to Bombay, which Raj always had a liking for, and a few days later, on 16 September 1937, Raj was to board the P&O liner, the *TSS Ranpura*, where cabin 416 was to be his home for the next two weeks on his way to Marseille.

Raj had barely slept the night before, dreams of him sailing out to the wide-open sea taunted him, causing him to toss and turn. He awoke abruptly from a nightmare in which the ship had sunk. Shaken, he decided he was better off staying awake. As he got ready, he realized he was unsure of what to wear for such an occasion. His choices were slim: he had only packed one small suitcase after all, the only suitcase his family owned. He settled on a heavy woollen blazer, woollen pants, and a starched shirt and tie.

Shortly thereafter, he, his father and a uncle made their way to the docks. Once there, Raj's eyes widened at the sight of the ship's size. He had seen pictures of ships in his textbooks before, but they did not do them justice. Raj suddenly felt small, and the reality of how far he would be from home started to sink in. The crowd around him didn't help, as they swiftly moved past him, bumping into him every so often as he stood staring up at the ship. Pulling at his tie, he realized the decision regarding his attire had been a poor one, the thick humidity steaming and choking him.

His concentration broke when he heard his father clear his throat. 'This trip I am sending you on is very expensive, son.'

Raj wasn't quite sure why his father would mention such a thing – after all, it wasn't Raj who had asked to go to England. It was his father's idea completely. However, he felt he needed to acknowledge what he had said. 'Yes, Father, and thank you very much for this opportunity. I will not let you down.'

Mohan Singh dismissed his words of gratitude with a wave. 'No, that's not what I meant. I want you to enjoy your trip.'

'Yes, Father.'

'Eat as much food on board as you possibly can.'

Confused, Raj looked to his uncle for some sort of clarification before turning back to his father, 'And how much food is that, Father?'

'Everything on the menu,' replied Sohan Singh, believing he was coming to the aid of his brother.

Raj was taken aback. His father had never mentioned anything of the sort when he went to Bishop Cotton School at the age of six. He knew it was an expensive school, but he hadn't been asked to eat everything that the school had to offer.

Mohan Singh looked at Sohan Singh before deciding to clarify his statement, 'No, son, I don't want you to get sick. But for instance, if there is a chicken dish and a fish dish, one is supposed to choose between them' – he took in a deep breath – 'well, what I'm saying is that if you have a hard time choosing – don't. Eat them both.'

Raj smiled. 'Yes, Father, I understand now. I will do my best.'

Mohan Singh nodded. 'Good.'

'Best of luck, Raj.' Sohan Singh grabbed Raj's shoulders. 'I know you will blow the British away with your brilliance.'

'Thank you, Uncle.'

Sohan Singh leaned in to whisper in his ear, 'Do me a favour and prove your Uncle Teja wrong.'

Raj laughed. 'I will try.' He then turned to his father and said, 'Goodbye, Father,' as he held out a hand to shake his.

Mohan Singh looked at Raj's hand for a moment. Raj noticed that he looked uncomfortable, as though he were no fan of the humidity either. But for the first time that Raj could ever remember, his father bypassed his outstretched hand, and though seemingly devoid of emotion, hugged him. Surprised, Raj stood stiff for a moment as his father finished the hug with a pat on the back.

Clearing his throat and standing up straight, Mohan Singh gestured towards the ship. 'On you go.'

# CHAPTER TWO

## *Kidlington, 1937*

Norah's feet hurt, her head pounded dreadfully, and her eyes felt sunken in from another tiring shift at the Radcliffe Hospital where she had been a surgical nurse for over two years. She unpinned her cap as she reached the front door of her home. She took a deep breath, knowing that on the other side of the door were her siblings, waiting to be fed, tutored in their schoolwork and then readied for bed. Same as any other day.

It had been nine years since their mother died. It was at the funeral that Norah had promised she would dedicate her life to taking care of her brothers and sisters. That day replayed often in her mind as she lay awake at night.

***

'I'm so very saddened by your loss, Norah,' said Lady Baines with a sad smile. Standing beside her husband, she was the picture of English nobility in an elegant black dress with her grey hair swept neatly into a matching felt cloche, and shielded from the rain by a cream-coloured parasol. 'I never realized your mother was so ill.'

Norah stood staring blankly ahead of her. She was unable to form any sort of reply. However, aware that some sort of acknowledgement was expected, she nodded ever so slightly.

Though her mother had been sick on and off for most of her life and had spent her last moments at the infirmary at the Radcliffe with the addition of birthing complications, Norah had never imagined or grasped the seriousness of her mother's affliction.

Her eyes were fixed upon the headstone that stood before her.

*Emma Elizabeth Eggleton*
*1885-1928*

She then came to focus on the five children huddled and sniffling next to her father. Peter, three, clung to his father's coat and buried his face deep within its fabric. John, nine, wiped his nose on the sleeve of his jacket. Beatrice, seven, and Muriel, twelve, worked desperately to soothe their seven-day-old sister, Betty, who couldn't be kept from letting out incessant high-pitched wails. Norah couldn't blame her – she too felt like kicking and screaming.

Norah's eyes gently closed for a moment and then reopened. They were her responsibility now. Fourteen years old and the eldest of six, Norah would have to be their mother, protect and raise them. All the intricate plans that she and Lady Baines had for her future – of leaving Oxford to become a concert pianist – would have to be forgotten. She had a duty to fulfil.

Norah felt a hand clasp hers. Her father, William John Eggleton, stood unshakeable in the sight of funeral attendees. It was at times like these when Norah believed his military training of looking unattached and unbothered took over. But she knew better. His hand tremored slightly.

He wasn't a very tall man. But with his broad shoulders and a thick well-groomed beard, he seemed very intimidating to the average person. To Norah and her siblings, however, he was just a big teddy bear.

'Mr Eggleton, we extend our sincerest condolences to you and your children.'

'Daddy' – Norah cleared her throat – 'I'm sure you remember Sir Athelstane Baines and his wife Lady Baines.'

Norah's father let go of her hand, removed his hat and bowed his head without uttering a word.

'This is not the way in which we would have liked to have met again, Mr Eggleton. However, I am sure Norah will be a tremendous tower of strength for you,' Lady Baines said.

Norah's father smiled softly. 'Yes, she has always had a way of becoming the responsible parent for us in times of need, hasn't she?' He gently laid his hand upon Norah's shoulder.

The countless days of taking care of her mother as she lay sick in bed, unable to attend to the family, or comforting her father when her mother had yet another bad day fighting her illness, circled viciously in Norah's mind.

'I would expect nothing less. Not having any children of our own, it has been quite the pleasure having her in our home for piano lessons after school. I must say, you have raised such an astonishing young lady.' Lady Baines shared a proud smile with Norah's father.

'Daddy.'

The four of them turned to see an exhausted Muriel rocking Betty, who continued with her screams.

'Ah, if you would excuse me for a moment' – Norah's father scooped the infant out of Muriel's shaking arms and into his – 'just wanting her mother, that's all,' he said faintly.

'Please do not hesitate to ever call upon us for assistance, Mr Eggleton.' Sir Athelstane removed his top hat and held out his arm as he added, 'With each passing day shall the sun shine brighter and the pain you endure dull in its sting.' He then placed his hat upon his head and with Lady Baines delicately holding on to the crook of his arm, strolled away.

Norah, noticing how small her baby sister seemed in her father's broad arms, and how stiff he looked as he held her, straightened her posture. 'Here, I'll take her, Daddy.'

'Thank you, dear,' he replied with subtle relief as Norah lifted Betty from his arms. 'It was your mother who was good at these things. I suppose that's where you get it from.' He kissed Norah on the forehead before walking over to the Methodist priest who had conducted the ceremony.

Norah choked back tears just as Betty's crying started to subside. 'Taking turns, are we?' She let out a chortle and reached up to remove a teardrop that fell on to her cheek. She wiggled Betty's tiny little hand. Her fingers curled tightly around Norah's. 'Don't worry' – she smiled gently – 'I'll be your mummy now.'

***

Only nine more years until her youngest sibling came of age and she would feel like she had accomplished her responsibility. Until then, it would be the same routine of feeding and bathing the children and keeping the house in order.

'Norah's home!' shouted her brother Peter, who held up a cricket bat in Norah's general direction as she opened the door.

Of all the children, Betty, now nine years old, Peter, thirteen, and Beatrice, seventeen, still lived at home. Although her father remarried four years after her mother's death, Norah still felt her siblings' welfare was her responsibility. Their stepmother seemed to only dote over her own two daughters.

'Norah! Norah!' Betty came screaming from her bedroom. 'Can we go play outside? Maybe a walk through the gardens?' Her big blue eyes shone up at Norah.

Norah's feet pulsed with pain. 'Oh dear, I'm afraid not tonight.'

Betty's gleeful face immediately drooped. 'But yesterday you said we could…' Her eyes threatened to overflow.

Peter dropped the bat.

Norah sighed. It was true, she had promised, if only to get Peter and Betty to hurry to bed the night before.

A low chuckle came from behind Norah in the living room. 'Not keeping the promises we make, are we?'

Norah's father was sitting in his chair by the window, reading the local paper.

Norah rubbed her forehead. She longed for sleep, but maybe a walk would do her some good, she tried to convince herself.

'Only teasing you, dear.' Her father stood up, folded the paper, put a hand into his trouser pocket and looked to his two younger children. 'Let's give Norah a break this evening. I'll take you to the park.'

Wide grins appeared both on Betty's and Peter's faces.

'Now, go on.' He playfully spanked their bottoms with the folded newspaper as they ran out giggling.

Norah walked into the kitchen to prepare supper.

'You know we are forever indebted to you, don't you?' her father said as he walked over.

Norah chuckled. 'I believe that is the only reason I keep coming home.'

He let out a deep laugh. 'We don't deserve you, dear.'

'Oh please, Daddy. It's my pleasure.'

Her father leaned against the wall and eyed her for a moment. 'No.'

Norah stopped measuring the flour for the dumplings to look up at him. 'No?'

'I can't keep allowing us to be a burden on you.'

'Dad—'

He raised his hands in protest. 'No, don't try to make excuses. Almost ten years and all you've done is put others before you.'

Even though she was twenty-four, his voice still moved her. Her eyes began to well, and she struggled to make eye contact with him.

'I think it's about time you set upon the life you want, not to be dictated by silly requests for walks after supper or chocolate biscuits if someone has been good.'

'The chocolate biscuits really benefit me though.' Norah smiled and her father reciprocated.

'You are truly one special young woman, Norah. There was a time in my life, right after your mother passed, when I didn't know how we would have survived without you. Truly.'

Norah sniffled.

'But now … now it's been long enough. As your father, I must put my foot down and insist you carry on and live your own life. Do what *you* want to do.'

'Daddy, I am doing what I want to do,' Norah insisted.

'Really? You've always dreamed of being a nurse and not attending university to become a concert pianist?'

It was true, once upon a time, she was on the path to becoming a professionally trained pianist. After one particular piano competition, she had been offered a scholarship to the Royal College of Music but she had declined in order to stay on in Kidlington with her family.

'You should be allowed to go to the Royal College of Music as planned. Don't waste those years you trained at Lady Baines's expense.'

It had been six years since she had stopped her lessons at Sir Athelstane and Lady Baines's home. Under the tutelage of one of the finest piano instructors in all of Oxfordshire, Miss Jessica Leach, Norah had practised and refined her playing skills. She adored her afternoons inside their home – very different from her own, and exceptionally quiet. Norah would pretend she was living out an upper-class fantasy. Their home was filled with the most regal and ornate furniture, succulent sandwiches and biscuits all delivered on silver trays by the staff of the house.

She could remember the very first day of her lessons and thought on it often.

***

When Norah arrived, she knocked on the large wooden door and waited patiently for it to open. After waiting for – what seemed to a twelve-year-old child filled with an extraordinary amount of eagerness and apprehension – an eternity, the door was opened by an elderly gentleman, who at first Norah thought was someone's father but turned out to be the butler.

The walls in the large reception area held portraits of stern-looking ancestors whose eyes followed Norah carefully, and in the corners of the room stood full suits of armour which looked as if they would jump to life at a moment's notice and chase her down the hallway with swords drawn.

Lady Baines guided Norah deeper into the mansion, and her flowing white gown swished into place as she stopped in the piano room. Norah stared in awe at Lady Baines' elegance as she stood there in silence awaiting further orders.

Norah exclaimed with excitement when she saw, behind Lady Baines, a grand piano with its raised lid. It sat by a window overlooking the most beautiful rose garden.

As Norah began to walk over to the piano, she heard her name. She stopped and turned.

'Yes, Lady Baines?' she asked quietly as Lady Baines pointed to a man and woman who were standing next to a couch. Norah's face fell; she had been far too preoccupied with the piano to notice that there were other people in the room.

'Come here, Norah. You know my husband, Sir Athelstane.'

'Hello, sir,' Norah replied and was quickly corrected by Lady Baines.

'Norah, when a lady is introduced, it is proper to curtsey and ask, "How do you do?"'

Norah nodded and tried again. She hesitantly curtsied and said, 'How do you do?'

Sir Athelstane bowed his head.

Lady Baines gave a warm smile. 'Much better. However, we must work on your diction. To become a concert pianist, you must talk like a lady, not like a commoner. I would also like you to meet Miss Jessica Leach, who will be your instructor.'

Norah clumsily curtsied towards a plump, middle-aged woman with a severe haircut and austere clothing. 'Miss.'

Miss Leach smiled brightly, which assured Norah. 'It's a pleasure, my dear.'

'We are all very excited to have you here, Norah,' Sir Athelstane said with his usual cheeriness. 'Now tell us, what are you going to play for us today, young lady?'

Norah felt her stomach leap. How silly of her! She hadn't prepared anything. She decided making excuses would not favour this company, so she opted to play from memory. 'Erm … Beethoven's *Für Elise*?' she mumbled.

'Dear, when asked a question one should answer with confidence. Shall we try again?' Lady Baines said.

Norah's cheeks turned pink. She was quickly rethinking her decision about attending these classes at their home. She didn't envision her experience being filled with continuous corrections on her etiquette.

Norah inhaled and mustered as much confidence as she could before speaking. 'Beethoven's *Für Elise*.'

Sir Athelstane raised his eyebrows and laughed while sharing looks with the others, 'My, quite the composition to choose, isn't it?'

Norah pulled at her dress and bit her lip. Maybe that was the wrong choice, she thought. But if it was, surely Lady Baines would have corrected her.

She was pleasantly surprised when Lady Baines simply gestured her to walk over to the piano.

Norah was about to sit down when she heard a clearing of the throat from the lady of the house.

'Norah, before playing, one must either bow or curtsey to the audience. In your case it would be a curtsey.'

Norah clenched her jaw, just lightly enough to keep them from noticing. She slid into a polite curtsey and then continued to her pre-playing ritual. She adjusted the seat; it was far too low for her and too far away to reach the pedals. Once in position, Norah took a deep breath, scanned the room and saw that they had taken their seats. Then she began.

Norah's fingers felt cold and tingled with nervousness, but with each note she played they warmed, and the room receded into the distance.

She closed her eyes. She was now far away, in a garden on a warm summer evening, the perfume of resident blooms and the sounds of buzzing bumblebees and the fluttering of butterflies filled her mind – it was a place she often thought of when in need of calming.

As Norah struck the last note, she let it hang in the air for a moment and sat back with her eyes still closed. It was quiet … alarmingly so. Her eyes opened, prepared for an empty room or even worse – an unimpressed one.

Suddenly, Sir Athelstane began to clap, followed by the ladies. Norah let out a sigh of relief.

'If I may…' Miss Leach said, looking to Lady Baines for approval to continue – she received a nod of encouragement – after which she turned to Norah. 'Norah, that was exceptional. In all of my years of tutoring, I'd be hard pressed to find another student who understood Beethoven as well as you evidently have.'

Norah's jaw dropped, but she closed it quickly when she saw Lady Baines lift her chin in disapproval at the sight. 'Thank you, Miss Leach.'

'If it's all right, I'd like to hear something else,' Miss Leach said as she rose to her feet.

Norah nodded. 'What would you like to hear?'

'What would you like to play? Anything you desire.'

Norah thought for a moment, and her favourite came to mind. She excitedly blurted out, 'I'd like to play Rachmaninoff's *Prelude in C-sharp minor*.'

Sir Athelstane and Lady Baines gasped in unison.

With a hand over her heart, Lady Baines stood up slowly. 'Dear, we do not have an appreciation for modern composers. To put it simply, we think them rather extravagant and atonal. Very different from the great classics, don't you agree? Is there anything else you would like to play?'

Thankfully, however, Miss Leach came to her rescue: 'If I may interject.' Sir Athelstane and Lady Baines looked at her with unblinking eyes. 'Rachmaninoff is an excellent composer. His *Piano Concerto No. 2* is simply marvellous, and the *Prelude* is elegant and romantic. I must insist you give him another chance to impress you.'

Norah smiled. She was sure she was going to get along quite well with her piano teacher.

'Very well then.' Lady Baines sat down accompanied by Miss Leach.

Norah faced the keys, and as with the other piece, the room simply vanished, replaced with the lovely dream of a garden as before. When Norah came to the end, once again there was no applause. This time Norah was sure she hadn't impressed them.

Finally, the silence was broken by Sir Athelstane. 'I guess we were wrong, Lady Baines.' His face was expressionless.

Norah wanted to slink away. Her heart thumped wildly. How could she be so ignorant and play a controversial piece for such a cultured audience? Surely they regretted ever believing she was talented, and they would revoke inviting her to take lessons in their home.

Sir Athelstane continued, 'This man Rachmaninoff is not so bad after all.' His mouth curved into a smile.

Lady Baines nodded in agreement. 'Indeed.'

Norah continued to impress them with her comprehension of various and vast compositions. She also, much to the amusement of Lady Baines, excelled in diction and etiquette. Around her family, she became known as the 'duchess', her brothers and siblings often scrunching up their noses at her accent or the way she held her teacup.

***

But that was all a distant fantasy now.

She missed playing the piano dearly, but what was she to do? The Royal College of Music in London was too far away. Norah's mind was brought back into the kitchen. 'I need to be at home,' she said.

Her father responded. 'But you don't.' Norah shook her head. He continued, 'I mean this in the best possible manner, but – we don't need you anymore, Norah.'

Norah choked with laughter and dabbed her eyes with a tea towel.

Her father walked closer, wrapped his arms around her in a hug and kissed her on the forehead. 'It's time now for your own adventure, Norah.'

# CHAPTER THREE

## *Bombay, 1937*

Picking up his bag, Raj boarded the ship. Upon the deck, he turned to wave goodbye. However, perhaps due to the size of the crowd, he couldn't spot his father or uncle. He remained on deck while the ship was pulled away from the dock by tugboats, unwavering in his efforts to find his father and uncle.

'Sir,' Raj's thoughts were cut off by a sailor, 'may I show you to your quarters?'

'Actually,' Raj smiled, 'I was hoping you could show me to the dining room.'

The sailor brought him to a large room lined with tables and chairs. Other than the wait staff, who were setting the tables with silverware and glasses to prepare for dinner, it was empty. Upon checking his wristwatch, Raj was embarrassed. It was only three in the afternoon.

He was about to close the door quietly and go, instead, in search of his room, when he was stopped by a waiter who was dressed in what Raj, at first, thought was a costume.

'Can I help you, young man?' he asked in a strong Yorkshire accent.

Raj stopped in his tracks. His heart began to beat faster as he thought up a quick answer. 'I was hungry,' he blurted out, afraid of what the man might say.

'That's why we are here, young sir.' He smiled at Raj and reopened the door.

'But I'm the only one in here. I don't think it's time to eat yet.'

'On a ship, sir, it's always time to eat.' The waiter showed him the way to a table and pulled out a chair for him.

Raj hesitated for a moment. He had never been the recipient of such treatment. He smiled as he thought about what his uncle Teja Singh had said about Indians being treated as second-class citizens. His uncle was obviously very wrong.

'What would you like me to bring for you?'

Raj wasn't sure what his options were, and the waiter, sensing his reluctance, offered some suggestions. 'It's not dinner time quite yet. But we have an assortment of sandwiches, soup and salads.'

'Yes please.'

'Yes please to which, sir?'

'Yes please to all.' Raj hesitated for a moment. 'Is that all right?'

'Of course, sir, it is,' replied the waiter, and walked off with the order and a wide smile on his face. 'We have a hungry one here,' he called out to the kitchen as he walked through the doors.

Raj's order arrived along with a small procession of kitchen and wait staff who wanted to meet the newest celebrity. He enjoyed his new-found fame and the delicious meals alike. And in the days thereafter, when he arrived for his meals, he was heartily greeted by the same staff. The others who dined at his table marvelled at his ability to down vast amounts of food and still remain active on deck.

Other than that, Raj spent his days playing bridge and chess, and engaging other passengers in deep philosophical conversations. Two weeks later, when the ship made its arrival in Marseille, he said farewell to the kitchen and wait staff who all bid him a warm goodbye.

As he turned to leave, he smiled as he overheard one waiter say to another, 'Wish there was always a chap like him on board. Makes life a little more fun.'

He hailed a taxi to make his way to the city centre, where he would board his next mode of transportation – a train that would whisk him off to Calais. As he sat in the backseat of the taxi, he took out the piece of paper that his father had given him, which outlined his itinerary. After Calais, he would take another boat to Dover, England, and then take a train to London. His instructions said that, once in London, he was to find the India House. There he would receive lodging for the night, and the next day he would take another train from King's Cross Station to Cambridge, where he would request admittance into Caius College.

Raj inhaled deeply. As exciting as this journey was, it was wearing on him, and he wasn't even halfway through. He neatly folded the paper again and placed it in his pocket just as the taxi pulled up to the station.

After finding the correct train and showing his ticket upon arrival, he found an empty carriage and plonked down in the seat. The train began to pull away from the station, and feeling he should make good use of this time, he pulled a chemistry book from his bag.

He intermittently took breaks from reading to gaze out of the window at the French landscape. Vineyards and rolling green hills flew past him. The train slowed as they came upon a village. Raj watched with amusement at a cowherd struggling to get his cows out of the way of a car that sat impatiently honking. The driver's arms flailed about as he shouted what Raj could only presume were French obscenities.

Yawning, Raj decided some sleep would do him good.

The train rocked after pulling away from another station, waking Raj. He stretched and apologized after accidently bumping into a passenger who must have boarded at a stop while he was asleep. He looked outside the window to see the morning sun peeking over the hilltops. Finding the time on his wristwatch, he realized he'd been asleep for six hours.

Two more hours until Calais, Raj thought, better see what food this train has to offer.

He stood in the doorway taking in the sight: the booths lining the dining car, tables decorated with the finest silverware Raj had ever seen, a small bar with shelves behind it displaying various bottles of liquor and wine. A tall and lanky bartender with a disappointed expression stood behind the bar, staring at Raj and making him feel unwelcome. Raj slunk into the nearest booth. An audible huff came from the bartender as he sauntered over to Raj.

'Bonjour, comment puis-je vous aider?'

Raj was impressed with how well-groomed the man was – slicked down black hair that parted in the middle and a thin sliver of a moustache with not a hair out of place.

'My apologies, I don't speak French.' Raj's hands started to sweat.

The man closed his eyes as he let out a deep sigh. 'How can I help you? Something to eat, oui?'

Thankful that he spoke English, Raj answered, 'Yes, may I have one of everything on the menu?' anticipating the same entertainment of kitchen staff he received while on the ship.

'Mon Dieu!' Gasping, the man screwed up his brows, obviously having never received such an ask before. 'No. You may not.' He shook his head sharply.

'I beg your pardon?' Raj asked, his face growing red.

'You may however have one thing from each section on the menu. Even that is crazy!' His eyes were wide open, and he threw his hands up in the air.

Raj thought for a moment. He had two choices, he resolved: either leave the car and say good riddance, or sit in the booth and down an obscene amount of food at the displeasure of this lanky and rude waiter.

After a few moments of watching the man's moustache twitch, he decided it would be way more enjoyable to hear the waiter huff and puff as he fulfilled his requests.

'Yes, I will have one item from each section.' Raj folded his hands. 'The largest portion of each, please.'

The waiter's mouth opened, about to shame him once again. However, thinking better of it, he picked up his jaw, lips pressed together tightly, bowed ever so slightly and walked briskly into the kitchen.

Although the portions weren't as lavish as the ones he had enjoyed on board the P&O liner, Raj deemed the whole dining process a success as he observed the waiter watching him eat every morsel set in front of him. While finishing the last course – a plate of assorted chocolates and cheeses – the train sounded, alerting its passengers and those waiting at the station of its arrival. Raj dabbed his mouth with a cloth napkin and pulled out a pocketful of francs, making the waiter gape.

He placed the money on the table, making sure to not overpay. 'Thank you for the, well … er … interesting service.'

He grabbed his suitcase and disembarked, and was thankful to be finished with that leg of his travels. Raj's unfavourable feeling towards the French was further bolstered in Calais when he waited on the dock to catch the ferry to Dover.

Passengers lined the customs office while a customs officer went by and inspected their luggage. When he came to Raj's suitcase, he asked the same question he was asking everyone else in French. Raj, unable to understand the language, answered with a simple yes.

The customs officer looked up from his notepad, clearly puzzled. A moment of silence followed, and the officer repeated the question to him, slower this time. Raj, still unsure of what was being asked of him, said yes again.

Raj gathered this was the wrong thing to do when the officer immediately threw his hands up in the air and walked away in a huff. The other passengers had their baggage delivered to the ferry while Raj remained with his in the customs shed.

A few minutes later, the same customs officer returned and asked him the same question, even slower this time, dots of saliva flecking his bushy moustache as he enunciated each word forcefully.

This time, Raj shouted out, 'Is there anyone here who speaks English?'

A young man with spectacles raised his hand. 'I work for Cooks. I speak English. How can I help you?'

Raj explained the situation, and the agent from Cooks then engaged the French official in a dialogue that became more and more heated until they were screaming at each other. Raj's mind went wild trying to understand what was unfolding in front of him, him being the cause of such a commotion.

'The French customs officer apparently asked you if you had anything to declare and you had said yes,' the young man began. 'He didn't know what to do, because everyone replies no, whether they have something to declare or not.'

'I see.' Raj looked to the customs officer. 'I don't have anything to declare. No.'

The custom's officer's brows lifted. 'Non?'

'No.' Raj emphatically shook his head.

To that, the officer let out a snort as he put a cross on his bag and gestured Raj towards the ferry. Raj thanked the Cooks agent and boarded, fully relieved to be finished with the encounter – and the country. But not before the Cooks agent demanded and received a fee of ten francs.

Raj spent the entire journey across the English Channel on deck, even though the water was choppy enough to make some of the passengers quite sick. But his excitement tied him to the deck. He did not want to miss a thing. He welcomed the cool breeze and mist that sprayed his face, forever focused on the horizon, squinting for the first glimpse of England.

Soon enough, the proverbial white cliffs of Dover appeared, at first as a faint outline, but as they got closer there was no mistaking what they were. Raj's heart was beating fast. Then the port of Dover appeared out of the ever-present mist over the English Channel, and the sound of the ship's claxon made him all but jump up and down with joy.

Not wanting to appear rude, Raj waited patiently on the deck while the gangplank was lowered and the first passengers disembarked. When it was his turn, he wasn't sure if he should run down to the English soil or walk nonchalantly. Wisely, he chose an intermediate path, then waited for a porter to carry his luggage down to the train whose engine was spewing smoke and soot into the air.

With a loud hiss of steam, the powerful engine was all an eighteen-year-old Indian boy needed to convince himself that England was indeed all that his teachers had told him it would be. Imperial, majestic and regal. Everything around him – from the regional accents of the workers to the King's English spoken by the most cultured passenger, from the name of the train, *The Golden Arrow*, to the engine driver who spent his time polishing the chrome pistons, and the young coal tender, not much older than Raj himself, with a dirty face to match his job description – it all shouted: *Welcome to England young man*, *welcome to England!* And Raj desperately wanted to shout back: *Thank you, thank you, thank you.*

An awestruck Raj stood staring at the train, which purred patiently on the tracks before him. Various Englishmen and women hastily bustled past him, anxious to get to where they were going. Unbeknownst to Raj, most had to swerve past him to continue on their way. He found out, however, when a harried businessman, top hat and all, bumped into him – 'Eh! Watch it now. Move along.'

Following the porter on to the train, Raj was shown into a carriage. He tipped the porter well, much to the latter's amazement and delight. But to Raj, that was the least he could do to show his appreciation for this voyage, a voyage he had anxiously been waiting for. He knew deep down inside his soul that this occasion, as mundane as taking a train usually is, unequivocally marked the start of a brilliant and joyous future.

Soon the train – with an almighty whistle and a heavy shunt which reverberated down the line of carriages – began to pull out of the station. With each mile that passed, India was one more mile behind him.

Raj opened the door to a first-class compartment. Two older gentlemen wearing what Raj assumed were very expensive suits looked up at him. Possibly noticing his hesitation, one of the men moved his briefcase and motioned for Raj to take a seat. Raj bowed in response.

They smiled courteously at him and continued their conversation with one another. Raj wasn't quite sure what he was expected to do, so he reached into one of his bags, pulled out a chemistry book and opened it. The two gentlemen paused to peer over at him.

'I'm going to Cambridge University,' he told them with a big smile.

The men nodded slightly in approval before resuming their talk. Raj turned to a random page, nestled deeper into his seat and consciously sat up straighter. After a few pages of inorganic compounds, Raj's focus turned to the window.

He wondered what might be happening back at home. He hoped that his mother wouldn't hold a grudge against his father for too long. He would see her during summer break, he was sure of it. However, he couldn't help but feel guilty; he knew she would sulk until his return.

'We are nearing London, young man,' said one of the older men, clearing his throat.

Raj closed his book and set it upon the empty seat next to him. His eyes went wide as he surveyed the structures outside the window, hoping to recognize some landmarks. Suddenly, the engine, with one last regal whistle, began to slow down as the train crossed the Thames. Raj began to make out buildings that stood looming over the city, the fog pierced by the train as it continued along.

Raj took out his itinerary once more; his plan was that, once he had arrived at Victoria Station, he was going to make his way over to India House, where he was to meet with the cultural attaché who had prior notice of his arrival.

***

'Why do you want to go to Cambridge?' asked the burly official upon his arrival at India House. 'You have been accepted at King's College, which is right around the corner. We can find you lodgings nearby.'

Raj, even though he would have liked to remain in London, felt he owed it to his father to go to Cambridge. 'No, I promised my father that I would go to Caius College and apply.'

'Caius College? Apply?' The official was stunned by Raj's naiveté. 'Young man, with all due respect, you have no chance of getting into that college. There is a long-standing procedure it seems you haven't followed. We received your marks by telegram and had made the application at King's College here in London for you, and they have accepted you. If you must, try Caius College next year.'

Raj's face fell, his thoughts of Teja Singh's opinion swirling to the surface. Maybe he was right, maybe it was a ridiculous idea to try to demand acceptance from such a prestigious school. However, Raj knew he was only here due to his father's request. It would be best to stick to the plan.

'I have to do this first. If it doesn't work, I will come back here.' Raj knew he had to try; what would he tell his father if he disregarded his wishes?

The official shook his head at Raj's stubbornness. 'Very well.' He added, probably looking forward to the day when Raj reappeared so he could patronizingly deliver the old I-told-you-so, 'For today though, why don't you take a bath and spend the night in the visitor's room, and then begin your journey to Cambridge tomorrow.'

Raj had been wearing the same clothes for a few days now. A bath sounded like a wonderful, and sensible, idea. He would need to look proper and clean for Cambridge. He was shown to a rather spartan room, and no sooner had Raj slipped into a lovely warm bath, looking out through the skylight at the blue sky over London, that he found himself falling asleep. It was the first time since he had left the shores of India that he was able to relax.

Realizing that, as relaxing as it was, it wouldn't be a good idea to nap in the bath, he got out and dried himself. Even though it was only early afternoon, clean and comfortable, he soon fell fast asleep on the soft bed.

An hour later, the slam of a door from the room above caused Raj to wake in a panic. For a moment, he was unsure where he was. Coming to his senses, he remembered he was in London.

Schoolteachers often taught lessons regarding London, which instilled a dream in Raj of exploring the city someday. It occurred to him that now would be the perfect time to go and wander about, taking in the sights he had only seen in textbooks.

He got dressed quickly, changing into the only clean clothes he had: another pair of heavy grey woollen slacks, a white button-up shirt, a Bishop Cotton School tie, and a heavy blue woollen blazer that was a bit large for him. His uncle Sohan Singh, who spoke to him about the importance of looking polished at all times while abroad, had gifted it to him right before he left. Raj walked down the ornate staircase to the lobby where he saw the same official from before.

'Going to do some sightseeing, are you?'

'Yes, before I go to Cambridge tomorrow, I want to see some of London,' Raj replied, eager to get going.

'Do you need someone to go along with you?'

'No, thank you,' Raj shook his head.

'Someone who knows their way around London, maybe?' added the official, not trusting a fresh-faced Indian boy to know the ins and outs of the city.

'No, thank you.' Raj waved goodbye as he walked out of the building and made his way to Trafalgar Square, and then on to Buckingham Palace and the Palace of Westminster.

Passers-by were amused by Raj, not just by how excited he was at each site but also by the way he was dressed. He suddenly became self-conscious as one local leaned in to whisper to their friend as they passed him. He began to pull at his clothes. There he was, an eighteen-year-old Indian, dressed for winter in September in England.

Hungry, and anxious to evade the staring eyes and pointing fingers, he ducked into a pub nearby.

'May I help you, young man?' asked the gruff publican, giving him a once over, which made him feel further out of place.

'Hoping to have some supper, please,' Raj said, clearing his throat.

The publican threw the towel he was using to wipe the counter over his shoulder and rolled his eyes. 'Over there.' He pointed to a table closest to the water closet.

'Would it be okay if I were to sit at one of these tables instead?' Raj asked, confused as there were plenty of tables empty. Besides one or two patrons at the bar, there was no one in the pub.

'If you want to eat here, that is the table available to you.' The bartender slid the towel off of his shoulder and began wiping a glass.

Hesitant, Raj sat down. He sat there for quite some time until a cook came out of the kitchen and slopped a plate down in front of him.

'Excuse me, sir, but I haven't even ordered yet. This must be for someone else.'

The cook wiped his brow, a spatula still in his hand. 'This is what we have. Either eat it or get out.' And he stomped back to the kitchen.

Utterly confused by the service, Raj wondered if that was just how Londoners were. He stared at the plate, unsure of what he was served. An overly dark piece of meat sitting in a light brown puddle with a side of peas – or at least that's what he believed they were. He lifted the rubbery meat on a fork and cautiously took a small bite. He chewed for what seemed an awfully long time before he was able to swallow. After taste testing each portion of the meal, he gathered he was served very burnt beef, cold and congealed gravy, and uncooked peas.

Raj didn't feel he should complain, so he finished his meal, or at least what he could without getting sick, and left highly disappointed and dejected.

He returned to India House and debated whether he should mention the meal to the official who welcomed him back, but decided against it. He went up to his room, climbed into bed and stared out the skylight at the night sky. His stomach growled as his thoughts drifted over to his mother's cooking. He missed it so, and wondered if all four years of college were going to be filled with inedible meals. His eyes welled up and tears began to streak his face. Curling up into a ball, he soon fell asleep.

'Sir?' Followed by a quick rap at the door made Raj's eyes flutter open. 'Sir?' came the voice again.

'Yes?' Raj cleared his throat as he looked at his watch. It was five in the morning.

'Thought you'd like to enjoy some breakfast before you went off to catch your train for Cambridge this morning.'

Afraid that the food was going to be like what he had experienced the night before, he wanted to decline, but so as to not seem rude he replied, 'Yes, thank you very much. I'll be right down.'

After splashing his face with cold water, brushing his teeth and changing into a set of clothes almost identical to what he had worn the day before, Raj hesitantly walked down the stairs to the dining room, wary of what might be on the plate.

'No worries about ordering here, sir. I scrounged up a right round and hearty breakfast. The best traditional breakfast the British have to offer.' The burly official beamed with pride as he set the steaming plate in front of Raj.

The plate was topped with piping hot sausages, two fried eggs, bacon, tomatoes with grill marks across the top, and baked beans all swimming around in a pool of grease. It was accompanied by two pieces of toast standing at attention in a silver-plated toast rack. The smell was certainly more appetizing than last night's supper, so Raj decided to have a taste. He started with the sausages, nibbling at the end, wary of it being overcooked meat again. But to Raj's delight, the sausages were juicy and packed with smoked flavours. He ventured next to the fried eggs and crisp bacon, then to the baked beans, and finally on to the grilled tomatoes. He ended the meal by wiping his plate clean with a slice of toast, devouring the entire meal within a matter of minutes. Raj was absolutely relieved that England did offer edible – even scrumptious – meals, and felt his mood improve. His excitement for his future here came flooding back.

'Off to university, are we?' said the ticket collector at the platform of King's Cross Station.

'Something like that,' Raj replied.

'Right.' The middle-aged man, with a large moustache and twinkling blue eyes, wearing his British Rail uniform proudly, looked at Raj quizzically. 'Well on you go then.' He pointed towards the train.

Raj thanked him and climbed aboard. Soon, the rocking of the train put him to sleep, though he awoke about an hour later as the train began to slow down. He peered out of the window and noticed the unmistakable outline of the city of Cambridge, with its myriad spires and ancient buildings. Once the train had pulled into the station, Raj left it carrying his small bag, and after asking for directions to Caius College, set out on his way.

***

He walked along Station Road and then turned right on to Hill Road and into the centre of the town. Even though it was early September, the sky was overcast, a stiff chilly breeze blew in from the east, keeping the temperature too low for Raj's liking. This time, he was glad to be wearing his woollen slacks and blazer. He played out in his mind how he hoped the conversation with the admission office would go once he arrived. The scenario always ended with an impressed master of admissions, who wouldn't stop remarking on his school marks. He picked up his pace when he saw Downing College and then Emmanuel College as he walked along Regent Street and then up Market Street, and then to the right of that, on Trinity Street, stood his ultimate quest, Gonville and Caius College. Raj stood outside the large ornate iron gates, paralysed by the rejection that might be waiting on the other side.

Through the bars of the gate, he saw students in dress gowns buzzing about and laughing as they made their way to their lectures. It was now or never. He took a deep breath as he reached out and pushed open the gates, which creaked at the movement.

With suitcase in hand, he walked slowly down the tree-lined stone path. Several students slowed their pace to take notice of him. Raj pulled at his blazer and straightened his tie, his outfit very different from the gowns they wore. The path opened into a large courtyard with an immaculate green lawn, which stood in the middle of imposing buildings. He wasn't sure which way he should go, and so he went up to the first person he saw, who appeared to be a professor.

'Excuse me,' he asked timidly. The man stopped and turned to face Raj. 'Excuse me, sir, but do you know where I can find the admissions office?'

'Why, it's the building right in front of you,' he replied, pointing to a doorway across the square.

Raj thanked him profusely and made his way to the office. Above a large wooden door were the words 'Office of Admissions'. Shifting his suitcase into his left hand, he meekly opened the door and peered around the corner, just in case it had opened to somewhere he shouldn't have been. A sizeable, ostentatious desk acted as a barricade to an office door, which Raj could only assume led to the master of admissions, and behind that desk was the gatekeeper – an elderly woman dressed in a very unattractive brown tartan suit, her grey hair pulled back in a tight bun, reading glasses that appeared to be attached to her nose, and a scowl on her very pale face. A slightly threadbare rug was thrown in front of the desk by someone who didn't care what it looked like. Two cane chairs next to a rigid wooden bench lined the wall, all looking as if they may have belonged to the original founders of the college. Raj gingerly walked up to the lady, who had not once paid him any attention, and asked to speak to the master of admissions.

'Is he expecting you?' she asked sternly, looking up at Raj for the first time.

Raj shook his head, 'No, madam, he isn't, but I was hoping to see him this morning. I was told he will see me because I come here with a recommendation from my chemistry teacher at Bishop Cotton School.'

'A recommendation for what, dear?'

'To receive admission.'

The lady's eyes widened. 'Admission? For this term?'

Raj nodded.

'Oh, dear, I'm afraid it's too late for that.' She folded her hands. 'The term has started. We have a protocol we ask all applicants to follow.'

Raj could feel his stomach drop, his heart began to race. 'I understand, madam, however, I have travelled a long way, from India, to be admitted to this college. I told my father I would try and so here I am. I would ask you to please let me at least speak to him.'

'I see,' the woman replied with a faint smile. She seemed as if she was intrigued by Raj's innocence and determination. 'However, unfortunately, we do not make any exceptions. I understand you have travelled a great distance, but this is how it is done at our university.'

Unwavering, Raj opened his suitcase to retrieve an envelope carrying his marks. 'Madam, please, these are my marks.'

Her lips pursed, she let out a breath and opened the envelope, fixing her glasses to read properly. Raj watched as her lips, starting off in a tight line, opened slowly.

'These … these are your marks?'

'Yes, madam.'

Searching excitedly for a pen and paper she replied, 'He is rather busy at the moment, but I will let him know you're here.' She asked for his name and the name of the chemistry teacher from whom he had received the recommendation. 'Take a seat. I will speak to Dr Rutherford.'

Raj sat down on the hard and uncomfortable wooden bench. He wondered if her reaction was a good sign and waited for what seemed a long time until she was followed back into the room by an important-looking man.

The man silently took Raj in. 'Did you apply to the college?'

'No, sir,' Raj replied standing at attention.

'Then how do you expect to be admitted?'

'I don't know, sir,' replied Raj, now sensing that it wasn't going to be as easy as he or his father had thought.

Dr Rutherford stood quietly for a minute. 'Where are the recommendations, young man?'

Raj handed them to the professor and stood there in silence while he went through them.

'Impressive, I must say,' he replied. 'The problem, however, is that there is no way we can accept you, since you haven't followed the proper procedure to gain admittance.'

'Can't you make an exception, sir?' Raj asked boldly. 'I have come a long way only to gain admittance to this school to continue my studies in chemistry.'

'I see that,' replied Dr Rutherford as he handed the papers back to Raj. 'But as I have said, you haven't followed the proper procedure, therefore you cannot and must not be accepted.'

Raj took the papers back but decided he should remain standing in the office. 'What's the proper procedure, may I ask, sir?'

'You have to sit an entrance exam. And it's a very difficult one,' piped in the elderly woman.

'I already sat that,' responded a confident Raj.

'Where, when?' asked a bewildered Rutherford.

'Here, sir.' Raj produced another set of papers from his bag.

Dr Rutherford thumbed through the papers in amazement. He handed them to the elderly woman, who upon reading them, handed them back to Raj. 'I must say, I am stunned,' he said. 'I have never, in all my years at university, seen such an incredible grasp of the subject.'

Raj beamed. At last, he was getting somewhere.

'However, even if you had followed the correct procedure, you have shown up too late. The term has started, and all lectures are at full capacity,' insisted Dr Rutherford.

The elderly woman nodded silently. Raj was absolutely sure that, after they saw his marks and recommendation, they would make an exception for him.

'If I may, sir,' the elderly woman began timidly, 'perhaps if a student were to drop, then the university would surely have an open slot to fill, correct?'

Dr Rutherford cleared his throat. 'I suppose if that were to happen, then, yes.'

Raj's heart jumped as a smile formed on his face.

'But I really doubt such a thing would occur.' He folded his hands. 'Now, if you would excuse me, I have other matters to return to.' He held out his hand.

A dejected Raj shook it. 'Thank you, sir.'

'Miss Abernathy, do you mind showing this young man out please?'

The elderly woman nodded in assent and Dr Rutherford went to his office and shut the door. Raj stood there, having a hard time understanding what had transpired. He didn't want to imagine the look on his father's face when he told him he hadn't been accepted. That the various expensive boat and train rides were all for nothing. He turned to open the office door and leave.

'Wait for a second, if you could,' said Miss Abernathy from behind the desk.

Raj stopped and turned to face her.

She could see the dejection plastered all over his face. 'Why don't you join me for some lunch on my break at noon, dear?'

Confused, but in no position to reject an invitation, he replied, 'Yes, madam.'

'Oh, please' – she waved away his reply – 'call me Gretchen.'

Raj nodded, though he didn't understand why she wanted him to join her for lunch.

At noon, on the dot, Raj met Gretchen outside her office. She had a large smile on her face when she saw him.

She shook his hand. 'A sandwich and a hot cup of tea, shall we?'

They entered a little café outside the college gates. Many students and professors occupied the surrounding tables. Gretchen ordered and paid for them both. Raj thanked her as he sipped his tea. Conversation was slim, and again Raj wondered why he had agreed to join her.

'Are you ready then?' she asked and looked at him. 'Yes, you look presentable.'

Confused, Raj followed her out. 'Sorry, madam – I mean, Gretchen, why would I need to look presentable?' he asked as they walked on to a bustling street.

'Well, I'm taking you back to the university. You're going to meet with the master.'

Raj stopped in his tracks, 'Madam – Gretchen – what do you mean I'm going to meet with the master?'

Gretchen turned to face him. 'I may only be the secretary to the office of admissions, but with that role comes the privilege of knowing the other secretaries, such as the one to the master.' She grabbed his elbow. 'Come on now, you have an appointment to make.'

Completely lost for words, Raj shook his head. He began to feel his journey to Cambridge was no longer foolish. 'I just can't thank you enough, madam.'

Entering the office, Gretchen whispered to Raj, 'Please don't get the wrong idea, Mr Kohli. Just because I'm taking you back to sit and talk to the master doesn't mean you will gain admission. In all of its 500-odd years, Caius College, and for that matter Cambridge, has not to my knowledge ever broken with tradition. So, your chances of gaining admission to the university are very, very slim. Especially this term. But who's to say you won't be the first?'

Raj smiled. 'Thank you.'

'Now, I have to get back to my desk. Best of luck, dear,' she said, taking his hand to shake it.

As she left, he sat down on another hard bench and watched the students as they strolled by outside the window. At first, they trickled across the grass square towards what Raj believed was the dining hall, and then there were more and more until the entire grass square was covered with students walking in every direction possible. Raj found a mathematical logic in their motion and wondered if he could derive a formula from it. He was so lost in his thoughts that he hadn't noticed the woman who had been calling his name until she tapped him on his shoulder.

'Mr Kohli, I presume. The master is ready for you.' She led the way into his office.

He made sure, one last time, that he looked presentable, as they passed a mirror in the hallway. Before him stood a large, beautifully polished, dark cherry door, which the lady opened and ushered him through.

'Mr Kohli – Dr John Forbes Cameron, master of Caius and Gonville,' the woman announced with a slight curtsey.

Raj's heart raced as he walked further into an extremely large, ornately decorated office. The walls were lined with shelves from ceiling to floor, filled with classic novels and textbooks. On a table to the left was a collection of what could have been ancient manuscripts, all neatly rolled and tied with bows. A fire roared beneath the painting of a scholarly-looking fellow holding a scroll, from what looked like the 1300s. And in front of Raj, standing behind a grand mahogany desk, sat the master.

'Ah, thank you, Miss Jones.' The master stood from his chair, his robes brushing the floor.

Raj approached him slowly. As he neared the desk, the master extended his hand and Raj took it. The door closed behind him, and Raj's heart began to pound even harder. Without a word exchanged, the master sat down behind his desk and pointed to one of two chairs opposite him. Raj sat. The master leaned forward, clasping his hands.

He smiled. 'It's a pleasure to meet you, sir.'

Raj couldn't ever remember being called 'sir' by someone of the master's stature before. He wasn't sure what to say.

Still in awe of where he was, Raj nodded his head. 'Thank you, sir,' he said finally. 'Thank you for seeing me, sir.'

The master sat back in his chair, 'Sit back and relax, Mr Kohli. Is that how you pronounce your name?'

Raj nodded his approval.

'I must say, in all the years I have known my secretary, she has never once come to me and lobbied for a student. In fact, I frown on that. However, having said that, when Miss Jones came to me this morning, I found myself intrigued by you. I talked to two chemistry professors, and they were both extremely taken by your understanding of the subject. I am myself a mathematician, and have had the honour of meeting and lecturing a man such as you from India who was a brilliant mathematician. I don't remember his name, it was a few years ago, and I tend to forget names that are hard to pronounce, but never faces, I always remember faces. So, when Miss Jones came to me with your case, it reminded me of him, and now that I've had the pleasure of meeting you, Mr Kohli, the similarities are striking.'

He stopped for a second, possibly to gauge Raj's reaction, but there wasn't any. Raj sat completely absorbed with what the master was telling him.

He continued, 'Over the years since the college was founded, we have developed an admittance process whereby we can select the students we want. We get hundreds of applicants every year, and we have a committee that goes over the applications with a fine-toothed comb. I don't believe there has ever been a time when a student just showed up at our doors and asked to be admitted, right out of the blue. And if they have, which is of course possible – I haven't been here for 500 years, even though I may look it – then I am sure they were sent packing.' The master stopped for a second and leaned back in his chair.

Raj remained expressionless. He wasn't sure what he should be feeling or if he should say something in his defence. He thought the best course of action was to do nothing until prompted.

The master continued, 'However, I have been informed that a rather nervous fellow has dropped out from the chemistry programme just moments after you showed up.'

Raj leaned forward. 'I don't know what to say,' he said quietly.

'Welcome to Caius, Mr Kohli,' the master concluded and thrust his hand forward for Raj to shake.

Raj shot out of his seat. 'Thank you, sir! Thank you! Thank you!' He took his hand and emphatically shook it.

Gretchen couldn't hide the shock Raj's news gave her. Over the next hour, she prepared him a list of the lectures he was to take. After finalizing the list, she led him to the dorm where he was to stay.

'Thank you so much, Gretchen,' Raj said, humbly. 'I owe it all to you.'

'It's my pleasure, dear,' Gretchen said with a wink as she left him alone in his new lodging.

# CHAPTER FOUR

## *Cambridge, 1937*

The door opened into a decent-sized room, larger than it had appeared from the outside, with cream-coloured walls and a bed on either side. A small wooden desk opposite the door was piled high with books. The bed closest to the window was already taken. Prompted by the sound of cheering, Raj peered outside the window to find out what the fuss was about.

An impromptu game of cricket on the courtyard grass was underway. Raj thought back to his days at Bishop Cotton School, where he loved to play. He didn't realize how engrossed he had been in watching the game, and failed to notice someone walk into the room until they knocked on the bed frame he was leaning against. Raj jumped and turned to face a man not much older than himself, but far better dressed, wearing a broad smile, a cigarette dangling from the corner of his mouth. Raj coughed as the smoke entered his lungs, and his companion immediately took the cigarette out of his mouth and put it out in the ashtray.

'Sorry,' he said. 'I guess you don't smoke.'

Raj shook his head and the visitor introduced himself. 'Colin, Colin Farnell.' They shook hands and Colin plonked himself in the chair across from Raj.

He was taller than Raj but not by much, and had sandy blonde hair. He was very pleasant, and Raj was relieved that he had been given a roommate who was so jolly. They talked for hours and they came to learn all about each other's families and most importantly their major, which was the same: chemistry. Raj found out in boarding school that chemistry was one of those subjects that you either loved and were good at or hated and dreaded the class. There was no middle ground. One could not be ambivalent about it.

A bell from the chapel tower rang and Raj wasn't sure what it was for.

'That's the dinner bell,' said Colin, seeing Raj's confusion. He continued, 'As the term has just started, we can go to dinner the way we are dressed. But in the future, one has to be dressed in robes.'

Raj was surprised. 'I thought those days would be over once I left boarding school.'

'No such luck here.' Colin laughed. 'You'll get used to it. I'm famished, how about you?'

'Famished, yes,' said Raj. 'But getting used to being treated like a child all over again – I'm not quite sure about that.'

Colin slapped Raj gently on the back. 'Come on, the food here is quite good, you know.'

They entered the dining hall and were immediately welcomed by the smell of roast beef and Yorkshire pudding.

***

Raj had a tough time falling asleep the night before his first lectures, not because of Colin's intermittent snoring but because his mind would not stop in its efforts of concocting outlandish scenarios of what tomorrow might hold. In one scenario, as he walked into the classroom, he was informed that Cambridge had decided to revoke his admission, and kicked him out in front of a class full of his peers. In another scenario, every time he found the door that opened to his lecture, it would suddenly disappear; he could hear the class being conducted but couldn't find the door to join. Each scene was more absurd than the one before, and although ridiculous they might have been, Raj tossed and turned.

Finally, the real moment came, and Raj walked into his first lecture – a chemistry lab with one Dr Thompson.

Not able to shake his nerves, Raj decided that arriving early would serve him and aid in settling his stomach, which was tied in knots. Several tables, able to seat two students at a time, lined the classroom. Raj was relieved when he saw the room empty and double checked his list of lectures to make sure he was in the correct location. As he walked in further, he realized he was not alone.

'Either you're very early or in the wrong location. If I were a betting man, I'd say the latter.' A man in his late sixties, with greying hair and a clean-shaven face, was measuring out some sort of liquid into a beaker at the front of the classroom. A blue flame quietly roared out from a Bunsen burner on the counter.

Raj hesitated for a moment, wondering if somehow at this university it was viewed as impolite to be so early. Considering all their other ludicrous rules, he wouldn't be surprised. 'No, sir. The former.'

The man stopped pouring and lifted his googles to take a look at Raj. His eyebrows drew together. 'Well, good thing I said *if* I were a betting man,' he replied and set his goggles back on his face. 'What is your name, young man?'

'Rajendra Kohli, sir.'

The professor looked up once again and nodded. He returned to his work. Raj watched as vapour curled inside the beaker before breaking free, causing puffs to burst out of the top as he poured more of the mixture in. The professor concentrated on the vapour with great intensity.

Raj found a lab seat not too far away and continued to watch as the professor transferred the beaker on to a stand with metal tongs. Raj curiously studied the professor as he went back and forth, examining a stack of papers that lay on the desk next to the beaker in order to adjust the composition of its contents.

Besides the bubbling from the beaker, the room ached with silence. Raj crossed and uncrossed his legs as he swore to himself that he wouldn't arrive this early next time.

'Damn!' The professor ripped off his goggles.

Raj saw the beaker was no longer bubbling. He cleared his throat. 'I recently read an article regarding the photochemical behaviour of aldehydes. I quite favour Norrish's explanation for the primary action of light.' Raj gestured to the beaker. 'If I were a betting man, I'd say you did as well.'

Dr Thompson blinked rapidly and cocked his head to one side, opened his mouth to respond and then shut it quickly, only to open it again, 'How did you…' He cocked his head to the other side as he stepped closer. 'That's precisely what I was just investigating. But what is so curious is how in the devil you knew that.'

Raj pointed back to the beaker. 'At first, I mistook the smoke for vapour, but then I realized it was a gas when it stayed in its state at room temperature. And because it's odourless—'

'Carbon monoxide, yes.' Dr Thompson eyed Raj. 'You're that Indian fellow that sauntered into the headmaster's office asking for admission to the university, aren't you?' A smile was beginning to form upon his face.

Raj wasn't fond of his description – sauntered – and wasn't sure if he should admit that he was, in fact, the student he was referring to. But seeing as how there weren't many Indian students, let alone ones that were studying chemistry at Cambridge, he responded, smiling, 'Supposedly, there is protocol that neither I nor my father were aware of.'

Dr Thompson nodded and let out a laugh. 'Well, I hear you come with high recommendations and quite the grasp of organic chemistry.' He lifted his chin and eyebrows. 'I look forward to finding out if that is true' – his chin fell – 'or not.'

At his last word, other students began to flow into the room and make their way to the open seats. The professor went to clean up his experiment.

'Oi, you're in my chair.'

Raj felt the sharp nudge of an elbow in his back. He turned to see a round boy with bright red hair and a matching splotchy face glaring down at him. Raj looked around. Other white fresh-faced boys were staring at him, obviously wondering who this newcomer was.

Raj picked up his books. 'My apologies. Didn't know there was loyalty to seats,' he mumbled under his breath.

The red-headed boy furrowed his brows and stepped closer, bumping into Raj, almost causing him to fall backwards. 'What did you say?'

'Oh, sit down, Harold, you royal git.'

Raj looked over to see Colin to his right. Harold's face ballooned and ripened into an even deeper shade of red.

'Raj, sit with me at this table,' Colin said as he led him over to an empty one in the middle.

A tall, freckled boy looked offended as they passed his table.

'Oh, Malcolm, I think you'll manage without me. Just know the thing with a flame – it's hot.' Colin rolled his eyes and turned to whisper to Raj, 'Am I glad that you're in this lecture. Harold thinks he's some sort of king just because his great great great great grandfather was. And Malcolm' – he rolled his eyes again – 'Malcolm is quite possibly the stupidest lab mate I've ever been forced to work with. I mean, I'm not a soon-to-be winner of a Nobel Prize, but at least I know what a Bunsen burner does.'

Raj did his best to hold his laughter.

***

The following days and months of the first term were pretty much all the same. Lectures from morning to evening, efforts to avoid Harold as much as he could – no easy task as they shared three classes. Nights were filled with studying. There was not much social time – with the exception of Sunday, when everyone was required to attend church, regardless of religious denomination. The rest of Sunday was free.

On numerous occasions, Raj had tried to make friends with those in his class but found it to be difficult. Most of his classmates looked down on him, and their dislike for him only increased when they realized he was far superior to them in his studies and was a favourite amongst his professors. Raj tried to not let it affect him negatively. However, it did make the university a very uncomfortable place to be.

Colin was the only one who wasn't intimidated and used Raj as a resource. Soon, Colin and Raj became very close friends, and they did most things together, especially on weekends, when they either toured surrounding colleges, walked around town or went punting on the river Cam. A couple of times, the boat they were in capsized, much to the delight of those sitting on the bank or in another boat close by. Neither of them was very good at punting, and it was mutually agreed that there were some things in life that were not meant to be – boating was one of them.

***

The end of the first term arrived, and after the final exams were over, Colin invited Raj to his parents' home in the countryside for Christmas. He was thrilled to accept the invitation, of course. India was too far to visit for the holidays, which meant he would have had to stay at the university. They both left in a car, with a chauffeur provided by Colin's father, and drove off into the frosty barren countryside for about an hour or so.

'There it is,' remarked Colin, pointing to a magnificent structure in the distance.

Raj's jaw dropped. 'That's your home, Colin?' He looked at Colin in amazement and then turned his attention back to the home, as the chauffeur turned left through a set of very ornate black iron gates with a crest on them, and down a long road lined by tall and very ancient chestnut trees. Occasionally, men who were either cutting the grass by the side of the road or working in the large flower beds, which also lined the driveway, doffed their hats as they drove by.

The car pulled into a circular driveway which wound around a fountain that had been turned off for winter, but Raj could imagine the long graceful sweeps and spray it would have created.

The car halted and Raj's door was opened. The chauffeur had to clear his throat dramatically to let Raj, who was still fascinated by the size of the fountain, know it was time to get out. As the front doors opened, they were greeted by a welcoming party of several butlers and maids.

Raj was further shocked when he heard the head butler address Colin as 'Your Lordship'. Raj shot a glance over at Colin, who smiled shyly and shrugged. Instantaneously, Raj fixed his tie. Never in his life had he been in the company of someone with a high title. He became quiet, unsure of how to act.

A moment or two later, the parlour doors burst open, and a very dignified couple, followed by a few large dogs, made their appearance. He was very warmly greeted by both parents and dogs, as well as by Colin's two very pretty sisters. Raj made sure he was on his best behaviour and bowed as he was introduced. When the over-the-top welcome was over, they were escorted into a drawing room fit for a palace.

The room was ostentatiously large. On the floor lay a colossal and intricate Persian rug, and on that several very comfortable looking leather chairs, a sofa with large, embroidered pillows and a substantial, elongated mahogany table that filled up the remaining space. Upon the dark, wood-panelled walls hung several portraits of very severe-looking men. All very posh, a far cry from anything he had ever seen in India. And as everyone was scurrying around, attending to various things, Colin and Raj were left alone for a minute.

'Didn't any of your ancestors smile?' Raj joked.

'I suppose not, maybe because they knew they would have to leave their fortune with their kin instead of burying it with themselves,' Colin said, joining in the joke with Raj.

'Your *Lordship*?' Raj questioned him.

'Does it matter?' Colin replied, and Raj shook his head. 'Let me ask you: if you knew, would you have treated me differently?' Taking Raj's silence as a yes, he replied, 'There you go!'

Raj stood up straight. 'Colin, the only lords I have ever seen was when I was in India, where the British are our rulers. I have never met one in person, and certainly never shared lodgings with one.' Raj scanned his mind for any occasion when he might have not acted properly or in a manner appropriate for such company.

'Well,' Colin said firmly, 'from now on, it's back to being Colin to you.' He hesitated for a second. 'Look here, Raj, I consider you to be one of my closest, if not *the* closest friend I have. I intentionally didn't tell you about my title, because for once in my life I wanted to be treated for who I am, not for who people think I am. I may have been born into a title, but you were born with brains far better than mine. Therefore, I'm the one indebted to you, for all the help you have given me in chemistry.'

'Yes, you're right.' Raj held back a laugh as he continued, bowing deeply. 'Your Lordship.'

Colin gave him a playful punch on the arm. 'Argh! If you let anyone at school know...'

Raj smiled. 'Your secret is safe with me.' He stretched out his hand, and Colin took it in a firm handshake.

On a couple of occasions Raj found himself alone in one of the rooms – such as in the library, looking at the books – when in walked Colin's two sisters, Margaret and Chantal. He felt awkward as they giggled on seeing him there and tried to engage him in conversation.

'Colin told us you're a genius,' said the prettier of the two, Chantal. 'Is that true?'

Raj began to turn red and shook his head violently. 'Colin has a habit of exaggerating.'

'Oh, you can tell us,' Chantal said, inching closer to Raj, which made him shift in his chair. 'I bet you are. Indians who attend university must be very smart.'

'Oh, do you know many?' Raj was intrigued.

'None,' they both replied in unison. 'You're the first Indian we have ever met.'

'But we've read about them,' Chantal said with wide eyes. 'Is it true you all live in huts and don't bathe?'

'Chantal! You can't just ask something so vulgar,' Margaret scolded her sister.

Chantal looked completely perplexed, 'Why not?' She turned to Raj, 'Clearly he is different from the rest – he goes to university for goodness' sake!'

Raj was thankful to Colin when he interrupted, 'It's time for Christmas dinner!'

Raj was sorry when Christmas came to an end, as he had never celebrated the holiday at home. It was a new, exciting and delicious experience. The food was especially appreciated by him. It was the first time he had tasted roasted turkey, with all its trimmings and stuffing. And then, to top it off, there was a plum pudding served by the butler, to the oohs and aahs of everyone as it came in flames along with a bowl of brandy butter. Nothing could have topped that, Raj thought, until tea the next day, which was accompanied by the most decadent of cakes – a Christmas cake with ankle-deep marzipan icing and a Father Christmas exiting a white ceramic chimney.

Unfortunately, time, as it usually does in these cases, flew by and they said their goodbyes, but not before Raj thanked Colin's parents for the Christmas gift they had given him: a slide rule, which was an instrument he never had the money to possess, and so he thanked them with much enthusiasm.

***

Once they were back and safely ensconced at the university, winter set in with a vengeance, and snow fell heavily, covering everything in a thick blanket of inconvenience. They could walk to most of their lectures along the hallways, Raj dressed in what sometimes seemed like everything he owned plus some of Colin's old scarves and gloves. But he was still uncomfortable and yearned for summer. The rooms had no insulation, or heat for that matter, other than very inefficient fireplaces which the two of them crowded around, trying to prevent the heat from escaping into the universe. Raj had experienced similar weather when he was in boarding school, but there had never been a need to go outside. Here, there were instances, such as going to the dining hall or lectures, for which Raj was ill-prepared.

One day, Raj was returning to his room from one of his lectures when it began to snow again.

'Blasted weather!' Raj shook off the snowflakes, which covered his head and the coat that he had borrowed from Colin.

'Not a fan of the snow, are we?' Colin laughed, sitting on his bed.

Raj clenched his jaw as he took off his boots – another item borrowed from Colin – which were soaked through. He waited for his toes to defrost in the warmth of the roaring fire. 'Not sure why anyone would be,' he huffed.

'Right. It's a dreadful thing, isn't it?' Colin mockingly agreed.

Raj rolled his eyes. 'Not as dreadful as this university, though.'

Colin perked up. 'What do you mean?'

'I mean, all the rules we have to abide by…' Raj scowled. 'I feel like I get a warning every time I step outside our room.'

'Got ejected from the dining hall for not wearing your robes again, did you?' Colin smiled.

'No, at least not today. I just received one as I crossed the lawn from my lecture to here! My fifth one this week, and all for stupid reasons.' Raj's eyes narrowed.

'Whatever for?' Colin shifted his legs so they were hanging off his bed.

'I wanted to take a shortcut on account of it snowing, and a professor yelled at me.' Raj threw up his hands. 'Can't walk on this grass, young man, this is for fellows only,' he mimicked. 'Felt like I was a child getting scolded by my mum!' Raj crossed his arms.

Colin nodded. 'Sorry, mate. But if you want to attend here, you have to abide. That's how this university is. Stupid rules and all.'

Raj raised an eyebrow. 'Well, what if I don't want to abide anymore?'

Colin's face contorted in confusion. 'And what? Get kicked out? You rebel, you!' He laughed.

Raj shook his head. 'No, I mean leave.'

'Leave?'

'Yes. Leave this university and go to another one. One that doesn't treat its students like infants.' Raj spat.

Colin's feet touched the floor. 'I see you're upset. However, if you left…' – he looked at the floor – 'it would be awful lonely here.'

Raj looked up at Colin as he sighed. 'It's not that I really want to leave. I just don't know if this was the best decision for me. I think you'd understand.'

Colin stayed silent and smiled sadly.

Raj continued to rub his hands together, trying to create some additional heat – any warmth was a blessing.

'Listen,' Colin began. 'How about you finish up this year, and if by the end it's still not your ideal, then transfer. But don't do it in the middle of the term. It will be a headache for you to find another university mid-year.'

Raj nodded. 'I suppose that makes sense. All right, I'll finish up this year and then evaluate my happiness.'

A wide smile spread across Colin's face. 'Good deal, old chap.'

***

As the days dragged on, Raj began to resent even more the pomp and circumstance required by one and all. The childishness of university rules, together with the unfriendliness of most of the students, with the exception of his friendship with Colin, made his life very solitary.

Raj finished his year with first place in his class, but also with a bitterness that couldn't be shaken.

And as the term began to wrap up with the end-of-year exams, he decided he would inform those who had made his time at Caius worthwhile: Colin, his professors and, of course, Gretchen. And though they were all very disappointed, they fully understood Raj's reasoning and wished him the best of luck.

'And where are you going to attend in the fall?' Gretchen asked while she took a sip of tea.

'I was thinking somewhere in London. I very much enjoy the city and believe I could be accepted to a college there.'

'Very well, then. I know wherever you choose, the school is very lucky to have you. Such a bright student you are.' Gretchen beamed.

'Thank you for always believing in me,' Raj said with a slight crack in his voice. He was sure going to miss her. She was one of the few who had showed him kindness.

Raj wasn't sure when the right time would be for him to let Colin know of his plans. He was afraid that, if he were to wait any longer, he would make matters worse. So, one evening, while both were practising how to write out formulas, Raj closed his textbook dramatically and pronounced, 'Colin, I have waited until the end of the year, and unfortunately, my feelings about this university have not changed.'

'Are you sure?' Colin asked.

'Yes, quite so. I am confident that I can find another university, one that treats its pupils as adults.'

Colin closed his textbook. 'Well then, I only ask one thing of you.'

Raj's eyes narrowed. 'Yes?'

'I think what you need is some old-fashioned fun before you start at another school.'

Raj leaned back in his chair, suspicious of what Colin was about to suggest – hopefully not punting again.

'How about,' Colin continued, 'you humour me, and we travel together this summer? We can take a holiday, gallivanting around Europe. You know, before we never…' He paused. 'We can go anywhere you'd like.'

Raj hesitated. 'Sounds fun. However, I told my parents I would be home for the summer.'

'Oh, come on now,' Colin said with a sly smile. 'You can spend the next summer with them. You'll have tons of time to spend together – you're family, for goodness' sake! You'll see them again. As for you and me, we only have limited time with one another. It will be our last hurrah!'

Raj felt a tug to agree. 'Well, even so, I don't have the money to do something like that.'

Colin waved Raj's comment away. 'No worries. It will be my treat.'

Raj's eyes went round. 'Really?'

'Oh, sure. It would be my pleasure,' Colin said. 'Come on, let's have a bit of fun. We're young chaps in university, we're allowed some fun every once in a while.' He winked.

Raj smiled. 'Well, then, if we're allowed…'

***

After Raj penned a letter to his parents informing them of his plans, the next few days were filled with planning their excursions across Europe. Upon Raj's interest and Colin's suggestions, they decided to visit Oxford, Ireland, Paris and Berlin, before stopping at London to drop off Raj.

Raj had not wanted to visit France after his initial impression of the people, but as an inducement, Colin had suggested Berlin as an added stop. Raj was hesitant after all the political unrest in the country, but when Colin reassured him that it was nothing to be worried about, he agreed. Raj counted down the days until they were to leave and, finally, the end of the semester came, and they woke up at the first sight of sunlight.

Raj enjoyed being on Colin's bill as they indulged in travelling in the finer carriages and stayed in luxurious hotels that Raj could never have afforded on his own. Their travels to Oxford and Ireland quickly passed by. In Paris, they spent their days exploring museums and landmarks, and their evenings in bars. On one occasion, much to Raj's embarrassment and Colin's amusement, Colin made up a story about Raj's heritage to a group of English-speaking French university students.

'Ladies, ladies,' Colin said before he took a sip of wine. 'Do you have any idea who this is?' He pointed a finger at Raj as he swayed.

The girls giggled and they shook their heads. Raj began to blush.

'This' – Colin hiccupped – 'is Raj Kohli, a *prince,* a *maharaja* from India.' He bowed and Raj almost choked on his drink.

One of the girls, with long blonde hair, turned her eyes to Raj. 'Are you really a prince?'

'Well, erm—'

'Why, of course, he is! Tell them, Raj.' Colin winked and took another large gulp.

Raj was hoping his face didn't betray how scared he really was to be talking to such a group of pretty girls. 'I am.' His voice cracked and he quickly took a sip of wine.

'You must own so many jewels, then,' a brunette with a red bow in her hair excitedly said as she leaned forward.

'More than His Majesty the King himself,' Colin piped up as the girls gasped.

'You govern subjects and everything?' a girl with yellow curls and big eyes asked.

'Well, his father, the king, does now. But when he is king, he'll rule over the whole kingdom.' Colin nodded emphatically as he put an arm around the girl with long blonde hair.

'And why are you in Paris?' the brunette asked as she daintily sipped her wine, causing Raj to blush.

'Just to visit—'

'Raj here is in Paris on official royal business. He needs to find himself a princess,' Colin whispered to the group, eliciting more gasps.

'Seems like a very important quest,' the brunette said as she smiled and scooted closer to Raj, who gulped.

'You're in so much trouble,' Raj said to Colin after the girls left. 'You're lucky I didn't tell them about you, Your Lordship.' Raj elbowed him.

Colin smiled, an imprint of a kiss in pink lipstick on his cheek. 'I'm just upset you never told me you're a prince,' he said with a wink.

They finished the last of their wine, roaring with laughter as they recalled the night's events to one another.

Soon, they were making their way to Germany. They spent their time exploring more museums and strolling in and out of squares, their holiday there being much tamer than their time in any other place. One afternoon, however, they heard loud chants coming from another square. As they followed the crowds, they came upon a massive audience, who listened intently to a speaker in military garb standing on a platform and speaking passionately. Raj became increasingly uncomfortable as he received unwelcoming stares from those around him.

'A political affair, you suppose?' Colin asked as he surveyed the shouting crowd.

Raj examined the gathering further, when he spotted another military fellow standing guard, wearing a red band around his arm with a tilted black swastika in the centre. 'Colin, I think I've heard about this lot from the newspapers and in lectures. I'm not sure we should be standing here.'

Raj was unsure whether Colin had noticed his discomfort but was thankful when he agreed to leave.

And as quickly the holiday began, it had found its ending. As the train headed for London, Raj found himself being whisked away again to his favourite capital, and as every mile passed, he became more confident that he had made the right decision.

'I hope you find what you're looking for, old chap,' Colin said with a sigh.

The plan was for them to say their goodbyes on board the train, and then Raj would hop off while Colin would continue to his home.

'I hope so too.' Raj laughed.

'Just don't go around making any other best friends,' Colin joked.

'Not sure I could even if I tried,' Raj responded with a smile. 'Thank you, for everything. My time at Cambridge was miserable, but it would have been absolutely hell if you weren't there.'

Colin kicked his feet. 'Well, then. Best of luck. Cheers.' And he stuck out his hand for Raj to shake.

However, Raj bypassed his hand and hugged him tightly. 'Farewell, Colin.' And then he added with a smile, 'Your Lordship.'

***

Unsure of the first step he needed to take in order to be accepted at a college in London, Raj did the only thing he could think of. A taxi dropped him in front of India House.

The lobby was just as he remembered it. High ceilings and large windows, with long golden drapes, marble columns and a large marble desk with, as always, the same official sitting behind it.

'Well, welcome back, sir,' the burly official said. 'Now, to what do we owe this pleasure?'

Raj set down his bag and shook his hand. 'It seems Cambridge was not the right fit for me. I've come to London to perhaps attend a university here. I remember you had mentioned one that had accepted me. I can't quite remember the name.'

'Yes. King's College, right across the way here.' He pointed out towards the window. 'I could set an appointment with the dean if you'd like. You'd have to interview, of course, but if I remember your marks correctly, and if you kept them high whilst at Cambridge, I don't see an issue with them accepting you once again.'

'Thank you,' Raj replied, then added after a pause. 'I've realized, even as I stayed here last year, I don't think I caught your name. My apologies, sir.'

'Not a worry. No apologies necessary. I'm Mr Dewan,' he said with a slight bow.

'Well, Mr Dewan, you were quite right about Cambridge. It was not my cup of tea. I look forward to a fresh start here in London.'

'London is lucky to have you, sir,' Mr Dewan replied, walking out from behind the desk. 'Would you be needing lodging while you are here? If so, we have the visitor room available.'

'That would be perfect, thank you.' Raj picked up his bag as he followed Mr Dewan to the room.

Raj stepped into the visitor's room, and as he did, he felt like he was stepping back in time to a year ago, eager to be accepted to a university and unsure if he would be. He was hoping this wouldn't become a habit. After Mr Dewan left, Raj was alone with his thoughts. He hadn't told his parents that he had left Cambridge, possibly out of fear of disappointing his father or because he just didn't know how to share the news. The new school year would start soon, meaning he would need to tell his father before he sent money for tuition.

Raj searched the wooden desk in the room and found some paper and a pen in the top drawer. He then began the search for the courage to write the letter to his parents.

*Dear Mummy and Daddy,*

*As you know, I have just completed my first year at Caius, as planned. I spent the whole year being studious and an exemplary student. You would like to know that I was very much the top student in all my exams and lectures. I even made a dear friend,*

*Colin, my roommate, and I am so grateful to have had your blessing in travelling throughout Europe with him this summer. It was an experience I will never forget.*

Raj felt a pang of guilt. It wouldn't be until next year that he would see them, and he wondered how his mother was doing.

*I'm sure you are aware that lectures at Cambridge are to commence soon for the new year. However, I must inform you that I will not be in attendance. I, along with my professors, have decided that my time at Cambridge must come to a close. The rules thrust upon each student are overwhelming and unbearable. I had decided to see it through to the end of the school year to see if things, or my temperament to handle such things, would change. Unfortunately, neither have.*

*I understand the disappointment you must feel, but I do intend to continue my chemistry studies and find acceptance at a reputable university in London. A university that would be impressive to all, held in similar regard to Caius. I have an interview with the dean at King's College tomorrow and am very confident I will be accepted. I will send word once I do.*

*I miss you both and hope you are doing well,*
*Raj*

He grew more nervous with every word he wrote, and he wondered if it was absolutely necessary for him to inform his parents. Coming to his senses, he reminded himself of the consequences of delaying it. He addressed the letter and gave it to the front desk to mail out.

The next day, Raj dressed as smartly as he could – with a tie and jacket and from Mr Dewan's directions – and made his way across the street to the dean's office. King's College had a less ancient appearance than that of Caius and looked more like a government building than anything else. This put Raj at ease as he stepped into the office.

'Mr Kohli, what a pleasure to meet you. I am Dean Hanson.' He shook Raj's hand. The dean was a middle-aged man, tall and lanky and dressed in an immaculately tailored suit. His office was lacking in size; however, every inch was covered with some sort of religious paraphernalia. A large wooden cross hung on the yellow wall behind his desk. Along with a picture of the Virgin Mary, his desk was covered in books and various papers. 'I have to admit, we were excited to learn that you were looking to transfer here, at King's. We remember your vast résumé from last year's group of applications. Although Cambridge might be impressed with your recommendations, we are more impressed with your vast knowledge of Christian studies.' Dean Hanson gestured for Raj to sit in the wooden seat across from his desk.

'Yes, I found the Bible lectures quite fascinating at boarding school,' answered Raj as he sat.

'I see, I see. It said in your papers, which India House provided, that you had' – the dean set his glasses on the end of his nose as he read a letter – 'received fourth place in the Biblical Knowledge Competition.' He put down the letter as he looked over his glasses. 'Is that right?'

Raj nodded. 'Yes, and I was the first Indian to do it too.'

'I would assume so.' Dean Hanson removed his glasses and placed them on the desk in front of him. Clasping his hands, he said, 'Being Indian, though, I suppose, you're not Christian? Were you raised Hindu?'

Raj shook his head. 'I'm a Sikh, sir.'

The dean nodded to say he understood as he leaned back in his chair. 'You know, we were founded as a religious institution, Mr Kohli.'

'I am gathering that, sir,' replied Raj as he looked at the cross on the wall.

'However, as time has progressed, we understand that staff and students of all cultures and religious backgrounds should be welcomed to our college. As we see it, learning from one another shall only make us stronger.' The dean continued. 'We at King's College would be absolutely delighted to have a brilliant student such as yourself in attendance.'

'Sir, thank you. I'm so pleased to accept.' Raj smiled and was thankful he didn't have to persuade this university, like he did Cambridge. He knew a bright future lay ahead.

Dean Hanson smiled and raised his chin as he continued, 'Usually, someone as well-versed as you are in the gospels would be well on their way to priesthood or a career as a religious instructor.' He eyed him for a moment. 'Is that your intention, Mr Kohli?' He didn't blink as he awaited Raj's reply.

'No, sir.' Raj was starting to realize why he was being accepted so easily here. 'Sorry to disappoint.'

The dean blinked, his smile disappeared. 'Very well, then.' He searched among the piles of papers for a clean sheet and placed his glasses back on. 'What are your subjects going to be?'

'Chemistry.'

'You have to choose three subjects. So, what are they going to be?'

'I don't know, other than chemistry.' Raj hadn't put much thought into other subjects.

'Okay,' replied the dean, 'let's make them up. First is chemistry, then physics…' He scribbled on the sheet.

'Sir, I apologize, but physics and I don't see eye to eye,' interrupted Raj, at which the dean nodded and continued.

'I doubt that. Let's just try, shall we?' The dean raised his eyebrows.

Raj somehow felt like it was not up for debate, so he politely nodded.

Dean Hanson continued, 'So, we have, chemistry, physics, and then one other…'

Raj stayed quiet, sure that Dean Hanson would pick the last for him.

'Ah, how about mathematics?' It was a rhetorical question, as he didn't wait for a response before jotting it down.

'Yes, sir,' replied Raj and got up from his chair. The dean shook his hand.

'You start Monday. Now, where are you living?'

'India House suggested a place in South Hampstead. The Greencroft Gardens, I believe.'

'A little far, don't you think?'

'I've already tried it, sir, and it's not too bad.'

'In which case, Mr Kohli, I will see you here bright and early Monday morning.' Dean Hanson stood up and held out a hand for Raj to shake. 'It was a pleasure to meet you. Welcome to King's College, young man.'

Raj apprehensively shook his hand with a nagging feeling that he was giving away his dignity to a university once again. 'Thank you for your time, Dean Hanson.'

The dean smiled and led Raj out of his office.

Raj left with a mix of emotions. He was thrilled to be accepted into the university, especially since it was located in the heart of London. He just hoped it wouldn't be a repeat of his former university experience. As he walked the streets, he took a deep breath, and as it was lunchtime, he decided that it was a good opportunity to go celebrate with a pint and a hearty meal. He walked into the first pub he could find – The Ploughshare – and ordered a pint of bitter along with a steak and kidney pie. After finishing his glorious meal, he made his way back to his new abode in northwest London.

# CHAPTER FIVE

## *London, 1939*

It had been more than a year since Norah found herself walking through the gates of St Mary's Hospital on Praed Street in Paddington to begin her new life away from home. She missed her sisters, brothers, father and friends who were back home in Kidlington, but she had longed for an adventure of her own. She had always put others first, and convinced by her father, believed it was now her turn to be made a priority in her life. Norah left her small village of Kidlington to move to the big city of London and continue her career in nursing.

Even though her family, along with Sir Athelstane and Lady Baines, tried to persuade her to attend training at the Royal College of Music, at twenty-five, she thought it silly to up and leave her career as a nurse.

At first, London was rather overwhelming. She wasn't used to a large city with all its hustling and bustling – everyone moved with purpose and haste. It was the opposite of her home village, where there was always time to stop and talk to the passers-by. But to do that here in London would be sheer madness. Even the hospital, at first, seemed to be so impersonal, with its imposing buildings and walls that came right out of a concrete factory, cold and grey. The Radcliffe, Norah's nursing school in Oxford, was the exact opposite, with its endearing staff and charming structure, possibly because it was so close to Norah's home and the warmth of Kidlington spilt over. But as time passed, she began to realize she would need to adapt to her new environment or else be miserable.

'Did you hear the radio programme last night, Norah?' asked Ruth, a fellow shift-mate who had transferred from Oxford to St Mary's around the same time as Norah. As they spent many a shift together, Ruth and Norah had become good friends. Ruth, with a slender face, natural pink in her cheeks, and short, light-brown hair was the perfect picture of young beauty. She reminded Norah of her sister Betty, and she proudly found herself falling into the role of an older sister to her.

'Not last night. Anything worth noting?' Norah began stripping the sheets off an empty bed.

'Norah! I can't believe you didn't listen.' Ruth stopped assisting as she leaned over the bed to stare Norah squarely in the face. 'It was only the address from Prime Minister Churchill himself.'

'Was it now?' Norah continued as she tucked in the corners of the clean sheets under the mattress.

'They're urging people to sign up and volunteer for the war, to do their duty for their country.' Ruth stuffed a pillow into a fresh pillowcase, pulling at its edges. 'You know, Mikey signed up last week at a volunteer station. He's just waiting to see where he ends up. Got me wondering if I should sign up as well.'

'Oh, Ruthie.' Norah gently creased the blanket so just enough of the sheet under it peeked out above. 'Do you really want to go to war?'

'Well, why not?' Ruth roughly fluffed the pillow between her hands, deep in thought.

'I just know the dread my family lived in every day when my father was away fighting in the Great War. My mother, especially, when we received a telegram saying that he was missing in action. It was unbearable.' Norah's eyes glazed over as the memory flooded in.

'I thought your father came home?'

Norah shook away the unwelcome memory as she blinked her eyes, bringing herself back into the present. 'Yes, it gave us quite a scare, until one evening, he just showed up at our door. Oh, how we all screamed with delight at the sight of him on the front step.' She smiled. Even though it was twenty-two years ago, it was as fresh as the day it happened. 'My two brothers are serving in the navy, actually.'

'See! It just feels wrong to sit at home while our efforts are needed abroad.'

'Matron Everton begs to differ. I heard she is proclaiming with all her might that we are very much needed at home. She will be a tough one to persuade otherwise.'

'Well, it's just not fair. Men shouldn't get all the adventure and glory.' Ruth plopped the newly over-puffed pillow at the top of the bed.

Norah patted Ruth on the back as she giggled. 'True. But why don't we see to the adventure we have right here at St Mary's first, shall we?' Norah waved Ruth out the door and turned back to the bed to fix the crooked pillow.

***

Almost a year into the war, and the hospital hadn't seen many casualties. However, in September of 1940 this all changed.

The German Luftwaffe began air raids in London, forcing civilians to find shelter. The closest place for the staff of the hospital was the Paddington underground station, and that was where everyone hurried off to, except those who were on duty. In the beginning, air raids started in the afternoons, dragging long into the night. A few weeks in, and the Germans began to bomb at night. London's night sky was stabbed with fire, while the day was drenched in dense smoke and debris.

Norah's shifts became longer and more frequent. She'd hardly had a day off in over two weeks and was feeling the repercussions of the lack of sleep. Finally, she was granted a day off by the matron and decided to take full advantage of the opportunity to see the world outside the hospital walls.

After picking up an egg-salad sandwich on Praed Street for lunch later, Norah was enjoying her day off at Hyde Park. As she sat on a bench and watched the ducks float on the Serpentine River, she was grateful she wore a scarf around her head and her thickest coat. The wind dragged in a chill that threatened to bring winter early and made her eyes water and the tip of her nose cold. Hoping to soak up the few moments she had to be outside, she forced herself to sit a while longer, while the last duck drifted around the bend. Eager to continue her day out, she persuaded herself that a walk around Kensington Gardens would warm her up. As she stood, she caught the eye of a man sitting on a bench to her right and reading a book. His green eyes flickered.

'Hello.' The man raised his hat and inclined his head slightly.

Norah felt herself blush. 'Hello,' she responded and quickly looked away so as to not give him the wrong impression. As she picked up her bag from the bench, the distant wailing of the air raid sirens sounded. Norah stopped as the sirens picked up volume closer to the park.

'Not now!' Norah found herself shouting at the sky, to which the man raised his eyebrows. 'Sorry.'

'No need to say sorry unless, of course, you are the one instructing the Germans to bomb our city.'

Norah forced a polite smile and began to look around for the nearest refuge.

'This way. The closest underground station from here is Lancaster Gate, we better hurry.' The man waved his hand for her to follow.

They ran and ended up following a huddling crowd into the tunnel. Each person claimed a lot of the cold ground as their own, as they laid their jumpers and coats down and sat or lounged upon them.

Soon, the sirens were drowned out by the boisterous booms and smashing of bombs. Norah watched as the lights zipped in and out and the tiled walls reverberated, releasing puffs of dust and dirt at each explosion.

Londoners were now over-familiar with the air raids – so much so that they came prepared for their captivity underground with playing cards, paper and pencils, and books and newspapers. Norah watched as a young mother tried to distract her little boy from the sound of the blasts by coaxing him to draw something on the paper she had pulled out of her handbag.

He pointed upward. 'Thunder, thunder,' he said and looked to his mother for approval.

The man from the park camped out across from Norah and didn't seem bothered by the noise from above. He was focused on the pages of the book he was reading. Norah squinted to see what book could possibly be so enthralling: *The Poetical Works of John Keats.*

He must either be bored or hoping to be put to sleep with a book like that, Norah thought to herself and laughed.

'Have you read Keats before?' the man asked when he saw Norah's interest in the title.

'Oh no, I haven't.' Norah pulled off her scarf, unveiling her hair. 'I'm afraid to say I haven't the slightest idea who he is.'

'Hmm, well would you like to?' he inquired.

'I'm not sure I would be able to understand it even if I were to read it,' Norah said. After completing her studies at nursing school, she had vowed to give herself a much-needed break from studying or reading any educational material. She realized she hadn't read a book in quite some time.

'It's not as hard as it seems,' he continued in his persuasion as he held the book out towards her.

Norah took notice of his light green eyes again; their twinkle complimented his shiny blonde hair and pleasant smile. He was well dressed, and his distinguished look gave Norah the impression that he was possibly in his early forties.

She nodded and took the book. 'Very well then, let's take a look, shall we.' She leafed through the pages until a poem titled 'Ode on a Grecian Urn' caught her eye.

'Ah, see that? *That* is a brilliant poem. My favourite by him, actually.' He excitedly creased the page's edge.

Norah took a moment to read the page. She started to giggle at her own expense – she couldn't understand what the poem was saying, even in the first few lines. 'I was quite right. I don't understand a thing!' she said as she closed the book and held it back out to him.

'It comes with time.' He smiled.

'How much time did it take you?'

'Unfortunately, I was born with the love of poetry. So much so that I took a profession that reflected my love.'

Norah's eyes widened. 'You're a poet?'

'Oh God, no! At least not of the same calibre as John Keats.' He knocked the cover of the book with his knuckles. 'I teach, actually. I'm a professor at the Royal College of Art.'

Norah's eyes lowered.

'I'm sorry, did I say something wrong? Should I have said Oxford instead?' the man asked, noticing the sudden change in her behaviour.

'No, I'm sorry.' Norah shifted her sitting position and fixed her dress. 'I was just reminded of a future I passed up on.'

'As a poet?'

Norah chuckled. 'Possibly.' She bit her lip as she continued, 'I was accepted at the Royal College of Music but decided not to go.'

'The tuba, no doubt?' he smirked.

She smiled. 'The piano.' She brushed away a strand of hair that had fallen on to her face.

'You must have been a brilliant player to be accepted there,' he proposed.

'I still am!' Norah teased. 'I was going to be a concert pianist. Though, I must admit, I haven't played in quite some time.'

'Hmm…' He sat back, possibly reminiscing on a future he had skipped out on as well. 'May I ask why you decided not to go?'

Norah scrunched up her nose. 'Oh, life got in the way. It has a funny way of doing that, you know.'

'I do know.' His thoughts seemed stuck on a memory. 'But all things happen for a reason.' He nodded to Norah.

'I suppose, or at least it's pleasant to think so,' she said as she watched the walls quake.

'I'm Norman, by the way.' He held out his hand. 'Norman Ashcroft.'

She slid her hand into his to shake. 'I'm Norah. Norah Eggleton.'

'Well, Norah, if it would be all right, I'd love to have you join me for a cup of tea sometime. We can work on that love for poetry,' he said, his hand still clasping hers.

'I'd like that very much.' Norah's eyes sparkled at the thought of afternoon tea with him.

As the bombing continued into the night, Norman and Norah found themselves talking the hours away. She told him of her home in Kidlington, and he of his in Burnsall. They talked about their family back home and how they missed them. They also discussed what brought them to London: for him, an opportunity to become a professor, and for her, her nursing career. And as the air raid ended, they scheduled a time to meet in a few days at the café in Paddington.

It was dark when Norah and Norman made their way out of the underground station with the rest of the refugees. They said goodbye and went their separate ways. Norah felt guilty as she made her trek back to the hospital, carefully stepping over debris from bombed brick buildings. Regardless, her smile couldn't be persuaded to leave.

***

'What's his name?' Ruth whispered as a wicked expression overtook her face.

Norah carried on down the hospital ward to check on each patient. 'What are you talking about?'

Ruth scampered next to her, trying to keep up. 'You've had a big, fat, jolly grin plastered on your face for a few days now. And I know that grin. That's the grin I had when I first met Mikey.'

Norah set a glass of water and a sleeping pill on a tray, readying it for a woman who had arrived two days ago with a bad burn on her face, another victim of the air raids.

'So, go on and tell me.' Ruth stood in front of Norah, her hands on her hips.

She fought her smile, but try as she might, it had a mind of its own and it bubbled up to the surface. 'Oh, all right then,' Norah whispered as she leaned closer to Ruth, making sure no one else could hear. 'I met a gentleman in the underground station—'

'How sad is that? Picking your mate now depends on who you meet during an air raid!'

'Shh!' Norah looked around, hoping no one was listening in. 'He's a professor—'

'A professor!'

'Shh! Ruthie, my goodness. You really don't understand what it means to be quiet, do you?' Norah smiled politely as a doctor walked by, eyeing them.

Ruth cupped her mouth. 'I'm sorry, I'm sorry.' She raised her hand to her heart. 'Please continue telling me about the professor. I promise I will be quiet now.'

Norah took a deep breath as she scanned the ward once more before she leaned in again. 'It's not what you think. He's an older man...'

Ruth's eyes got wide, and Norah quickly put her hand over her mouth to stop her from what would have been an exclamation of some sort.

'I've been meeting him at a nearby café every so often. He teaches me about poetry and we just talk. We're just friends, and that's all.'

Ruth's eyebrows drew together.

'Seriously. We simply enjoy each other's company.' Upon seeing Ruth roll her eyes, Norah added, 'I swear. Nothing more.' Norah slowly removed her hand from over Ruth's mouth.

'And he feels this way as well?' Ruth asked.

'Yes.'

'He's said this to you?'

'Well' – Norah smoothed her uniform – 'not exactly, but I don't imagine he feels the opposite.'

'And why wouldn't he?' Ruth pursed her lips. 'You're an attractive, available woman. Men only care about those things. You're a ripe candidate.'

There was silence for a moment while Norah tended to each patient. Ruth picked up the chart that hung at the end of the bed. 'That's how it starts, you know' – she raised her eyebrows – 'simply enjoying each other's company.'

Norah, realizing the conversation wasn't going in her favour, just shook her head and sighed.

***

Norah looked forward to the times she would meet Norman – invariably at the Paddington Station tea shop. Each time he met Norah, he brought along a different poetry book from which he would read a poem and then explain its meaning. Norah was in awe of his knowledge.

'I never thought of poetry before in the same way I think of it today,' Norah said as Norman finished reciting a poem and lifted his cup of lukewarm tea to his lips. 'I can't thank you enough, Norman. You have opened my eyes to a whole new world.'

Norman beamed and shrugged as he took another sip of tea. 'Thank you. I have always loved poetry. Even as a child I found it to be expressive, and I was habitually entranced trying to get into the mind of the poet. And, Norah, I really enjoy reading and explaining poetry to you.'

Norah's cheeks turned pink as she tried to hide her smile in her teacup. It had been a year and a half since Norah's last relationship, and she knew she was due one, but the thought of commitment made her a bit nervous. She finally had a life of her own after moving away from home; she wanted to soak up every last bit before having to share it with someone again.

'Has Ruth given any more thought to signing up for the war?' Norman asked as he set his teacup down.

Norah welcomed the distraction from her thoughts. 'Yes, she informed me last week that she has decided to sign up.'

'Hmm.' Norman bit the inside of his cheek, deep in thought. 'You don't suppose you'll join, do you?'

Norah laughed. 'I'm not sure, actually. Haven't given it much thought. Even though it would be fun to live a little and see the world.'

'It's not fun, Norah. Not fun at all.' Norman's face grew stern, and Norah knew she must have said something wrong.

'I … I didn't mean that war is fun…'

Norman sat back in his chair as he looked out the window. 'I haven't told you this before, and I don't quite like remembering it. I try most of the time to forget I ever did, but I've seen war before, first-hand.' He locked eyes with Norah. 'I was an eighteen-year-old boy fighting in the Great War. The ugliness and barbarity of human nature…' His voice trailed off and his eyes glazed over. 'At first, when I had volunteered to fight, I was excited about going. Oh, how I was going to see the world! Not just excited, but in fact, I looked forward to the day I would be deployed. As a poet, I even romanticized death, although I had never, in actuality, witnessed it. That was until the first day, when I took my place together with my regiment in one of the hundreds of trenches in a field filled with a painful mixture of ankle-deep mud and human blood. And the stench … the ever-present stench of death.' His eyes searched the memory. 'It was there that I realized I no longer lived in a world that I had fantasized for myself, but in fact in a world that was real and deadly. At the end of the first day of fighting, when all the guns had fallen silent, I sat down in that ankle-deep mud and…' His voice trailed off again. He was silent for a moment. 'I stayed there until my commanding officer found me curled up in the foetal position, simply afraid to move.'

Norah wasn't sure of how to respond. Instead, she watched the pain of the memory flicker across his face.

'Don't go.' His eyes locked with Norah's once again.

'Don't go where?' she asked, even though she understood what Norman meant.

'Don't go to war, Norah. It's ugly and will scar you for life.'

'Why do you think I have any intention of joining up?'

'Because in the short period we have known each other, I have learned you are a strong and caring young woman who, I would bet, would have a hard time not devoting her skills and life for the betterment of others. Even when it would possibly mean making the ultimate sacrifice.'

Thoughts of her father telling her to stop putting others before her lit up in her mind. It felt all too familiar.

'Norman,' began Norah, 'I am honoured you would say, or care so much to say, such kind words, but right now I have no intention of going anywhere. I can assure you my services are needed badly here at St Mary's.'

Norman smiled sadly. 'I do hope you're right.'

Norah reciprocated his smile, and he opened the poetry book once again and leafed aimlessly through the pages, looking for an appropriate poem to recite to an eager Norah, who sat across the table from him.

# CHAPTER SIX

## *London, 1939*

Before Raj knew it, it was the middle of the term, and even though he was doing very well at King's, it was lonely back at his flat. At the end of a long day, all he could do was hit the books once again. He would eat out only now and then, because to do so more often would have been too expensive. But how he longed for a home-cooked meal! If he ever had an extra pound or two to spare, left over from what his father sent for tuition, he would enjoy some fish and chips from the corner shop, which would mean both a delicious meal and a look at the day-old newspaper the haddock was wrapped in. That way, he'd be able to stay almost up to date with current affairs without having to pay for the news. Raj chomped down on another steaming hot bite of fish as he craned his neck to read a piece that wrapped the bottom. His chewing slowed down as he ingested every word that detailed the latest on the Nazis.

It was now the winter of 1939, and the war had begun. The entire population was glued to their televisions and radios every free hour. Patriotic music was blasted from what seemed to be every rooftop. The constant buzz of the possible draft filled the conversations of all young men, including Raj. He wasn't sure whether he would be subjected to the draft, being an Indian, but he pledged to himself that, if the situation called for it, he would volunteer. Up to that point, the lines to sign up at local enlistment centres were extremely long, and those who were in university appeared to be given a pass.

In comparison to Cambridge, Raj much preferred his time at King's. His professors and lectures were interesting, and he even came to like the playful rivalry he had with his lab partner, Alan Gilchrist. They would often compete for first place in class and would tease the other when they overtook them in placement.

Raj was looking forward to the day's lecture, as they were to receive their marks from their most recent exam. He was certain Alan would beat him on this one.

***

'He died?' Raj looked up at his professor and then at the empty stool to the left of him.

'Yesterday. He took his own life.'

Again, Raj looked up at his professor and then at the empty stool. He didn't know what to think, let alone say. Words failed him. His brain went on strike. He was numb. He swallowed hard, blinked faster than normal and turned his attention to the other students in the laboratory. All twenty of them had the same look on their faces as Raj did. Surreal. It couldn't possibly be true. There must be some sort of mistake, Raj thought. Nobody commits suicide – that only happens in stories, not in real life. There was silence in the laboratory.

Raj looked at the professor. 'Died?' he asked, not wanting to believe what he or the others had heard twice.

The professor didn't answer.

Raj continued, 'How?'

'Jumped off a bridge,' he replied as if he, too, was in shock. Maybe he was. Maybe he too had thought people committed suicide only in books.

'Which bridge?' asked another of the students.

'Does it matter?' replied the professor, thinking they had spent far too much time on the subject.

'Why?' Raj further inquired.

'There were problems at home, I believe, Mr Kohli,' replied the professor.

Raj was hoping to feel relief after hearing that information, but he didn't.

'All right, gentlemen.' The professor was ready to move on.

Raj didn't want to, but felt he had to – he promised himself that later he would find out more. At the end of the lab period, a couple of the students, who knew that Raj had been closer to Alan than they, suggested they go out to the closest pub and drink to his memory. Raj wanted to decline as he didn't think that drinking a few pints of beer was appropriate, however, he went along anyway.

The pub, The George, was crowded – as expected on a late Friday afternoon. The usual locals were there, crowding around the ancient bar, which was marked with beer stains and the odd burn here and there from a cigarette butt. No matter how often it was wiped down or polished, the marks remained. The building had stood on that ground for the last 180 years and had always been a pub. The name changed as the owners changed, but the atmosphere never did. It couldn't change, it was ingrained in the velvet curtains and the near-threadbare carpet.

Raj's small group – not everyone had enough saved to spend at the pub, so they stayed back – pushed their way as politely as possible through the crowd. When the first student reached the hallowed bar, he ordered for everyone. Money changed hands and then the student body turned around in perfect formation, spilling the least amount of beer possible. They made a beeline for a table at the far end of the room, furthest from the roaring fire, around which some person lacking any decorating skills whatsoever had arranged a few mismatched chairs in a haphazard manner. The student body didn't care – they were there that night to drown their sorrows, both real and imagined, and drink a few beers in honour of their dear departed fellow student. They pondered any changes to their lives in the light of the ever-expanding war.

The first few minutes passed in silence, after a toast was given in honour of Alan by the one person who held the esteemed position of being at the bottom of the class.

'It never ceases to amaze me, Mr Stubbs, why you keep insisting on giving your pea-sized brain a workout for which it is so ill-equipped,' one of their professors would say each and every time he returned the offending student's test, which made Raj wince. Raj believed there was no need to show such contempt, especially as a professor.

'Why don't you give the next toast, Raj?' said another member of the group. 'You knew him better than any one of us.'

Before Raj could answer, another student piped up. 'Are any of you thinking of joining up?'

'Joining what?' asked Stubbs, showing genuine ignorance.

'The bloody army, you idiot,' replied Timothy with a laugh.

Raj glared at Timothy, promising to say something if he continued in that vein.

'Oh, *that* joining up,' replied Stubbs. 'No, why would I want to do that?'

'Well, I'm really very relieved to hear that, because I would pity anyone you shared a trench with.' The others laughed.

'Is that really necessary?' Raj asked Timothy pointedly.

'Is what?' Timothy responded, confused.

'Here we are drinking to honour a fellow student, while you put down another. It would do you some good to show respect to all, not just the ones you choose,' Raj remarked as his heart thumped and his hand curled into a fist.

Timothy's gaze fell to his beer as he replied with only silence. The rest of the group followed suit.

The silence was finally interrupted. 'What about the toast, old chap? It's your turn,' said the same person as before.

The others had moved on and were waiting for the next toast as a justification to continue their merriment. Raj felt pressured and knew he had to say something.

He raised his glass, and in a voice that the others strained to hear said, 'Alan was a friend of mine. Not a real friend of mine...'

'I'll drink to that!' interrupted a nondescript member of the student body.

A series of loud shushes made him apologize, and Raj continued, 'I met Alan when I first came to King's, and I remember well that he saw me looking lost in a hallway. I was trying to find the lecture hall and he came over and took me there. He was a very gentle soul, and he will be missed.'

Raj raised his glass, but the rest lowered theirs in sadness, probably because they felt they had been extremely flippant in their approach to Alan's death. They finished their beers in silence, and with heavy hearts left the pub, making their way back to their rooms.

Raj, though, remained behind and sat down on one of the empty chairs and squeezed his eyes to prevent a tear from rolling down his face. He raised his glass to his face to help hide his sadness from any witnesses. After taking a long swig, he put the glass down on the table and looked around the room, as if he were looking for something, though he knew not what. His eyes fell on a pretty woman, maybe in her late twenties or early thirties, sitting alone at the end of the bar closest to him.

She looked over and smiled from across the room. The thought crossed his mind about how nice it would be to talk to someone who maybe didn't know what the periodic table was. As he was contemplating how he would meet the challenge, he nearly choked on his beer when he saw her walking over to him.

'Would you like another pint, love? You look like you could do with one,' she asked in a slight cockney accent.

Raj instinctively jumped up and replied in a very garbled voice, which made the woman smile even wider. He was stunned. No woman had ever asked him that before, and he subsequently panicked. She sensed his nervousness and turned to the publican and ordered two pints of bitter.

Raj, flabbergasted, stammered, 'Th—thank you.'

'Oh, my pleasure, really,' she replied as they sat down at the table, their beers in front of them.

At first, there was an uncomfortable silence. Raj was still too afraid to start a conversation, but luckily, she wasn't.

'Are you a university student?' she asked, leaning back in her wooden chair.

'I am, yes,' he replied. 'I'm sorry, I—I don't know your name.' Raj could feel his hand shaking and he hesitated to pick up his glass in case it was obvious to her.

'Esther,' she replied. 'And yours?'

Esther had a lovely smile, he thought. 'Raj,' he said, his voice cracking with nervousness.

'And where are you from. I'm assuming not from around here?'

'India.' Raj's mouth went dry.

'Raj, it's okay, you can relax. I'm not going to bite you,' she said with a slight laugh, eliciting one from him as well.

Esther was very well dressed. Much better dressed than most of the women in the pub.

Raj mustered up all his strength. 'Are you a university student as well?' he asked.

'Oh, good heavens, no,' she replied. 'I never went to university. Couldn't afford it. My parents aren't that well off. When I turned seventeen, I went to work at Selfridges, and I've been there ever since.'

Raj felt a little disappointed by her answer. He had imagined that she came from an educated background.

'What do you do there?'

'I manage a department,' Esther replied.

In the two years Raj had been in England, he had never been out on a date with a woman, or even for that matter, been out with a group in which there were women – besides the time with Colin. Even then, Colin did all the talking. He so wished Colin could be there to speak for him. Naturally, Raj wasn't sure of himself – and it showed.

'Have you been to this pub before?' he asked, now getting a little braver.

'Oh no,' she replied, and Raj was a little taken aback. He wasn't sure if he had said the right thing, or if he had offended her. He wanted to immediately apologize, but Esther continued.

'I don't live around here. I actually live in Middlesex. I'm here because I was supposed to meet a friend for a drink after work. But he never showed up.'

His loss, Raj thought.

'What happened to your friends?'

'I believe they decided the night was over,' replied Raj with a faint smile.

'And you didn't, I see.'

Raj nodded. 'We came here to drink ourselves silly because a friend of ours committed suicide.'

'Oh, my goodness,' replied Esther. 'I'm so sorry to hear that.'

Esther's face grew solemn, and it was obvious to Raj that she was taking pity on him. 'What are you doing for dinner?'

'Nothing,' Raj replied and then added, 'probably just go back to my flat after getting some fish and chips.'

'In that case, why don't you and I go and get something to eat?'

Raj bit his lip; there was no way he could afford to take anyone out on his miserable budget. 'I really need to get back soon, I have a chemistry exam next week, and I'm not at all ready for it.'

Esther smiled even though he was sure he had disappointed her with his response. He believed she knew he wasn't being quite truthful, but she let it slide.

'So, you're reading chemistry, are you?'

Raj felt a little more at ease. He nodded.

'My, you must be a very bright chap! Chemistry wasn't one of my strong subjects in school.' She took a sip of her pint. 'Well, I will leave you be.'

Raj stood as Esther got up from the table, leaving behind a half-finished drink, and shook Raj's hand.

'I hope we bump into each other again one day.' She flashed a smile once more, and Raj could feel his palms getting sweaty.

After she left, he sat down again feeling completely deflated, and leaned back in his chair. By this time, however, the pub had filled with more people and he decided to leave. When he walked out into the cool air, he was half expecting Esther to be standing there waiting for him and was disappointed she wasn't.

'Pretty arrogant of me to think that,' he mumbled to himself.

***

For the next few weeks, Raj had difficulty concentrating on his studies. His thoughts kept replaying the night he met Esther. In fact, on several occasions, he went back to the same pub hoping she would be there, only to sit alone and jump every time the door opened.

He was now almost certain that he had offended her that evening, after declining dinner with her. There was only one course of action: go to Selfridges and apologize to her, even though he knew that wasn't the real reason.

On a day when his lectures finished early, Raj caught a bus that dropped him off on Oxford Street, not far from Selfridges. Once there, he had to gather up enough courage to walk in and talk to her. Then it dawned on him. Raj didn't know her last name, and he certainly didn't know the department she worked in. He stood outside planning his next move. He looked up at all the floors and knew he had a challenge before him. He liked challenges. So, he let out a deep breath and opened the front doors.

As soon as he walked in, he was greeted by a pack of women walking around perusing racks of clothing.

Oh dear, he thought to himself, what have I got myself into?

Then he had an idea. He walked up to the customer service desk and waited his turn to speak to a well-dressed elderly lady behind a counter.

'Excuse me, madam,' he asked very politely, which made the lady smile. 'I'm looking for an employee by the name of Esther?'

The elderly lady smiled. 'Love, we have many Esthers here. Do you happen to know her last name?'

Raj sheepishly shook his head.

'How about a department?'

Raj again shook his head. 'I'm sorry, I'm taking up far too much of your time.' He turned to leave.

'No, love, you're not. I'll tell you what. This seems to be very important to you. How about I give you the departments the Esthers we have work in. It's kind of tedious, because you'll have to go to each place.'

'Oh!' blurted out Raj, remembering something. 'She manages a department.'

'Now why didn't you say that in the first place? That must be Esther Hoey. She manages the lingerie department. It's on the third floor.'

The blood drained from Raj's face. He had never walked into a women's clothing department in his life, let alone the lingerie department. He didn't know what to do. He took a deep breath, thanked the lady, and walked up the wooden escalator to the third floor.

He looked at the information board and followed the signs to the lingerie department. And then he found himself standing at the entrance. His heart was racing. His palms were sweaty. He hurriedly wiped away the sweat that ran down the sides of his cheeks and walked gingerly into the department. Before he could change his mind and run out, a very pretty woman stopped him in his tracks.

'Can I help you, sir?'

'Erm, no, thank you,' replied Raj instinctively. 'No, I think I'm in the wrong department.'

'Well, maybe I can help you. What department are you looking for?'

'I don't know the name of it,' replied Raj in a high-pitched voice, 'but I know it's not this one.'

The young woman's giggle echoed in his mind, which confirmed his hurried decision to leave.

'Raj?' came a woman's voice.

Raj swallowed and turned around, coming face to face with Esther Hoey. He smiled and his face flushed. Sweat began to pour down his face. His hands began to shake, and soon his entire body trembled with fear. Esther, however, looked very pleased to see him.

'Come to buy some lingerie, have you?' She smiled from the corner of her mouth.

Raj immediately felt like a fool. 'I'm really sorry. I've never been to a lingerie department in my entire life.'

Esther interrupted him with a whisper. 'Would you like to look around? Maybe you can get an idea of what to buy me some day.'

Raj's mouth went dry and his mind failed to formulate a response.

'I'm teasing you, Raj. Just having a bit of fun.' She playfully hit his arm.

'I hope it was okay for me to come here?' Raj sighed, glad his mind was working again.

'Of course,' she replied and looked around the department. 'I wondered if I would ever see you again. Come, let's get a cup of tea in the canteen.'

Esther led him out of her department and into the store café. They enjoyed many cups of tea and talked for hours. And thus began Raj's first romantic relationship.

***

Raj and Esther saw a fair amount of each other, mostly on Sundays though, because he couldn't afford to slip in his studies. A few months into their relationship, Esther would share the mattress on the floor in Raj's flat when she had a day off, or they would stay at her home on Judd Road in St Pancras. Her home was much nicer than his bare-bones flat with no heat, private bathroom or kitchen. Esther liked to cook, and Raj loved having a home-cooked meal. They were sitting down for one of those meals on a Sunday evening when Esther brought up a conversation that nearly had Raj choke on his peas.

'You know, my parents have asked when we're planning on getting married.'

Raj took a sip of his drink to keep from coughing, 'Really? They have?'

Esther dabbed the corners of her mouth with her napkin. 'Yes, silly. We've been together now for five months. It's only appropriate to assume.'

Raj had never dated anyone before, let alone someone outside his culture. This was all new to him. 'I haven't even met your parents.'

Esther looked away, drew her eyebrows together, and pushed her peas into a pile with her fork. 'You haven't, have you?'

'No. Every time we're supposed to meet them, you always say they called to cancel.'

Esther gave a tight-lipped smile. 'Yes, they are always so busy.'

Raj wondered if she was telling the truth.

'Have you thought of it?' Esther put down her fork.

'Thought of what, Esther?' Raj continued to eat the roast chicken on his plate.

'Marriage, Raj.'

Raj had almost forgotten. He cleared his throat. 'Not really.'

Esther frowned. 'Really? Nothing? Not at all?'

Raj set down his fork. This was going to be a conversation whether he wanted it to be or not. 'I'm a second-year university student with no job. Forget about someone else, I barely have the wages to support myself. As much as I do love you, I don't think it's responsible to be married. Not yet, at least.'

Esther's eyebrows perked. Obviously, some part of what he had just said caught her attention. 'Yet? So, you mean there is a possibility? You do want to marry me, Raj?'

Raj weighed his thoughts as to how to respond. 'One day, yes. When I have saved up enough.'

'I'd like to marry you too, Raj.' Esther leaned over to kiss him. As Esther picked up her fork, her mood picked up as well. 'I've always thought Kensington Gardens would make for a wonderful place for a wedding.'

***

As their relationship intensified, so did the war.

The daily bombings carried out by the Luftwaffe had most of London scurrying to the underground stations for shelter. When the all-clear was sounded, little by little the inhabitants of the city reappeared to assess the damage to their homes and the many historical sites around them.

On a warm June day, when the crowds were exiting the underground stations once again, amid the sobs and cries from those who saw what was left of their neighbourhoods, Raj, who was now on summer vacation, passed by a recruitment centre. He hesitated for a moment pondering his next move, and decided the time wasn't right to join the British army. He had his reasons. He had to finish university for one.

'Aren't you going to join the queue?' He heard a familiar voice and felt a tug at his sleeve.

He stopped next to a grinning Roger Stubbs. 'I didn't think you were going to join the army, Stubbs.'

'Changed my mind. Want to help my country. You should too, Raj.' Stubbs beamed.

Raj examined the line that stretched down the street and around the corner. There must have been a hundred or so behind Stubbs.

'I wanted to join as soon I heard Timothy and William signed up.'

'They did?' Raj wondered why they didn't tell him.

'Didn't you know, mate?'

'No, no I didn't. When did they do that?'

'Last month. Right after lectures were over. I found out by accident when I met with Professor Langley, who wondered if he would have enough boys to teach next term. It seems as though you and I are the only ones who haven't signed up yet.'

Raj's mouth fell open. He shuddered to think if he had showed up for classes in September only to find out he was the only one. His gaze turned to the line that kept advancing at a slow pace. Stubbs was about fifteenth in line.

'It doesn't hurt that the pay is good too.' Stubbs winked.

Raj's last conversation with Esther regarding marriage rang in his mind. 'How much pay?'

'Starting at two shillings a day, but obviously increases as you go up rank. And that doesn't include all the provided meals!'

It wasn't the way Raj had hoped to receive a wage, but maybe it would be enough to make Esther's wedding plans a reality faster than expected.

'Keep my place in line, Stubbs. I'll be right back,' Raj declared.

Stubbs looked bewildered as he watched Raj run to a nearby telephone box.

'Esther?' said Raj into the receiver, covering his left ear to better hear her. 'Esther, I'm going to join the army.'

There was a scream from the other end. 'Why would you want to do that?'

'Don't worry, Esther. Soldiers receive a wage, and with it I'll be able to save enough for us to be married.'

There was silence on the other end, as Esther contemplated this.

'You'll come back to me?' she asked.

'As soon as I can.'

'You promise?'

'I promise, Esther,' he insisted.

'Okay…' Esther's voice cracked. 'I guess. I'll be waiting for you. I love you, Raj.'

'I love you too.' Raj placed the receiver back in the cradle and ran out of the telephone box, nearly knocking over an elderly man in the process.

'Here I am,' Raj gushed when he met up with Stubbs at his place in the queue.

In very short order, Raj found himself inside the building, where he was asked to enter a room. Once in there, he came face to face with a stern-looking elderly nurse who had probably come out of retirement to help with the war effort. She looked disdainfully at Raj.

'Strip,' she said, watching him carefully.

'Now?' asked a very bashful Raj.

'Now,' she demanded. 'That's if you want to go ahead with joining the army.'

Raj did as he was asked, and once he was standing there naked with just the nurse in the room, he began to regret his decision. She carefully looked him over and noticed that the toes on both his feet were curled inwards.

'Your toes! They're like a monkey's,' she said, giggling to herself, apparently pleased with her sense of humour.

Raj swallowed. His toes were curled due to his parents' insistence over the years that his current shoes were big enough for him and that he didn't need a new pair. Over time, in order for him to be able to fit into his shoes, his toes had adapted.

'He's Indian, sir,' the nurse piped up – obviously something she deemed important enough to share with the doctor as soon as he entered to begin his examination.

The doctor looked up and eyed Raj, 'Indian?'

Raj silently nodded.

The doctor reciprocated Raj's nod and continued with the examination.

The nurse suddenly looked offended. She turned to the doctor and asked, as if Raj wasn't in the room, 'Are they allowed to join the British army?'

Raj's breathing slowed and his heart thumped loudly.

The doctor shrugged. 'Not for us to figure out. We just examine their health. Let the army officials see to it.'

The nurse opened her mouth, about to contest the doctor's line of thinking. However, the doctor's composure dissuaded her. He tilted his head and peered over his spectacles towards the floor.

'Your toes…'

But before he could finish, Raj replied, 'Yes, we're fascinating creatures. They're like that so we can hold on to branches better.' He glanced over at the nurse, who narrowed her eyes at him.

The doctor, though, burst out in laughter. 'Go on, sir,' he replied. 'You've passed. Good luck and thanks for signing up.'

The ancient nurse pursed her lips at him, and Raj grinned. He grabbed his clothes and dressed quickly as the nurse reluctantly directed him to the next room.

# CHAPTER SEVEN

## *London, 1941*

Soon, the German bombers had to contend with the Royal Air Force, and sometimes, instead of hurrying to safety, some Londoners would stand outside under the clear blue skies and watch Spitfires dart around the sky, attacking bombers. A loud cheer would go up when one of the German enemy aircraft burst into flames. It became quite a sightseeing sport until the bombing stopped in 1941, when the Battle of Britain had been won by the Royal Air Force. London and other cities such as Coventry began to dig out from under all the rubble.

The last two years had been filled with more of the same: Norah and Norman continued to meet for tea and ventured out for supper once in a while. On occasion, Norman would surprise her outside the hospital after a shift. Norah always loved those times and welcomed them as an escape from what she had to witness while at work. And although they spent numerous hours together, they remained simply friends. Norah would sometimes wonder why it hadn't advanced beyond that, only to convince herself that – contrary to how it looked in her mind – he must not think of her in a romantic manner, and even though she was tempted at times, it wouldn't be polite for her to instigate.

The number of casualties from the bombings grew, as did the number of surgeries each day. At each patient's tearful eye and bandaged wound, Norah was finding it harder to stay hopeful and harder to supress the internal debate of whether or not to sign up for the war.

Norah ventured around Central London to witness the vast amount of damage done to buildings that had been built centuries ago. She would walk over Westminster Bridge towards Waterloo Station and survey the devastation from the South Bank. The indiscriminate bombing of civilians. Norah's heart ached and it would hurt every time a new bombing victim would enter the ward. Burned flesh, missing limbs. Men, women, children.

One afternoon, when Norah received a letter from her brother John – a sailor – detailing his duty in the war and the fighting he had been a part of, she felt an overwhelming sense of purpose and dedication to serve. It became obvious to Norah that, as much as she loved London and wanted to stay at St Mary's, and how much she respected Norman, her skills could be of better use closer to the front.

After her shift, she and Ruth went down to the local recruiting station arm in arm and volunteered.

*The posting came through. I was summoned to the matron's office where she sat sternly behind her desk as always, dressed in her nursing uniform that was so well starched it crackled as she walked, so as to try and distinguish herself from the rest of us mere mortals …* Norah began to write in a letter to her sister, Muriel.

'Sister Eggleton,' she said in her all-too-familiar officious voice.

'Yes, matron,' Norah answered quietly as the matron held up a piece of paper which she then thrust towards her in one swift move. 'Here are your orders,' she added, motioning with the paper as if to say, 'Take it.'

Norah eventually leaned forward to accept it with her right hand.

'Orders, matron?' Norah asked, even though she knew what they were.

'Yes, Sister Eggleton. You applied for a commission in Queen Alexandra's Imperial Military Nursing Service, and the paper you have in your hand is to say that you have been accepted and are to report to Glasgow next month.'

'Next month!' Norah answered, somewhat surprised. It didn't give her enough time to do all the things she needed to do before she left. Norah wanted to go home to Kidlington and say goodbye to her family. She would be pressed for time, but she'd make sure to do it. And while all these thoughts were whirling around in her mind, she realized that something the matron had said didn't make sense. 'Glasgow?' she said out loud, 'why am I going to Glasgow?'

The matron smiled and motioned to Norah to read the paper, which she was about to do in her presence when the matron said, 'Sister, you can go now.' As always, she finished with a dismissive wave of her hand.

Norah left the room. The dismissive waves were comforting, the fake smile was not. Once Norah had closed the door behind her, she opened the paper and read it slowly. When she was done, Norah couldn't help but let out a cry of joy, to the horror of the matron, who poked her head around the door to her office to see what the commotion was. Norah realized she was being posted to a hospital ship. She was to report to Glasgow in mid-June, when the ship's refitting had been completed. She was elated that she would be joining her brothers Peter and John on the high seas.

'Ooh, wouldn't it be just lovely to bump into them at some port? Rule Britannia, and all that,' Norah said out loud, knowing that the matron was within hearing distance.

Norah folded the paper into a neat and tight square, put it in her pocket and tapped it for reassurance.

Soon, her excitement dripped away as she realized not all who would hear her news would be as happy as she was. She knew that, if she was going to tell Norman, their afternoon tea would be the time to do it.

Her shift ended and she began her journey to the café. As soon as she opened the door and spotted Norman sitting at their usual table, her heart sank. She knew telling him the news wouldn't be easy.

'Well, I knew it was only a matter of time,' he replied as he turned to look out the window.

'I'm sorry, Norman.' Norah fiddled with her hands in her lap. 'It's just that, having been in the surgical ward here at St Mary's, I have seen … rightly or wrongly, only time will tell, I feel that I owe it to my country to offer my skills and knowledge. Seems a little idealistic, I agree, but it would make me feel better. I'm needed at some base hospital somewhere, wherever the hospital ship takes us.' She took in a deep breath and gauged Norman's reaction. There wasn't any.

After a few moments of uncomfortable silence, it was Norman's turn to say something. 'I'm not upset, Norah. I just want you to be safe and carefree, without a mind that plagues you with awful memories.' He reached into his bag, pulled out the book of John Keats' poems and handed it to her. 'Here, this is yours now.'

'Oh, Norman, I couldn't possible take this from you. It's your favourite.'

He held up a hand. 'I insist. Maybe when you're off in a faraway land, you'll find it in your cabin trunk and remember me.'

Norah smiled softly as she rubbed her fingers over its worn cover. 'Thank you, Norman. I will certainly treasure this and return it to you when we next see each other.'

Norman forced a smile as he lifted his teacup in a toast. 'May war be good to you, Norah.'

With that, he ordered two more teas and the remainder of their time together was no different from the numerous other times they had met. Norman read Norah a poem, and they discussed the meaning of it. Soon, it was time for Norah to leave.

'Well, I better go and pack.'

'Right, the high seas are waiting for you, after all.'

Norah stood and Norman followed suit. They briefly hugged, and Norman gave her a kiss on her cheek. 'I do hope I'll get to see you again one day.' His green eyes glistened, and Norah wondered if they were filling with tears.

'You'll be the first to know when I'm back,' Norah reassured him as she returned his kiss on the cheek.

Norman stood and watched her walk out of the tea shop. Curious, Norah turned to take one last look at him. She saw him sit again, his head in his hands.

***

Norah returned to her room at the hospital to prepare and pack for a quick journey to Kidlington – to say goodbye to her family before embarking on her new future in Glasgow. Her room wasn't a big one, but it had been her home for about two years, and she had grown fond of it. There was a large window that looked out over Praed Street that Norah often peered through to people-watch. She had brightened up the white walls with some reproduction artwork by painters like Franz Hals. The bed wasn't overly comfortable, and sometimes when she plonked herself down on it, the frame would rock, and she was sure that one day the springs would give out and she would find herself on the floor. But luckily, that never happened.

'Norah!' A series of short rapid knocks came upon her door.

'Yes.' Norah opened it to see an emphatic Ruth holding a letter.

'Is it true? Are you being posted to a hospital ship in Glasgow?' Ruth asked as she entered Norah's room.

Norah shut the door. 'Yes. I received my letter from the matron today.' Norah eyed the letter Ruth was holding. 'Is that your posting?'

Ruth excitedly nodded as she waved the letter above her head. 'Guess who else is being posted to a hospital ship in Glasgow!'

Norah gasped and covered her mouth. 'Really?'

Ruth nodded again. Her eyes shut as her smile overtook her face.

'I am so happy! We'll sail the seven seas together!' Norah took Ruth's arms as they bounced up and down.

The rest of the night, as Ruth and Norah dreamed up what the service would bring and what places they might see, Norah's nerves began to play up. The fantasizing was nice and fun, but she knew the reality of war would be far from it.

***

The train to Kidlington travelled awfully slow for an eager Norah. She twisted her pips straight on her uniform and couldn't wait to know what her father thought. She was to meet him at the bus station where they'd walk to the pub, The Railway Hotel, owned by her stepsister Frances and her husband Cyril, to indulge in a toast or two.

'So, how do I look?' Norah did a twirl and posed as she stood in front of her father.

He clasped his hands in front of his chest, 'My, you look rightly smart. I'm so proud of you, dear.' He hugged her tightly. He let go to take another look at her before hugging her again.

She hooked her arm in his as he carried her bag and led the way to The Railway Hotel, on the banks of the Oxford canal.

'There she is!' erupted her brother-in-law Cyril, upon her entrance to the pub.

'Oh, Cyril!' They hugged and exchanged kisses on the cheek. 'Where's Frances?'

'She's around here somewhere, probably nagging someone.' He raised his eyebrows and rolled his eyes. 'Always nagging.'

'I heard that,' Frances said as she came sweeping into the room. 'Norah! My goodness, it's so good to see you. And look at that brilliant uniform.'

Norah smiled and playfully curtsied in response.

'Take a seat, take a seat.' Cyril waved them over to two empty seats at the bar. 'Now what will we have? A shandy, no doubt?'

'Of course,' Frances piped up. 'It is Norah we're talking about, isn't it?'

Norah smiled. 'Yes, Cyril. I would love a pint if you wouldn't mind.'

Cyril nodded as he pulled four glasses up from under the counter and began to serve out healthy pours. 'So, Norah, are you excited about going to war?'

'Excited?' Norah's father jumped in. 'War isn't about excitement. At least not in how you're asking. War is tough. It's character building.' He lifted a fist to his chest.

Norah wondered if her father had a similar experience to that of Norman's and shuddered at the thought.

'Yes, and we all know Norah dear needs more character building.' Frances winked. 'Now, before you take a sip' – Frances slid two frothy glasses of golden bubbly shandy over to Norah and her father – 'let's cheer to the brave and gallant Miss Norah Eggleton!'

The crowd joined in. The clink of glasses being pushed together in a toast rang throughout, as voices shouted 'Hear, hear!' all around them.

Norah took a large swig.

'My, take it easy, Norah.' Cyril laughed. 'I'm sure you'll be partaking of quite a bit of that while on board.'

Norah's father laughed. 'The only good thing about war' – he took a big gulp of his drink – 'is the drinking.'

Norah turned to her father.

'Dad,' she said, putting her glass down on the bar, 'may I ask you a question?'

'Of course, dear, fire away.'

Norah hesitated for a moment, not quite sure how to approach the subject that was uppermost in her mind. She took in a deep breath. It was now or never.

'Dad, when I was in London, I met a man, a professor.'

Norah's father smiled, and Norah quickly continued before he dared to think she was about to announce an engagement, 'He was in the Great War…'

Before Norah could finish, she saw her father's demeanour change – his smile disappeared, and he quickly took a sip of his beer. Norah had a feeling she shouldn't finish her question, however, she needed to know.

'Dad, you've never really talked about your experiences. I would, if it's all right with you, like to hear about, you know, the war.'

Her father's eyes lowered, and he nodded. 'The Battle of the Somme…' he replied. His was looking deep into his beer, which he held tightly. 'The first real action I saw was on 23 July 1916. It was horrible, Norah, really, really horrible.' He stopped for a second. 'I was lucky. My brother, your uncle…' He stopped in thought. He spoke with such hesitation and relief that Norah knew he had never spoken of this before. 'All I remember of battle is the screams.' He blinked quickly, as if he could still hear those screams to this day and was actively working to be rid of them. He cleared his throat and sat up in his chair. 'After that, I did everything I could to stay alive. All I wanted to do was to come back to England, to your mum and you kids. That's all I wanted. But I had to go for another two years before I could do that. Two years of the same evil. I was captured. I think by then I was exhausted and just gave up.' He took a big gulp of his beer and put the glass back down slowly on the table.

Norah bit her lip and felt a shiver run up her spine as she asked the next question: 'Where were you captured?'

A smile spread under his beard. 'Aye, in Craonne, but not for long. I escaped.' He let out a laugh as his mind thought back to those days. 'Can't keep a good man down, can you?' He took another sip of beer and shifted his stance. 'Cyril, can you fill my glass? I'm going over there to talk to Norah.'

Cyril filled the glass and Norah followed her father to a table away from the bar. When they sat down, Norah's father began.

'I joined up because I was the ultimate romantic. It sounded fun and patriotic. Of course, your mum was dead against it. She certainly didn't want me to leave her behind with young children.' He smiled sweetly. 'Can't say I blamed her. You were only five or so. But I was determined to go, as was my youngest brother, your uncle Harold.' William paused for a moment and Norah could swear she saw his eyes tear up. She was about to change the subject when he continued, 'Shot in the head, was our Harold. Shot in the head.'

Norah sat there and allowed her jaw to drop. 'Dad, I'm so sorry, I didn't mean to stir up any bad memories.'

But maybe William thought it was the right time and decided to continue, even though Norah knew it pained him to do so. 'He was only nineteen, Norah. Only nineteen. I tried to get him not to join up – he was fifteen when he did. I didn't find out about his death until after I came home. He's buried in a cemetery at Pozières, in France…' He took in a deep breath and held it. He smiled sadly at Norah. 'Do you mind awfully if I don't continue?'

Norah nodded. 'I'm so sorry you had to endure all that,' she said breathlessly.

He rubbed her back and smiled. 'You just take care of yourself, dear.'

With that, they both got up and walked over to a little group that had formed by the bar.

'Just be careful, won't you?' Frances put her hand on Norah's arm.

'Don't worry. I imagine we'll be out to sea, far from any action.' Norah's hand rested on Frances's.

'Aye,' said Norah's father. 'But the Germans have a navy and planes. I'm sure they would love to bomb a hospital ship.'

Norah's mouth fell open. 'They wouldn't do that. That's silly.' Norah looked to Cyril and to her father, searching for some reassurance.

'She'll be all right,' Cyril interrupted as he put a hand on William's shoulder. 'She'll come back to us, won't you, Norah?'

William smiled sadly, 'I do hope so.'

The conversation then turned to more mundane and less stressful topics, such as a local farmer who had been chased by a cow, tripped and fell, and was butted by it. Everyone laughed at his expense, and the farmer, who was sitting at the crowded bar, raised his pint of bitter in acknowledgement and pointed to the large bump on his forehead. That elicited even more laughter, and Norah, who had begun to think a little about the prior conversation, relaxed and ordered another pint of shandy.

'It's probably the last one I will have in a long time.'

'There will be one waiting for you when you return, Norah,' replied Cyril, and he clapped his hands to silence the now rowdy crowd. When they were quiet, he raised his glass and proposed another toast to her. He looked at Norah. Frances stood next to him, his arm around her. 'Norah, there isn't one person I have ever met who hasn't liked you.'

The crowd agreed.

Cyril continued, 'We wish you the best of luck, and may God go with you on this adventure. We will wait for your safe return. Just know that you will be in our hearts and prayers each and every day. God bless you, Norah, we are so very proud of you.'

But there was none prouder in that room than Norah's father, who put his arms around her and held her close to him. 'I love you, my daughter.'

Tears welled up in her eyes and began to flow down her cheeks. 'I love you too, Dad,' Norah said as she pressed her face deeper into her father's chest.

# *Part Two*

# CHAPTER EIGHT

## *Cheshire, 1941*

The spring of 1941 found Raj standing with the other recruits on the parade ground while bitterly cold winds blew through them on their way across the country. Raj's hands froze, his toes froze, his mouth refused to cooperate, and all because he had decided to volunteer to fight. Even though his flat in Russell Square had no heat, he would have much rather stayed indoors than be battered by those evil winds blowing in from the Irish Sea. Even the supply of warm clothing didn't help.

As he marched on the parade grounds, thoughts of Esther overwhelmed him. He missed her and he couldn't wait to be back in her arms, and better yet, in her home where she had heating. He began to daydream about home next. It had been three years since he'd been in India, and as time went on, he felt more and more homesick. He hadn't divulged his decision to volunteer for the war. He liked having a life of his own, not having it dictated by his parents, but he also knew that keeping the important decisions he'd made a secret was not a habit he wanted.

That afternoon, Raj sat down on his creaky cot in the barracks and wrote the much overdue letter to his father.

*Dear Father,*

*As you probably already know, war has broken out in Europe and Britain has declared war against Germany…*

He thought about making up a lie saying that he was drafted, but then told himself not to hide behind lies or secrets anymore. He would tell the truth, and as concisely as he could. The quicker, the better.

*Many of my fellow peers in university have joined the war effort as volunteers. I too have been moved to do so. I joined a queue at a recruiting station. I am now a private in the Cheshire Regiment, at the regimental headquarters not far from the Welsh border. I receive very good meals and pay and have every intention of returning to university after the war. I hope you can understand my decision.*

*Please send my love to Mummy.*
*Raj*

He didn't realize he'd been shaking until he put down his pen. He swiftly addressed the letter, and before he could change his mind, brought the letter to the censor's office and left it there in the in-tray. He prayed he wouldn't receive a reply from his father.

About a month into Raj's training, he was ordered to the office of the colonel.

'You're a university chap, aren't you, Kohli?' he began.

'Yes, sir.'

'What were you reading?'

'Chemistry, sir.'

'Chemistry!' the colonel repeated, rather surprised.

'Yes, sir.'

'And now you're a private in the Cheshire Regiment?'

'Yes, sir.'

'Well, that won't do. We are going to make you an officer cadet.'

'Yes, sir.'

'Is that all you have to say, Kohli?'

'I had enlisted, sir, because I wanted to help out the war effort,' said Raj.

A slight smile slipped from under the colonel's well-waxed handlebar moustache.

The colonel stood up and extended his hand. 'You leave this evening.'

Raj packed his belongings and left the barracks while the other recruits sat and watched in silence. It was obvious that all this had been prearranged – outside was a lorry waiting to take him away. He jumped in the back, and soon they were hurtling down the streets on the outskirts of Cheshire to the railway station. There, he was presented with his tickets and travel orders.

And yet another adventure in my life has begun, Raj thought with a deep sigh.

***

He found himself at the gates of the Aldershot army barracks, where he was dropped. On the other side of the gates stood cadets running drills and commanders barking orders. He hoped to go unnoticed as he entered the gates and walked to the quartermaster's office.

The quartermaster, Sergeant Major Samuel Blacksmith, was one of those men who leaves an indelible impression on anyone they meet. He was tall, about six-feet-five, with a broad chest. His uniform was heavily starched. He wore a line of ribbons, including one for gallantry. He occupied a large amount of space in a not-so-large office. He was clean-shaven, with short blonde hair, and piercing, bright blue eyes. He also had a booming voice, as one would expect. When he walked, he picked up his regimental stick, slammed it under his left arm and thrust out his chest. He was sitting behind his desk looking through some papers, when Raj walked in and saluted him smartly.

He stood up and took a deep breath. 'Cadet Kohli, right?'

'Yes, sir.' Raj wasn't sure if that was the right way to address him.

'Well then, Cadet Kohli, one does not salute when one is not in uniform.' He paused for a second to judge his reaction. 'Is that clear?'

'Yes, sir.'

'Good.' He sat down again. He pointed to the chair opposite him. 'Please, sit down.'

Raj complied, kicking himself for his stupid mistake.

'Okay, Cadet Kohli, why don't we have a little chat now.' Sergeant Major Blacksmith leaned forward, his arms on the table, his fingers interlocked. 'We heard about you coming here, and I don't want to be rude … but we've never had someone like you here before.' He hesitated for a second and leaned even closer. 'How many pounds of rice do you eat a day?'

At first, Raj didn't understand what he was asking. But the words 'like you' echoed in his mind and it clicked. He did his best not to laugh as he answered.

'Oh, Sergeant Major, you don't have to worry about that. I eat the same amount as everyone else.'

The sergeant major sighed and sat back, dragging his arms along with him. 'Thank you, Cadet Kohli. We were in one hell of a fix trying to think of where we would get that from.'

Raj forced a smile and a nod.

'You may go now, Cadet Kohli.'

'Thank you, sir.' Raj made for the door.

'Cadet Kohli,' the sergeant major bellowed.

'Yes, Sergeant Major?' Raj turned around in near panic, not knowing why he had been addressed in such a loud voice, to find the sergeant major standing, towering over his desk.

'Cadet Kohli.' His eyes squinted as he took a good look at Raj. 'Tell me, did you shave this morning?'

Raj wanted to feel his face to make sure he did, but then he remembered. 'Yes, Sergeant Major, I did,' he said hesitantly.

'In which case, Cadet Kohli,' his voice reverberated off the walls of the office, 'next time stand a little closer to the razor, will you?' He sat back down.

Without another word, Raj left the office.

This will be fun, he thought as he inhaled deeply and walked off to find his barracks.

***

On Saturday, 30 November 1941, Raj was commissioned as a first lieutenant and waited to be assigned to a regiment. Days passed and cadets trickled out of Aldershot to their assignments. Raj was left wondering if he had been forgotten, until he received a call summoning him to the colonel's office.

The colonel was looking out the window, his posture impeccable as he stood up. He didn't move when Raj walked in.

'Lieutenant Kohli.'

Raj saluted. 'Yes, sir.'

'We have debated for some time as to what to do with you.'

Raj blinked. He didn't understand.

'Since you being' – his mouth hung open as he searched for the right words – 'not English ... we were not sure if we should allow you assignment in one of our regiments.'

Raj fixed his stance, preparing himself to hear the worst – that they were releasing him from the military.

'But until we decide just what to do with you, you have been assigned to Lincolnshire to receive machine-gun training,' he said, his fingers twitching. And with a nod, the colonel dismissed Raj.

It was as if the commanding officers were playing 'hot potato' with him, confused and uncomfortable with having an Indian among their ranks.

Raj participated in the short two-week course on machine guns, and once he had completed it, he felt honoured when he was asked to stay on as an instructor. It was there he discovered his love for teaching and leading.

However, after a month of instructing, it came to a sudden halt.

One day, Raj showed up at the firing range and found his commanding officer, Major Richards, giving a tour to a visiting colonel. Upon laying eyes on Raj in his uniform, the colonel gawked.

Raj immediately saluted him, but the colonel did not return his salute.

'What is he doing here?' he asked Major Richards with disgust.

Major Richards cleared his throat. 'Sir, he is one of our machine-gun instructors. One of the finest.'

'And he speaks English?' the colonel asked incredulously.

'Yes.' Raj could feel his face getting hot. 'Sir,' he added.

'Hmm. I see.' The colonel eyed Raj, his nose high in the air. 'Surely we have qualified British commanders who can instruct.'

Raj looked at Major Richards, wondering if he would have the guts to object, but he didn't.

The colonel leaned forward, his hands behind his back as he spoke to Raj. 'We cannot have you instructing our officers,' he said, his voice growing louder.

Raj's students, who were standing close by, perked up, obviously eavesdropping.

'Sir,' replied Raj calmly, 'it wasn't my choice, I was posted here. It is your prerogative to have me reassigned.'

'Certainly.' He then turned to Major Richards. 'Please see to it right away that he is reassigned back to where he came.' His eyes turned to Raj. 'After all,' he continued with a sly grin, 'you chaps have an army of your own.'

Raj's hand curled into a fist and he took several breaths to fight the urge to punch the colonel square on the nose. Maybe it will reset his constant need to hold it high above everyone else, Raj thought. Instead, Raj saluted and turned to walk to his quarters.

He almost turned right back around when he heard the colonel shout after him, 'Go on. That's right, pack your bags and get out of here. Go back to your jungle hut!' He let out a loud laugh, hoping the others would join in, and Raj smiled when they didn't.

Raj waited in his quarters until the next day, when he received orders to report back to London. A ship was to take him from Glasgow to Jhelum. Raj was reminded of his uncle Teja Singh's remarks about the British and nodded along. He would be happy to return home.

He summoned a jeep and jumped in. The corporal driving the jeep was surprised to see Raj with his kit bag.

'Where to, sir?' asked the corporal, who looked at a stoic Raj for an answer.

'The railway station, Corporal,' replied Raj as he bit the inside of his cheeks.

'Yes, sir,' the corporal said as he shifted the jeep into gear.

They drove in silence. As they turned the corner and saw the railway station ahead, the corporal hesitated before speaking.

'Lieutenant, if I can just say, it was very much known around camp that you were the best instructor they have ever had. For my part, sir, you are the epitome of an officer and a gentleman, and I would be honoured to serve under you.' He swallowed.

Raj kept up his stoic expression and hoped the corporal couldn't notice the shaking in his voice, 'Thank you, Corporal.'

When they reached the station, the corporal refused to let Raj carry his bag. He walked with him on to the platform, which at that time of day was crowded with commuters. He put Raj's bag down, came to attention loud enough for everyone on the platform to notice, and saluted him. Raj extended his hand, and the corporal shook it. He then turned and marched out of the station, letting his words – 'One damn good officer that lieutenant is' – trail behind him. Raj quickly boarded the train to escape the onlookers' stares.

***

The train ride was unbearable. Raj wasn't in the mood to be left alone with his thoughts and longed for it to be over. Finally, the two-hour journey came to an end and Raj stepped on to the platform and out on to the cold rainy streets to hail a taxi.

Raj returned to his flat in Russell Square feeling rejected. He didn't want to be alone. But all his friends were gone. They had all left to fight. He hadn't spoken to Colin in quite a while, and for a moment he toyed with the idea of calling his house. But just before dialling the number he backed away, afraid of any bad news that might be transmitted to him. He walked along the streets. It was the end of December and the cruel British winter was now in full force. The cold wind blew through him, sudden snow squalls blacked out the landscape, and all this helped in making Raj feel even more isolated than he was. He decided there was one person still around.

'Is Esther here?' Raj stood in the doorway of the lingerie department, in his crisply ironed uniform, well-polished shoes, and a wide grin on his face – a far cry from the first time he appeared in the doorway.

'Esther? Yes, who may I say is asking?' The young sales associate eyed him.

'Erm … Yes, Raj.' He took off his hat.

The sales associate nodded politely and disappeared behind a door. Soon, Esther appeared through the same door and for a moment seemed to be glued to her spot.

'Raj?'

He smiled and tugged at his uniform.

'What are you doing here?' Her eyes shifted as she looked around the department. She unglued herself and walked over to him, bringing the volume of her voice down. 'I never thought you would come back. To me that is.' She quickly flashed a smile.

'I told you I would.'

'Yes, you're right. I should never have doubted you.' She stepped backward and smoothed her dress. 'Well, come on, Raj, let's go get a cuppa, shall we?' With wary eyes she led him to the canteen.

Raj wasn't sure why she was acting the way she was, her eyes continued to dart about even as they sipped on their tea. He figured that she was upset since he hadn't written to her. He had every intention to but struggled with what to say. She probably thought he had left for good.

'I missed you, Esther.' Raj tried to assure her of his affection towards her.

'Oh, you too, Raj. I didn't know when or if you'd be back.' She sipped her tea and fixed her necklace.

'Is everything all right?' he asked. She didn't seem the same.

'Yes, I'm so sorry, Raj. Just caught me off guard, seeing you here. It's been six months. I hadn't heard from you.'

Raj nodded. 'I know, maybe I should've telephoned you.'

She smiled nervously. 'So, tell me, how is training? And what's next for you?'

'Well, I was hoping to fulfil my promise to you.'

Esther straightened her posture. 'And what's that?'

'To get married.' He made to stroke her hand, but she pulled away quickly. Raj slowly placed his hand back in his lap. 'Did I do something wrong?'

'Oh no, dear. It's just … isn't it in bad taste to show affection while in uniform?'

Her hands moved up to her neck, fixing her necklace.

'I suppose you're right. My apologies.'

Raj lowered his head.

'Won't you be sent off to war?'

'I have no idea where they'll send me. But I do know that I only have a short while here before I am to be stationed in India. Most likely be sent to the front lines after that.'

Esther covered her mouth. 'Oh goodness, Raj. But if you go to the front lines, then what will happen to me?'

Raj wondered why she didn't ask about him going to India and when he'd be leaving. 'Stay at Selfridges, I guess.'

'But I get to be the wife of an officer?'

Raj's spirits picked up, as did hers. 'Yes.' He smiled. 'Would you like that?'

She smiled back. 'Yes, of course. But when?'

'As soon as we can. Not enough time to plan for Kensington, but I thought it wouldn't matter … The magistrate's office will do fine for me.' He leaned over the table towards her.

She looked at her wristwatch. 'Well, I can't right now.' She tried to muffle her smile. 'I've been away from my department too long. I've got to go back. Where are you staying in London, now that you're no longer a student?'

'Same address in Russell Square.'

Esther got up, straightened her dress and began walking away while Raj was still seated. 'Oh, I'm sorry, love,' she said when she realized what she had done.

'It's all right. I've got to get going myself.'

'We'll meet later?'

'Yes, shall I come over to your flat once you're done with work today?'

'Why don't we meet at your place instead?'

Raj thought he saw her mouth twitch.

'Esther' – he let out a laugh – 'you know my flat doesn't have any heat.'

'Oh, I don't mind.' She dismissed his comment with a flick of her wrist. She leaned in to whisper to him, 'Forces us to hold each other closer then.' She winked.

There was the Esther he remembered.

'All right.' Raj stood up. 'We can talk about when we should get married tonight as well.' He grinned.

Esther gave him a tight-lipped smile in response, as she turned her gaze to two nearby employees, who quickly looked away and began to hurriedly whisper to one another.

'Goodbye,' she said and disappeared out of the canteen.

Raj made his way down the wooden escalator and on to Oxford Street.

It was an unusually warm day. The sun was out, and even though there was always the fear of the air-raid warning sounding, the street was filled with people.

Raj sat down on a bench in Green Park and closed his eyes to soak up some of the unusually bright sunshine and to map out his life, or at least the next few days.

'What should I do?' Raj asked a crow that landed on the bench not far from him. It didn't respond. 'Just as I thought. You're no help.'

It was less than six months ago that he had been sitting in a lecture hall while his life revolved around chemistry. And now? Well now, he was a lieutenant in His Majesty's Royal Army, on his way back to India to fight in the Punjab Regiment. After that, he wasn't sure what would happen. His stomach fluttered at all the unknowns that seemed to be presenting themselves. He smiled. Yes, so many unknowns, but he did know that he had a woman who loved him and whom he would marry soon.

'I'm going to be married.' He shared his smile with the crow before it cocked its head to a side and flew off.

He watched it land in a nearby tree.

'Yes, well I should be going too.' Raj chuckled.

He got up and made his way to catch a bus to Russell Square.

***

Raj and Esther agreed to a date, and on a Monday at 10 a.m., Raj in his uniform and Esther in a pale blue dress and holding on to Raj's arm, walked into the magistrate's court in St Pancras. During a break between cases, they were married by the magistrate. From there, they went to Fortnum Mason for lunch and accepted the many congratulatory words from the other patrons. They had a lavish lunch, after which they walked out into a cloudy and chilly day and sat down on a bench in Green Park. Raj could swear it was the same bench he had sat on a few days before. He looked for the crow, but it didn't appear.

A few days later, when Raj and Esther were staying over at his flat in Russell Square, a letter arrived from Somerset House.

*Dear Lieutenant Rajendra Shamsher Singh Kohli,*
*This letter is to inform you that your application for a marriage certificate to a Mrs Esther Hoey dated Monday, 20 January 1941 is in review. Our records indicate a current marriage listed for Mrs Esther Hoey to a Mr George Baker of Middlesex. Your attendance is required at the magistrate's office in St Pancras at your earliest convenience for approval or nullification.*

*Sincerely,*
*Robert Grant*
*The Office of the Magistrate*

Raj blinked. This can't be real, he thought. There must be some mistake. There must be another Esther Hoey. An error on the part of the magistrate's office, no doubt. Raj paced the length of his flat and decided he needed fresh air.

Esther had left for work earlier. In fact, she had worked an awful lot since he got back. He went out and walked until he decided he needed to sit down and contemplate his next move. There was no one he could talk to. As if by some inexplicable force of nature, Raj found himself back in Green Park, on the same bench as before.

It was another unusually sunny day, and he closed his eyes again to shut out the world so he could think clearly. The crow returned. He got up and made his way to the nearest telephone kiosk.

'Is Esther there?' he asked of the woman who answered the phone.

'May I ask—'

'Please. I need to speak with her now,' Raj interrupted.

'Hold on a tick, will you? I'll get her. She's on the floor with a customer.'

Raj heard the receiver being placed on the desk. His heart began to beat faster. He was in uncharted territory. He didn't know what he was going to say to Esther when she came on the phone.

'Hello?' Esther's voice answered.

'Who is George Baker?' Raj breathed into the phone.

A silence. 'Raj?'

'Tell me, who is George Baker?' he demanded.

'Love, why don't we talk at home?' Her voice was sweet, obviously trying to placate him.

'Esther, answer me. Why did I receive a letter today saying that you're currently married to a Mr George Baker?' Raj asked sternly.

Her voice cracked 'Oh, Raj…'

'So, it's true?' Raj threw back his head and let out a breath.

'Raj. Let's just talk at home, shall we?'

'Why didn't you tell me?' The pitch of his voice was rising.

'It's not that simple,' Esther whispered. 'I don't love him like I love you…'

Raj closed his eyes. 'We are to never talk again. You hear me?'

'Raj—'

'No. No more. This was all a mistake.'

Raj hung up and stared at the receiver. Esther had taken up too much of his life. He couldn't wait to go back to India and his family.

# CHAPTER NINE

## *Glasgow, 1941*

As Raj arrived at the docks in Liverpool, he straightened his uniform and inhaled. He boarded the *SS Newfoundland* and looked back at the shore. The once-cherished moments spent in London were now tainted. He was relieved to be leaving for India. Maybe he would be granted leave from Jhelum and could visit his family. These thoughts rekindled hope.

He squinted up at the sky as the clouds rolled back to unveil the sun, which was stretching its rays, unfurling its welcoming warmth upon all creatures below. Raj smiled as he felt the promise of better days ahead of him.

The voyage across the oceans was going to be a long and arduous one. The convoy, of which the SS Newfoundland was a part, would have to criss-cross first the Atlantic Ocean and then the Indian Ocean to avoid the ever-present German submarines.

Raj couldn't wait to be back on Indian soil and could often be found counting the minutes down. He spent most of his time stretched out on the deck, lying back in his chair, reading a book he had found in the ship's library.

Until a few days into the journey.

A loud explosion rocked the ship violently, knocking him off his chair. He immediately jumped up and felt the ship beginning to list.

As he attempted to regain his balance, a command crackled over the loudspeaker, 'Torpedo to the engine room! Everyone, abandon ship!'

Raj was thankful that most of the passengers were military personnel and there was no sense of panic.

One young sailor joked with another while waiting in the neat queue that formed outside the life raft. 'Finally, something worth telling my grandkids one day,' he snickered.

When it was his turn, Raj climbed down the rope ladder, which was frayed and soggy from the spray of ocean water, and into the rocking lifeboat. When it reached capacity, it pulled away from the side of the ship, rowed by four sailors.

'Oi! Hurry up!' one sailor shouted to the others. 'We need to get as far as we can from the ship before she sinks!'

They worked tirelessly until they were far enough away. Everyone's eyes doubled in size and their jaws dropped in awe as they watched that creaking metal giant, the *SS Newfoundland*, disappear under the waves in the blink of an eye. Raj watched in horror as a nearby lifeboat was sucked under and swallowed whole by the suction created by the sinking ship.

One by one, the sailors in Raj's lifeboat took their caps off and held them to their hearts.

'I bloody told them to move away…' The sailor's whispered words drifted out into the quiet stillness around them.

Raj wondered if it was a sign that he wasn't meant to return home, but then, in the distance, he saw the distinctive outline of a smokestack belonging to a battleship as it steamed towards them. Each passenger in the lifeboat struggled to determine if the fast-approaching ship was of an ally. A collective sigh of relief was heard when, high above them, they spotted the British flag waving boldly.

Lifeboats took turns climbing aboard to waiting cups of tea and biscuits. Once the last person made it on board, the ship began its passage to Liverpool.

A week later, they were offloaded, and Raj received subsequent orders to again board a ship and make his way back to his home country. As Raj sailed, the memory of the torpedo strike receded, rushing to the surface only when he caught glimpses of shadows beneath the water, but to his relief they only turned out to be shoals of fish swimming at high speeds just below the surface.

To occupy his mind, Raj read and re-read every book in the ship's library. Fear subsided when the ship hit the calm waters of the Indian Ocean with its myriad awe-inspiring flying fish.

Everyone on board, including the sailors, was weary and prayed for Ceylon to appear on the horizon. A few days later, the cry went out and everyone ran to the front of the ship to get the first look at their destination. Raj was thrilled to see land.

A few hours later, the ship docked in the Colombo harbour. Raj's sea legs fell upon dry land and manoeuvred around the sailors and various dock workers to find the harbour master's office, where he would receive his next orders. When he opened the door, he was met by a British major in his tropical uniform, sporting an overgrown handlebar moustache.

'Lieutenant Kohli?' asked the major in a supercilious tone.

'Yes, sir,' Raj replied with a salute that was not returned.

'Here are your orders.' And with that, he handed Raj a manila envelope, turned and walked out of the office without uttering another word.

Raj studied the envelope. 'But excuse me, sir…' He opened the door to shout after him, 'Where do I catch the ferry?'

The major stopped but refused to turn around as he shouted, 'Good God! What do you want me to do, hold your hand and take you there?' He scoffed and continued on his way.

'He is a bad bugger.'

Raj closed the door to find the harbour master standing in the inner office.

He pointed in the direction of the departing major. 'Don't worry,' he said in his heavy Sinhalese accent that took Raj aback – it had been a long time since he had heard such a thick accent. 'Major Thompson thinks he is God. Nobody likes him, probably not even his mother.'

The harbour master laughed at his own joke and Raj smiled, not wanting to be rude. He put his arm around Raj's shoulders and led him outside.

'Just follow that road there.' He pointed to a dirt path which disappeared into a clump of trees with wildly overgrown branches. 'That will lead you directly to the ferry.'

'Thank you, I appreciate the guidance,' Raj replied as he opened the screen door to the outside.

'One day, we will get rid of these buggers.'

Raj turned to see the harbour master with his hands on his hips, smiling. Raj politely bowed in acknowledgement and continued out the door and on to the path to the ferry.

Raj waited until he was aboard the ferry to read his orders in full detail. He was to catch the train in Ramanathapuram and then make his way up the country to join his new regiment, the Third Punjab Regiment. He laid the document on his lap as he looked out the window. It would be his first posting as an officer where he would command troops. His knee bounced up and down.

Was he ready?

***

Several days later, with transfers in Bombay and Delhi, his train pulled into Jhelum.

Raj was greeted by a sergeant and a couple of jawans, who saluted and asked, 'Sir, no bags?'

'Unfortunately, my belongings are lying safely at the bottom of the Atlantic Ocean.'

The jawans winced.

Raj continued with a request: 'I will be in need of clean clothes and a range of toiletries at the earliest convenience.' Luckily, he was given soap and a toothbrush, and was able to borrow a razor from the sailors on the ship.

Raj was pleased that the drive to the Punjab Regimental Centre was quick as the sergeant drove sharply through the traffic. After going through the gate, he was taken directly to his room.

'Sir, lunch will be served at 12 p.m. in the officers' mess,' the sergeant said, and with a quick salute was off.

Raj opened the screen door, which led to his room, and after a quick scan decided it would probably be the best place he would get to sleep in for many years to come. The sagging of the bed, the burn marks on the chair, and the desk needing to be propped up against a wall for support – these were minor inconveniences.

At 12 p.m. sharp, Raj opened his door and could hear loud conversations emanating from the officers' mess. With one final check of his uniform, he opened the door and walked in. The conversations immediately stopped and hung in mid-air as the crowded hall collectively stared at him. Raj's face felt hot. He wasn't sure why he had become the centre of attention. Was his uniform too conspicuous because it was what he had been given at Aldershot?

For a brief second, he debated whether he should turn around and bolt when, thankfully, a grey-haired British colonel walked over and shook his hand.

'Welcome, Lieutenant Kohli. We are very excited to have you here,' he said, warmly.

Suddenly, as if on cue, the several distinctly varied conversations started up again and the colonel clapped his hands to silence everyone so that he could introduce Raj.

'Officers, may I introduce Lieutenant Kohli. He comes to us from England, where he served and trained in Aldershot and Lincolnshire,' he announced. He turned his head to Raj and quietly said the rest directly to him: 'I was downright giddy upon hearing of your assignment to us. With your education and training, you don't belong here. And for our sake, I hope the Royal Army never realizes their mistake in sending you away.' He laughed, patting Raj on the back.

Raj was about to thank the group for welcoming him when an Indian lieutenant colonel named Anup Chowdhry, jumped up. 'Well, hope you don't think that makes you better than the rest of us here,' he remarked with a sneer.

'No, of course not,' Raj replied as he watched the lieutenant colonel clench his jaw and grit his teeth.

Raj made sure to limit his interaction as much as he could with Chowdhry, and soon found himself immersed in regimental life, enjoying the day-to-day.

However, it became painfully clear to him – and to the lieutenant colonel – that the senior British officers held a certain amount of reverence for Raj. They often tried their best to commandeer Raj to do coveted jobs, such as being on the viceroy's contingent. On another occasion, he was asked to help with propaganda in order to recruit soldiers.

Raj, unfortunately, could see Lt Colonel Chowdhry's ever-growing jealousy bubbling, and prayed he wouldn't see the day it boiled over. So Raj was relieved to find out that his request to take leave to visit home had been granted – he needed a break from the bitterness that radiated from Chowdhry.

***

Raj was sitting in the train compartment at the break of dawn, when the train slowed down to pull into the Dehradun station.

With one final whistle, the engine stopped abruptly, and he looked out of the window to see if his father had arrived. Raj left the compartment after giving his luggage to a coolie and tried unsuccessfully to stroll nonchalantly out on to the platform in his uniform.

Standing at attention was Raj's father, looking distinguished, as always, in an off-white poplin suit with a matching tie and shirt, his beard well-groomed and his turban tied immaculately. Nothing had changed. Their eyes locked and Raj's began to mist up even though his father stood unmoved. Instinctively, Raj bent at his waist to touch his father's feet out of respect, but no sooner had he begun than his father put his arm on Raj's shoulder.

'No, son. Please stand,' he said as he pulled Raj into a brief hug.

When they let go of each other, Raj saw, standing right next to his father, his uncle Sohan Singh. He too was immaculately dressed in a similar suit with a matching tie and shirt, his turban neatly folded. Before Raj had a chance to bend down to attempt to touch his feet, Sohan Singh had his arms around him in a tight hug. 'Welcome home, Raj!' he exclaimed.

As soon as the car pulled up in front of the house, Raj saw his mother standing in the veranda with tears streaming down her face, flanked by some of the servants. She couldn't wait, and even before the car had stopped, her head came in through the window as she showered Raj with kiss after kiss, knocking his hat on to the seat. Raj didn't protest. He finally managed to exit the car after his father came around from the other side and gently pulled her away. Once he was out of the car, though, she hugged and kissed him on both cheeks, and that would have continued had it not been for Sohan Singh who, in his jovial manner said, 'Give your son a chance to breathe.'

With tears of joy still streaming down her face, she reluctantly did so. Raj knew what was coming next and she didn't disappoint.

'Puttar, you must be hungry,' she said in Punjabi.

For a second, Raj allowed himself the joy of letting those words, which he had longed to hear for so many years, echo in his mind. He smiled and followed her indoors, with his uncle and father in tow, to a table filled with all his favourite foods from childhood.

Everyone sat down to a meal that lasted a good two hours – during which they enjoyed chicken curry, dal and an assortment of perfectly cooked vegetables, washed down with glass after glass of lassi – and Raj revelled in telling stories of his time in the military.

'Can you imagine, they asked me how much rice I ate every day when I got to the officer candidate school?' Raj recounted, eliciting laughter from everyone.

'And what did you tell them?' asked his uncle.

'I told them I ate English food.'

'You should have told them you didn't eat rice, but needed ten parathas every day,' his mother joked, not wanting to be left out, starting another round of laughter.

But exempt from the vocal merriment was Raj's father, who ate quietly until he cleared his throat and turned a stern face to his son. 'Raj, we are all proud of you. But I need your assurance that you will return to university once your war duties have been fulfilled.'

Raj, whose stomach ached from all the laughter, now experienced a sudden change in mood. His smile faded into respectful, sombre composure. 'Father, I'm not sure when the war will be over—'

'I said *once* your duty to it is over. Not by a certain period of time other than when it is over. To attend university was the only reason you were sent to England.'

Raj glanced at Sohan Singh to gauge his reaction, but unable to read him, Raj answered, 'Yes, Father. When my duty is done, I will return to university to complete my studies.'

Lunch was over and the entire party, with the exception of Raj's mother, who left with the servants for the kitchen, walked into the living room and collapsed on the numerous padded chairs, divans and sofas. Soon the idle chatter diminished and the weight of the rich food upon the stomach was felt by one and all. There was no use fighting the effects, and one by one, they fell into a sound sleep.

An hour later, the delightful aroma of samosas and pakoras being fried made its way into the living room and encircled every sleeping person's nose, making them open their eyes to a blurry world filled with the sights and sounds of tea being prepared.

One by one, the sleeping figures rose and made their way to the dining room. Raj shook his head in disbelief at the number of plates, each piled high with all his favourite desserts and snacks.

'Mummy, you really outdid yourself,' Raj said, as he put an arm around his mother's shoulders.

'Oh, puttar, it is nothing,' she said.

After Sohan Singh and Raj's father made their plates and exited to the living room to enjoy the snacks, Kundun prepared a plate for Raj.

'Really, I can do that myself, Mummy,' Raj laughed. He knew she was thoroughly enjoying herself, now that she was able to take care of him once again.

'Please, it's my pleasure,' she answered as she smiled and scrunched her nose. 'Now, puttar, I was talking to Dr and Mrs

Sharma, and they tell me that their daughter Sita, who is very pretty, has come home from a trip and they thought it would be a good idea if we all meet.'

She must have noticed his eyes roll, but continued undaunted, 'She's very fair, and you know her father is a very wealthy doctor. We all think she would make you a very good wife. And the dowry would be big.'

'Mummy, I haven't been home for a full day yet and you're already trying to get me married?'

She shook her head. 'Puttar, you need to get married. It is the respectable thing to do.'

'I agree.' Raj's mind flickered with thoughts of his marriage to Esther, and how disappointed his mother would be if she found out. 'But I have told you many times that I want to marry a woman I fall in love with, someone who makes me happy.'

Her gaze lowered. 'But this is the way it is done, puttar.'

'Yes, and are you happy?' Raj blurted out, but then wondered if his question was out of line.

Kundun glared at him. 'It's not about happiness. It's about tradition.' Her eyes were wide and her gestures were growing more dramatic.

As Raj bit into a piece of burfi, he thought maybe she was right. He hadn't had much luck on his own, that was for sure. Maybe he had everything backward, every decision he seemed to make ended up going severely wrong. Maybe he was being too idealistic about how his life should go. Maybe it was better to let someone make them for him…

He swallowed and nodded. 'Okay, Mummy. I will meet with—'

Before he could finish, she jumped in, her eyebrows rising high in excitement, 'Puttar, make sure your uniform is nicely pressed. Ask the ayah to iron it for you. I think it's very creased. You don't want to give Dr and Mrs Sharma the wrong impression when they come over today.'

Raj nearly choked on an onion pakora. 'What do you mean, today?'

'Well, I invited the Sharmas over for tea, and they will be here in about fifteen minutes.'

'But, Mummy, you only informed me of this a moment ago.' His mouth hung open.

'You're lucky I told you at all.'

She turned to one of the women servants who was scurrying around with purpose. 'Shanti, please take Raj to his bedroom and make sure his uniform is pressed.'

Without another word, Shanti grabbed Raj by the arm and pulled him out of the kitchen. Raj did not protest – it was useless.

A few minutes later, Raj appeared at the kitchen door in a very neatly ironed uniform, with a proud Shanti standing next to him. His mother approved. There was a knock on the front door. The door opened to reveal Dr and Mrs Sharma with their daughter, her face covered with the pallu of her blue-and-gold sari.

Kundun shooed him away from their sight, enthusiastically waving with the back of her hand. 'Go! Go! We will call for you later, so you can make your entrance,' she hurriedly whispered.

Raj watched the next few minutes unfold through the slit of the open door. The Sharmas entered the veranda and were ushered into the house by the head servant. After they had found their places and a couple of minutes had passed, Raj's mother entered the room followed by servants bringing trays of cups and saucers. Tea was served, and as they filled their plates with the offerings, Raj's mother began her task of telling them all about her son. Not a single thing was skipped; in fact, all points were exaggerated upon. Everyone seemed duly impressed.

His eyes fell upon Sita, who still hid behind her silk sari, her black, shiny hair poking through the gaps.

'He will make a very good husband. He has a bright future, having got his degree from Cambridge.' Raj listened to the conversation in abject horror. She did, however, correct this record slightly. 'Well, he will be going back after the war to finish his degree in Cambridge.' That correction was met with their approval.

'Well, where is the young man? I believe it's time to meet him,' Dr Sharma said as he looked around the room.

Raj froze. He knew it was time for his grand entrance. After one final look in the mirror, to make sure his uniform looked immaculate, Raj appeared at the doorway to the living room.

As he entered, a collective gasp rang out from the Sharmas. Raj felt his hands go clammy, not sure what to make of their response. Was it good? Were they expecting him to look different? Maybe he shouldn't have worn his uniform.

The next few moments felt like an eternity, as silence ensued. Finally, Dr Sharma got up from his chair and held out his hand to Raj. Raj hesitantly clasped it and they shook hands. He could hear his mother let out a sigh of relief.

'Come sit, Raj.' Kundun ushered Raj into a seat next to Sita.

He nodded to Sita as he sat, catching a glimpse of her glimmering light brown eyes. Everyone settled down to continue talking, eating and laughing. By this time, Raj's uncle and father had joined the group.

As the conversation progressed, Raj spotted, out of the corner of his eye, Mrs Sharma hurriedly gesturing at Sita to pull her sari off her face. Receiving the message, Sita discreetly pinched the fabric, letting it fall from her head. Her long, golden earrings twinkled as the sari fell. His mother was right, she was beautiful. Her skin was fair, with hues of pink from make-up, which complimented her gentle eyes. Her hair was bound in a braid that fell softly over her front to her waist.

Raj realized he was staring when his concentration was broken by Mrs Sharma. 'Are you staying in India for a while?' she asked, and Raj noticed how different her daughter looked from her. She was plump and severely unattractive.

He cleared his throat rather exaggeratedly. 'No, I have to return to my unit in Jhelum in about a week. And from there we will, in all probability, be sent to the front lines to fight.'

He saw his mother wince – obviously not the right thing to say – but he was far from hearing the same wedding bells as they were. There was a war to be fought.

'But after the war, will you be coming back to India?' Mrs Sharma asked, trying to pin Raj down.

'I don't know how long the war will last.'

'Surely, not much longer.' Kundun tried to ease the direction of the conversation.

'Well, no one can say for sure when it will be over,' Raj corrected her. 'But even so, I have given my word that I will return to university to finish my degree when it is over.'

'Cambridge?' asked Dr Sharma.

'King's College, London,' replied Raj, but then remembered what his mother had told them and quickly added. 'It's also possible I will return to Cambridge.'

He saw his mother's tense shoulders fall a bit. 'Shall we leave these two young people to themselves for a few minutes,' she said.

Dr and Mrs Sharma wagged their heads in agreement. As they walked down the stairs into the garden, Raj heard his mother begin, 'Did you know that Raj is a miracle? He was not supposed to live past six days. A hakim just happened to stop by our house…' They nodded along, eyes widening at every sentence.

But back in the house, Sita and Raj sat for a moment in thick silence until Raj realized he would have to be the first one to speak. 'I guess now is our only chance to get to know each other,' he said with a laugh.

Sita blushed and nodded at the floor.

Raj waited to see if she would respond, but after another moment of silence, he decided that if there was going to be any conversation, he would need to lead it. 'So, my mother says you've just returned from a trip. Where did you visit?' Raj hoped this question would prompt an interesting dialogue. He was wrong.

Sita shifted in her chair and bowed her head towards the ground as she spoke. 'Yes, I was visiting my cousin. There I was learning to sew and cook.'

Raj took a sip of tea and nodded politely. He pulled at the collar of his uniform and wished desperately that their parents would return from the garden soon.

Sita looked over her shoulder, obviously sharing the same thoughts.

Raj said, 'Arranged marriages are loads of fun, aren't they?' He chuckled.

Sita's eyebrows furrowed. 'What do you mean?' she asked.

Raj, realizing his humour was lost on her, shook his head and longed even more for his mother to return.

Sita's eyes fell, but suddenly she perked up. 'Tell me, is England as wonderful as they say?'

Raj sat up. Maybe the conversation wasn't dead after all. 'It's spectacular,' he began. 'London, especially. I find it difficult not to be inspired by all the history and art that lives among its streets.' Raj could feel Sita's eyes on him.

'I'd love to visit one day. But I don't think that's possible.'

'Why not?'

Sita giggled. Raj was waiting for a further reply, but there was none. Apparently, her laughter was her answer.

Sita wagged her head. 'You speak like them.'

Raj's eyebrows drew together, not understanding what she meant. 'Like them? Like whom?'

'The British.' She smiled.

'Oh…' Raj didn't know what to make of her comment. 'I guess I learned it from my teachers.'

Sita twisted her pallu as silence filled the room again.

Raj let out another deep sigh. 'Sita, you are very beautiful…'

Sita smiled and giggled, and her earrings jingled as she did.

Raj blushed as he continued, 'And you seem to come from a wonderful family. I'm just not quite sure if this is something I'm comfortable with.' Raj examined Sita's response as her eyes didn't meet his. He decided to shift his approach. 'I mean, I'm not sure of when I will return from the war. When I do' – he paused – 'or *if* I do, I wouldn't be opposed to meeting again. That is, if you have not been married off. Wars are very unpredictable. I know my involvement already has been nothing short of it … What I'm trying to say is, I don't want you to wait around for me.'

She pulled at her sari, her eyes glistening.

Raj's eyes searched hers. 'I hope that wasn't harsh of me to say.'

Sita kept quiet.

'Sita, I'm…' he wanted to continue in his explanation but stopped when he saw the families making their way back to the house. Sita covered her face again. Raj was sure it was to hide how upset she was. He had only spent five minutes alone with her, and had already managed to offend her. He shook his head, disappointed by how he had handled things.

'And how are things with you two?' asked Mrs Sharma with folded hands.

Not wanting Sita to answer, Raj decided to jump in. 'Everything went well.' He shot a glance over at Sita but couldn't tell if what he had said met with her approval. He continued anyway, 'I was telling Sita that, after the war, when I return to India, we will definitely meet again and figure out how to proceed.'

No sooner had he finished his sentence than Dr Sharma puffed out his chest. 'Wonderful! The Kohli family and the Sharma family will soon be united.'

His announcement brought about hugs and joyous cries from the mothers. Raj nervously bowed in Sita's general direction, hoping she would forgive him. And amidst the goodbyes, Sita leaned towards Raj and gently whispered in his ear: 'I will pray that you make it back home safely.'

Later that night, while Raj lay in bed, he tried to convince himself that an arranged marriage wouldn't be all that bad – they would just have to get over the uncomfortable silence. He finally succumbed to sleep and was left dreaming of what other sweets and savoury treats lay waiting for him tomorrow.

***

After ten days of constant pampering by his mother, and a seemingly endless stream of visitors who came from all corners of Dehradun to pay their respects, Raj's leave came to an end. Having said goodbye to one and all, he left for Jhelum.

His mother clung on to him until he closed the car door. With a great amount of trouble, he worked to settle the lump in his throat that leaped up at every utterance of goodbye from his sobbing mother. He observed every angle of her aged face, trying to memorize every line in great detail before the car pulled away.

He cast away the thoughts that roared wildly in his mind, telling him it was the last time he would see her.

# CHAPTER TEN

## *Jhelum, 1942*

Upon his return to Jhelum, Raj didn't have very much time to get used to regimental life before he was told that he would be departing once again.

Raj was not excited to see the lieutenant colonel – a dislike that was soon reinforced.

'How did you get this posting?' An angry Lt Colonel Anup Chowdhry shouted from the doorway of Raj's quarters.

'Excuse me, sir?' Raj asked with innocently raised eyebrows after he saluted – a salute which Lt Colonel Chowdhry did not return.

'This posting, Lieutenant,' he enunciated every word with immense distaste. He vigorously shook a letter above his head which looked as if it were about to burst at any moment from the rage that boiled inside. 'I received this letter today. It says that as soon as you return from leave you are to report to Delhi to be part of the viceroy's bloody detail!'

Raj blinked a few times, working to comprehend what the lieutenant colonel was saying. 'I'm sorry, sir. I haven't the faintest idea of what you're talking about.'

'Sure, play ignorant.' Lt Colonel Chowdhry scoffed. 'I see you talking with the British officers,' he spat. 'You don't wear a turban, you sport an English haircut and speak like them. You try to pretend you're one of them. But you'll never be.' He narrowed his eyes and gritted his teeth as he leaned forward.

Raj bit his tongue, his nostrils flared.

'It's a shame that it's being denied,' Lt Colonel Chowdhry said, standing up straight, gripping the letter. A sly smile crept over his lips. 'A better posting for you will be with the front-line troops of the Punjab Regiment.'

Raj's face fell. He wasn't sure how Lt Colonel Chowdhry could countermand orders from Delhi. But that was not for him to question.

Chowdhry's smile grew at Raj's silence.

'Sir,' Raj finally said, clenching his jaw, 'I am here to follow orders. So, if I am posted to the front lines, I will go.'

Raj's obedience seemed to infuriate the lieutenant colonel even more. Raj watched as a look of disgust flickered across his face. 'You think you should be sitting in my chair, don't you?' His words were sharp and pointed.

Before Raj answered, he carefully considered the words he would use. Raj knew that Lt Colonel Chowdhry's suspicion of him was unfounded, and he was only acting out of jealousy and spite.

'With all due respect, sir,' Raj began, 'it took you eighteen years to get where you are. I have a strange feeling it will take me much less.' Raj saluted the lieutenant colonel, pushed past him out of the room, and marched down the hall, his boots clicking loudly against the concrete floor.

***

In June of 1942, Raj was again on a train, but this time to the port of Karachi. He was exhausted by all the postings and transfers –

before he could settle into one location, he was transplanted to the next. Where did he belong?

With the rhythm of the train's wheels drumming on the tracks and the subsequent ship's passage across the turbulent sea, Raj's heart raced. He had been in the military for a year now, and this was the first time he would be in battle. Of course, he had volunteered knowing that the probability of him being sent to the front lines was, in all actuality, high. He had even counted on it. But now, as the ship began to dock at the port of Alexandria, the reality of it all became ever so clear. His mind disobeyed his silent pleas not to dwell on what could happen, but the imagined scenarios intensified, each one more excruciatingly morbid than the last.

Raj stepped off the ship and was driven to a reinforcement camp near the pyramids and sphinx of Giza. The golden-bricked giants stood imposing, scattered throughout the desert. Raj took off his cap as they drove by, in awe of human capability.

The jeep drove along the dust roads, and although the drive produced a breeze, it didn't shelter them from the ruthless sun. The heat was suffocating, and the air even smelled hot. Sweat formed along Raj's forehead and dripped into his eyes, causing them to sting. The tires kicked up sand, and tired of wielding his arm for protection from it all, Raj eventually pulled the handkerchief from his pocket to tie around his face.

Upon reaching camp, Raj found his new living quarters: a poorly ventilated tent. He hadn't been in his tent for very long before he heard a voice from outside, addressing him.

'Lieutenant Kohli.'

'Yes, I'm here,' Raj replied, not knowing who was calling him.

'Colonel Evans here, please join me outside in this damnedest of ovens.'

Raj walked out and saluted the colonel. 'Come on, Lieutenant, let's go to my makeshift office.'

Raj followed the colonel to his tent and sat down in a canvas chair, while the colonel walked around to the opposite side of a dilapidated cane desk.

'Lieutenant,' Colonel Evans said, 'welcome to Egypt. You better get used to heat, even though I'm sure it gets up in temperature where you're from in India as well.' He gave a friendly smile. 'I've been informed you are a trained machine-gun officer,' he continued, his neck pushed forward and his nose scrunched, awaiting Raj's reply.

'Yes, sir,' Raj responded.

'Where did you do your training? Mhow?'

'No, sir.'

'I'm not aware of another machine-gun school in India, Lieutenant.'

'It wasn't in India, sir.'

'Not in India?' the puzzled colonel asked. 'In that case, where, Lieutenant?'

'Lincolnshire, sir,' replied Raj to the colonel's utter amazement.

'Lincolnshire! What the devil were you doing in England?'

'That's where I was commissioned, sir.'

Colonel Evans stroked his bristly moustache. 'Where, may I ask, did you go to officer candidate school?'

'Aldershot, Colonel.'

The colonel's eyebrows knitted. 'Are you a King's Commissioned Officer then?'

'To be truthful, Colonel,' Raj paused, 'I'm not sure what I am.'

The colonel gave him a crooked smile. 'Was your commission announced by the war office in *The London Gazette*?'

'No, it wasn't. That's why I'm not sure what I am.'

'Well, just know that whatever you are, it's all very impressive.'

Raj bowed slightly. 'Thank you, sir.'

'And the Middle East Training Centre in Palestine needs someone with such qualifications and experience as yours.'

Raj didn't respond. He had just been transferred there, he had just put down his kit a moment ago, and now it sounded as if he was being moved again. He wasn't looking to pack up and leave once more.

Colonel Evans nodded. 'Well, thank you for stopping in. I look forward to meeting you again in the future.'

'Sir.' Raj saluted and left the tent.

***

A few days later, Raj received orders to join the 3/1st Punjab Regiment, which at that time were stationed just outside Cairo.

Upon his arrival, Raj went to meet the men he was to command. His uniform was drenched in sweat and clung to his skin. He found his men lying on the sand under man-made shade, made from a stretched tan cloth held up by leftover tripwire tied to a nearby tent. Some napped, while others swatted away persistent, buzzing flies.

'Good afternoon, men.' Raj spoke in Urdu, in his most commanding voice.

The men squinted up at him, and when their eyes finally adjusted to the sun's brightness, they jumped up one by one, saluting and standing at attention. 'Sir!'

He smiled as he surveyed them. Most of them were Muslim, some Sikh like Raj, and others Hindu. But all were Punjabi. Some had turbans and neatly trimmed beards. Their faces were young and betrayed discomfort, with redness and sweat.

Raj saluted the group back. He paced in front of them, stopping in front of a particularly young soldier whose beard wasn't as full as the rest. 'How old are you, jawan?' Raj asked.

'Eighteen years old, Sahib,' the young soldier replied with a crack in his voice as his face twitched nervously.

Raj examined his hyperextended salute, his fingers dry and cracked, sand and dirt trapped under his nails.

'At ease,' Raj directed and watched as the soldier let down his salute with a long breath. 'What is your name?'

'Mohammad Raffa, Sahib,' he replied and wiped a line of sweat that fell from his brow.

Raj looked out at the rest of the group. 'I am Lieutenant Kohli, and I will have the honour of being your commanding officer. I look forward to getting to know each of you personally.'

His words were met with smiles and appreciative nods as a line formed to shake his hand. At each handshake, Raj's smile grew. He finally felt like he belonged.

***

The desert sun was at its highest point but was soon hidden behind a heavy curtain of blowing sand. Raj hoped it wasn't an omen for what was to come. As each day passed, the time when he and his men would see action against the mighty German Africa Corps in Gabr el Abidi, Libya, drew nearer. Rommel's vaunted Africa Corps, troops hardened by years of battle in that part of the world, waited for the attack they knew would come at some point.

Raj and his troops prepared for battle with various strategic training exercises. The tension was high, and conversation became minimal as they all thought on what was to come. As Raj instructed his men, chills ran through his body. Just past the colossal sand dunes and a few hundred yards away, stood the Germans – no doubt preparing as well.

The wind had subsided and much of the pyramids and the sphinx was visible again, though with an additional layer of sand.

'Good show, don't you think?' A major stopped and stood watch over the soldiers as they practised using their bayonets, shouting at each thrust into the surrounding, and now slayed, air.

'I think so,' Raj said with a salute.

The major saluted back. 'I don't mean to interrupt. I had the intention of introducing myself earlier. I'm Major Charles Boulter.' He held out his hand for Raj to shake.

'Nice to meet you, Major.'

'Looks like you've got a good company on your hands here.' Major Boulter tilted his head forward, towards the men, then squinted up at the sun. 'It's a hellhole here, isn't it?'

Raj laughed. 'I don't think anyone could mistake this for paradise, no.'

Major Boulter smiled and nodded. 'The only thing making this bloody place bearable is the Scotch. Granted, we are the ones who brought it here, but nonetheless it is here and ready for us to consume at the ready. I hope you'll join the rest of us officers as we drink ourselves silly, trying to forget this godforsaken sorry excuse for a country. Really, I'm not quite sure why we don't just let the Germans have this territory,' he joked, a boisterous laugh escaping him.

Raj joined his laughter but was soon interrupted by a saluting jawan.

'Colonel Dalton Sahib wants to see you,' he relayed to Raj.

'You had better go,' Major Boulter said with a slap on Raj's back. 'Depending on what he says, we can have a whisky waiting for you when you get back. Scratch that – no matter what he says, we'll have a whisky waiting for you.' He ended with another laugh.

Raj smiled and excused himself to follow the jawan to the colonel's tent.

Raj opened the flap of the tent slowly and found Colonel Dalton inside, not at work but lying in his cot with his feet up, reading *War and Peace*. The light of the sun was mostly blocked out by various large drapes that hung across the ceilings and sides.

'You called, sir?' asked Raj.

The colonel did not look up from his reading and instead pointed to a chair at the foot of the bed.

'Sit down, Kohli.'

Raj did so and waited patiently to be addressed. Colonel Dalton, a rather large man, with sand-coloured hair and red cheeks, put his book down, swung his feet over the side of the cot and sat up. 'You're a lucky chap, Kohli.'

Raj waited for the reason as to why.

'You're going to Palestine.' Colonel Dalton hesitated for a moment and then continued. 'That's right, we are going to be fighting in bloody Libya, and you're going to rest your feet in Palestine.'

'I'm sorry, sir?' Raj replied, hoping the colonel would explain further.

'You have been informed that there is need for a machine-gun instructor at the school in Palestine by Colonel Evans, have you not?' Colonel Dalton lit a cigarette.

Raj responded with a quick nod.

'So, off you go. Have a fabulous time in the sun under the date palms, instructing soldiers on how to fire that bloody useless weapon. But please, just think of us now and then, will you?' Dalton said sarcastically as he took a long drag of his cigarette and lay back on his cot.

Raj closed his eyes. He couldn't believe his luck – or lack of it. He was exhausted from being transferred from one camp to the next. Couldn't he just pick a unit and stick to it? Along with disappointment, anger began to seep in. He clenched his fists as he thought about his men receiving the news about him leaving right before they went off to battle. They would feel betrayed. They would be sent to the front lines to die, while he would be running off to safety. It wasn't fair.

'Sir, I want you to know that this is not my choice.' Raj stood up.

The colonel lowered his book to look at Raj. 'You can go now, Lieutenant.'

'Sir, if it means anything, I really do not want to go to Palestine, I would like to stay here.' Raj stopped for a moment to gauge a possible objection from Colonel Dalton.

When the colonel continued to read, Raj decided to add to his statement. 'Sir, if it's all right with you, I'd like to go into battle with my men for a couple of days and then go to Palestine.'

Colonel Dalton looked strangely at Raj over the rims of his reading glasses. He shook his head and went back to reading.

Raj continued to look for an excuse that the colonel would buy: 'Sir, what if I get some mysterious illness that only lasts two days?'

Colonel Dalton didn't budge and continued to read. Raj responded by not budging, as well. He wasn't going to take no for an answer. Dalton clicked his tongue, sat up and closed his book. 'And what happens if you get killed in action? Then what?'

'Then we would have nothing more to worry about. You could tell the divisional commander that I succumbed to the illness.'

The colonel ripped his glasses off his face, obviously wanting to retort but not sure how. Defeated, he began to read again. Raj, deflated, saluted quietly before leaving the tent.

The colonel grunted after Raj: 'Kohli.'

Raj opened the tent flap again, his heart pounding, readying himself to be cited for insubordination.

'Yes, sir,' he answered.

'Have you ever read this book, Lieutenant?' he asked, waving it in front of him.

Raj shook his head.

'Well, hopefully you will, one day,' Colonel Dalton continued with a tight-lipped smile.

'Yes, sir,' replied Raj, then added curiously, 'Why, sir?'

'Because then you will find out that you need to concentrate on the damn book to understand it, and because of you, I can't bloody well do that.'

'I'm sorry, s—sir,' stuttered Raj, wondering how to proceed.

Dalton let out a deep sigh. 'Okay, Lieutenant, you will have your wish. You can stay for our first battle, but after that' – he lifted his eyebrows high – 'you must go to Palestine, or I will get into trouble.'

Raj couldn't believe his ears. He began to smile, and instead of saying anything that could possibly aggravate the situation and have the colonel change his mind, he saluted smartly and left.

'Damn book,' Raj heard him say, followed by the sound of what seemed to be a book thrown at a tent wall.

Raj left for the mess tent in search of Major Boulter and a stiff drink.

'Ah, there he is,' Major Boulter shouted as Raj walked in. He immediately found an empty tin cup and gave a generous pour to Raj. 'Now it's time for that damn Scotch!'

The alcohol did its work, each sip easing the tension within Raj's body. But he tightened up again when Colonel Dalton came stomping in and swigged brandy straight from the bottle.

'Damn book,' he mumbled under his breath in between swigs.

The other officers heartily laughed and joked, pushing out of their minds what was to happen on the battlefield in a few short hours.

Their time, however, was interrupted when Colonel Dalton stood up. He lifted his bottle and proclaimed, 'Here's to Lieutenant Kohli who, after our action against the Nazis in Libya, will be whisked away to bask in the hot Palestinian sunshine, no doubt followed by some hard drinking in the bars of Tel Aviv in the company of some exotic women. Lucky bugger.'

'Is that true, old chap?' Major Boulter put down his cup, followed by the other officers who eyed Raj curiously. 'You're leaving?'

Raj was lost for words and took a sip of his Scotch to gain courage. 'I'm being summoned to Palestine to instruct—'

A chorus of collective groans came from the surrounding officers.

'Bup, bup, bup,' Colonel Dalton stood. 'No moping about. Let's give this man a proper send-off by beating the goddamn Nazis!' He raised his nearly empty bottle in Raj's general direction.

The crowd raised their drinking cups and bottles in response with a roar.

Colonel Dalton gritted his teeth. 'Let's give them hell tomorrow, boys!'

***

Raj left the tent, wary of drinking too much. He wanted to prepare and be in tip-top shape for the coming battle. It still being the middle of the day, he went to spend the rest of it with his men.

'Lieutenant Sahib,' said Mohammad Raffa. 'Is this your first time in battle?'

Raj wasn't sure what the right answer was. He hesitated before telling the truth. 'Yes, it is.'

The young jawan smiled at him and wagged his head. 'Me too, sir.'

Ghulam Husain, another jawan, held out a tattered photograph to Raj. 'This is my family. My wife and three girls.' He smiled as he pointed them out individually. 'I keep the photo in my front pocket, so they are always with me. Do you have a wife, Sahib?' Ghulam asked as he cupped his hand in the sand and watched a steady stream of it slip out of his grasp.

Raj thought about Esther. 'No, no I don't,' he answered.

Jawan Nur Shah piped in, 'Oh Sahib, that won't do. You must get a wife.'

Raj let out a laugh. 'You sound like my mother.' He thought of Sita. He thought that the polite thing to do was to write to her, but it didn't feel right. He wondered if he should put his feelings aside and force himself to go along with his mother's wishes. Perhaps being in love didn't matter. His mother did say that the feeling of love would come after…

The conversations continued, and as the day turned into night the conversations turned morbid. The idea of death danced about the edges of the camp.

Eventually, the men gave in to sleep but Raj stayed awake, running the plan of attack over and over in his mind, until, finally, it was time.

***

It was 2.30 a.m., and under the cover of darkness and in all quietness, the 3/1st Punjab Regiment manoeuvred to surprise position from the north in coordination with other battalions. Unfortunately, the Germans were waiting, and before any of the Indians were ready, they found themselves being ferociously attacked. Hours of bombardment by heavy artillery followed by an all-out assault by tanks and infantry had the Indians suffering tremendous casualties.

Raj, who was being held in reserve – the colonel not wanting him to be exposed to any real fighting – was livid when he saw the bodies, wounded and dead, return. His eyes were on fire when he stood next to Colonel Dalton. He had stood there behind a sand dune in relative safety with the colonel, watching the action, and more angrily, watching the troops – who, just a few hours ago, had been sitting and talking to him about their homes in the Punjab and the dreams they had upon their return – being carried back on stretchers, their bodies covered with blankets.

'Sir,' Raj was animated. 'Sir, I can't just stand here and watch this carnage. Can I at least help in the attack?' Colonel Dalton didn't reply. 'Sir,' implored Raj for the umpteenth time, 'I can't just stand here.'

Finally, the colonel looked over at him with sadness painted on his face. 'I could really use you, but I just can't do that.'

Raj suddenly had an idea. 'Sir, what would happen if you were doing something else, and when you looked up to talk to me, I wasn't here.'

Colonel Dalton laughed. 'First you interrupt my reading of *War and Peace*, and now you want me to be guilty of dereliction of duty?' He paused for a minute. 'Lieutenant, you're a Sikh, aren't you?'

'I was born one, yes, sir.'

'What the hell does that mean?'

'Sir, both my parents are Sikh, but I went to Bishop Cotton School in Shimla. I had no exposure from then on to Sikhism. I never had long hair, nor do I follow any of the religious customs.'

The colonel shook his head. 'You were born a Sikh though, right?'

'Yes, sir,' replied Raj, unsure of why the colonel needed to know.

'They say there are no better fighters than the Sikh, don't they?' The corner of the colonel's mouth twisted into a smile.

Suddenly, Raj understood the colonel's line of questioning. 'Yes, sir!' he nearly shouted, his heart racing, the adrenaline in his blood racing through his veins.

'Okay, Lieutenant. But please, for the sake of my army career, stay alive.' The colonel was about to continue, until he looked him over, searching him up and down. 'Kohli, where is your weapon?'

Raj shook his head, 'Don't have one.'

As Raj ran up to Major Boulter, he could hear the colonel finally process his reply. 'I beg your pardon?'

The major looked back at the colonel, who simply shrugged. 'Okay, Lieutenant, I want you take these men' – he pointed to about a hundred or so being held in reserve – 'and attack here.' He pointed to an X on his map.

Raj couldn't believe he was so anxious to go into battle. The troops collective nervousness was palpable. Raj sat down next to them and briefed them on the assault they were about to engage in.

Instantaneously, the battle cry of the Punjab Regiment was sounded. Led by a very determined Lieutenant Rajendra Shamsher Singh Kohli, the troops made their way down a steep sand dune and into a hail of bullets – baptism by fire.

Bullets whizzed through the men and hit the sand, cutting them down in their tracks.

Suddenly, Raj heard the retreat whistle blow.

'Retreat! Stop! Return to camp!' Raj screamed so loud his throat throbbed with a sharp pain.

He waved his hands, leading his men back behind the sand dune before he lost all of them. The bullets were spraying around them continuously.

Breathing heavily, Raj peered over the dune through his binoculars. The moon lit up the dead and wounded strewn across the desert, their blood darkening the white sand.

Raj's sight fell upon an outline. Sepoy Mohammad Raffa was lying in the sand, his steel Brodie helmet resting a few feet away from him. Blood steadily flowed from his head, a bullet wound on its side. His chest rose and fell ever so slightly.

'Take these,' Raj ordered, thrusting his binoculars at Havildar Major Mir Ahmed.

'Where are you going?'

'Out there,' replied Raj, pointing to where Sepoy Mohammad Raffa lay, and hastily threw off his kit.

'Sir, no,' he warned Raj. 'He will be dead soon.'

Raj ignored the havildar major as he began to slither down the side of the dune. He needed to keep his body as close to the sand as possible. The sand got into his mouth as he shuffled along. It was plastered against his sweaty face and fell from his eyelashes into his eyes, scratching them every time he blinked. He wouldn't pay any attention to it, he couldn't – there was no time. He was focused on his mission, and second by second, inch by inch, he came closer and closer to Sepoy Mohammad Raffa. A couple of inches more, and he would be there.

He reached forward. His outstretched fingers clawed and found the sepoy's leg. 'Keep your head down,' he said.

The sepoy quickly nodded in compliance, the light from the stars above reflected in his glistening eyes, and he tightly closed his lips to keep silent, even though his body trembled.

All around him, the Germans continued their attack. In the distance, flames shot up from the surrounding buildings.

Raj pulled at Mohammad Raffa's trousers and began to drag his body back towards the top of the sand dune. Raj gritted his teeth, his eyes bulged, he could feel his muscles tearing as he used every ounce of strength he had to pull the sepoy to safety. A stray bullet whistled past him and penetrated the sand to his left with a dull thud.

A hand stretched out from the top of the dune and tugged on his arm.

'Let me help, sir.' Havildar Major Ahmed leaned over.

Between the two of them, they pulled Mohammad Raffa into their territory.

Raj yelled for a medic and one ran over. Raj grasped tightly on to Mohammad's hand as the medic attended to his wound, which was caked with sand and blood. The sepoy whimpered. At the touch of the medic, Mohammad instinctively flailed his legs and shoved his hips in the air. His sharp screams pierced the night air. Havildar Major Ahmed shone a flashlight from above, helping the medic see. Mohammad's dirty face was streaked with tears.

'Kohli!'

Raj turned to see Colonel Dalton over by a tent, standing with his hands on his hips. Raj squeezed Mohammad's hand before getting up to meet the colonel.

'Lieutenant, if you were supposed to be here, I would recommend you for a Military Cross. But because you aren't here, I can't.' He released his hands from his sides. 'But I can give you a handshake.' Dalton stretched out his hand and Raj shook it. 'That was the stupidest and bravest thing I have ever seen anyone do. Now, I need you to leave before the next attack. You are to go catch a lorry. It will carry you to Palestine through allied territory.'

'Yes, sir.' Raj nodded earnestly and saluted him.

Once Raj had packed up his meagre belongings, he made his way back through the lines and to the lorry. He climbed into the back, and with much crunching of gears, began his journey. The rocking of the truck put him to sleep almost immediately, and there he remained in the comfort of his dreams until he reached Jerusalem.

# CHAPTER ELEVEN

## *Glasgow, 1943*

On 15 June, Norah arrived in Glasgow, where even in the middle of summer, it looked as if it were recovering from a bout of incessantly dreary winter, with its dark grey clouds threatening to pour down at a moment's notice. It was chilly to say the least, and the barren hills and valleys looked depressing without a coat of summer greenery. Even the numerous lochs looked dark and unwelcoming. There was a nasty, lazy breeze coming in off the Irish Sea. Norah clutched her coat tighter as the wind whipped around her. She pulled her scarf up around her bare neck and tucked her nose deep into its folds, hoping to find some sort of relief.

She was directed to the hospital where she was to meet her new matron and the staff of nurses, doctors and orderlies she would be serving with. She waited in line to check in with a uniformed nurse who would provide more information on the exact services needed of her on the ship and where her living quarters would be.

The line was quiet. Norah could only imagine everyone was as anxious yet excited as she was. She kept biting her lip in anticipation and found herself peeking around the person in front of her periodically to gauge how long it would be until she reached the front.

'Name, please,' the nurse muttered mechanically.

'Norah.'

The nurse looked up over her glasses. 'Last name.'

'Oh, my apologies. Of course, you would want a last name. How silly of me. Eggleton. E-g-g-l—'

'Here are your instructions.' She held out a letter while simultaneously crossing off Norah's name from a list. 'Stand over there, in that room where everyone else is, until you are instructed otherwise.'

'Norah!' came a shout from the common room, at which the nurse rolled her eyes and pursed her lips.

'Erm, thank you, sister.' Norah, put off by the nurse's demeanour, took the paper and looked around for who called her.

'Oh, Ruth, it's so good to see you, dear!' Norah and Ruth hugged. Suddenly conscious of the lack of talk in the room and how any sound reverberated off the walls, Norah whispered, 'I was wondering when I would get to see you.'

'So exciting we get to serve together, isn't it?' Ruth squeezed Norah's hand. 'I had to say goodbye to Mikey three weeks ago.'

'Oh?' Norah looked around, hoping they weren't disturbing the room.

'Yes, he got posted to a hospital ship as well, but to one called the *St David*.' Ruth's smile faded into a pout.

'I'm so sorry to hear that, dear.' Norah then remembered that she hadn't read the paper she was given. 'Does this give us details about our ship?' She began to skim the document. 'The *Leinster*, eh? Oh, it says it was a troop carrier that has been retrofitted into a hospital ship. How about that?'

'Yes, interesting. Hope it's been fitted enough. Mikey said in a letter that his ship severely lacks space for patients.'

'Oh, goodness.' Norah wondered if that would be the case for theirs.

Norah surveyed the room. Lining the walls stood her new family. Most nurses looked young, coloured with naiveté and nervous anxiety. She wondered if that's how she looked. The doctors in the room were of different ages, and most of them looked calm, not the slightest bit unnerved by the reason they were there: to attend to the wounded of a gruesome and bloody war.

'Attention, everyone.' A pleasant, smiling matron stood at the front of the room, her hands clasped. She was short and plump, wearing an immaculate uniform with bright shining buttons and a stiffly starched headdress, along with the most well-polished shoes Norah had ever seen. 'Thank you all for being on time. Welcome. I am Matron Geraldine Edge, and I will be leading you on the *Leinster*. You should have received your document detailing your position and lodging on the ship. If you have not received it, please visit Sister Cornwall at the front. If you have, please line up outside with your things. Each of you will be bussed to the docks in a moment. Once you arrive at the docks, follow the orders of the sailors to the *Leinster*. From there, find your cabin and join the rest of the crew and staff in the mess deck promptly at 1630 hours. There, we will enjoy our first meal together. Now, if you will, please line up outside.'

The crowd of staff turned and made their way to the door. Norah and Ruth followed suit, and Norah felt a little like they were cattle being herded when Sister Cornwall started shouting from behind the group as a bottleneck began to form at the door: 'Come on now, hurry up! Get yourself outside! Get in line!'

Norah was thankful that Sister Cornwall wasn't the matron and was hoping to have limited contact with her on the ship.

Norah and Ruth, along with ten others, piled into an ambulance while the rest of the lot waited their turn. It wasn't long before they reached the docks and piled out in front of another sister barking orders.

'This way to the *Leinster*! Get your bags and watch your step! Quick now!'

Standing at firm attention at the end of the dock was the liner. She was freshly painted white with a bright red stripe across her body, interrupted by a red cross close to her bow. Thick black smoke emanated from her funnel and numerous little lifeboats were tied to her, skirting her terrace. She was pointed towards the open sea, ready to head across the dark waters as her passengers loaded on through the fuel doors.

Ruth and Norah boarded with the help of two young sailors who held out their hands for them.

'It looks like my quarters are this way.' Ruth pointed down the hallway.

Norah took out her letter as she read the door closest to her. 'I think I'm the opposite way.'

Ruth frowned. 'I was hoping we'd be closer together.'

'Me too, but I'm sure it won't even matter. We'll see plenty of one another,' Norah said as she squeezed Ruth's hand. 'Let's see to our rooms and I'll meet you at the mess with everyone else.'

Ruth nodded and went to look for her cabin. As she passed by each cabin, Norah kept checking for the number corresponding with the one printed on her sheet.

'Ah, here we are.' Norah stopped at a small door listed as B7-29.

As an officer, Norah had her own cabin, though it wasn't very much. She twisted the handle, and it creaked open to a humble room that was cramped with a cot and tiny bedside table. Its small porthole barely lit up even that tiny room.

'I've seen larger cupboards,' she remarked to herself.

Upon entering, she realized that the walls were painted a putrid shade of green. The only upside she could find was that it had its own bathroom. Norah dumped her kit bag containing all her personal items on her cot and began to set about trying to make the small space as homey as possible.

The poetry book Norman had given her stared up at her from amongst the pile. For a moment, she stood there staring back, worried that if she were to open it, it would remind her how far she was from home. Looking to keep any emotions from bubbling up, she placed the book in the drawer of the bedside table and closed it.

She hung up her uniforms on the rod provided next to the bathroom, and pulled out the large drawer under the bed, into which she unceremoniously dumped her remaining items. 'I'll get to them another time,' she said and closed the cabin door behind her to make her way upstairs to the mess.

When Norah opened the door to the mess, she was immediately struck by the buzzing of various people talking. She suddenly became aware of how she had walked in alone.

Maybe I should have waited for Ruth before coming in, she thought.

She scanned the tables to see if Ruth was already there, but if she was, she was unable to spot her in the crowd.

'Sit here, dear.' An older woman with light blonde hair pinned up neatly patted the chair next to her.

'Oh, how nice of you. Thank you,' Norah said with a smile as she pulled the chair to sit down.

'I'm Olivia and this is Anne,' she pointed to the young woman sitting next to her.

'Hello, pleasure to meet you. I'm Norah.'

They exchanged smiles.

Anne leaned over. 'So, what are your thoughts about being on a ship, Norah?'

'I'm rather excited,' she replied.

'Hmm, I guess I am as well.' Anne nodded in agreement.

'It looks as if I'm the only one not,' Olivia said, raising her eyebrows.

'And why's that?' Norah inquired.

'I don't like being away from home, dearie. I'm much older than you lot. I'd rather be there, enjoying the company of my dog.'

'I can understand that.' Norah didn't like thinking about how far away from her family she'd actually be. London was far enough from Kidlington in her mind. 'May I ask why you signed up for service then?'

'One day, my brute of a husband and I had quite the row, and he said he'd be better off without me. Next day, I went to the recruiting station and joined up. I told him: "We're putting that to the test!" I'm thinking a few months of me at war will straighten him up.' Olivia laughed, causing Norah and Anne to join in. 'Gives me a right good laugh every time I think of him fumbling to make supper on his own. Or the hell it would give him to fold his own knickers!' Olivia's face reddened, trying to catch her breath as tears streaked down her face.

As their laughter faded, Norah was left with an aching side. She surveyed the room once more and saw other laughing faces, new people to meet who would soon become her best friends and family.

She grinned. It was going to be a real adventure – one she could finally call her own.

# CHAPTER TWELVE

## *Jerusalem, 1943*

Raj awoke to the sight of what could have easily been mistaken for a Hollywood set. He almost expected Victor Mature or some other star to make an appearance. The buildings and people carried on untouched and unfazed, as if there were no war raging on in other parts of the world.

His encampment was to the west of the city, on the road to Tel Aviv, a short drive from Jerusalem.

Once Raj had reported to the commander, he dropped his bags in his tent and started his exploration of the land in earnest. As a boy, he had studied these ancient ruins from the crisp pages of a book and was in awe that he now actually had the opportunity to step foot in them.

On his first day instructing at the Middle East training camp, Raj was introduced to his students as an expert on the Vickers medium machine gun.

'And what makes this gun so special, Lieutenant?' a sceptical gunner asked.

'This' – Raj ran his fingers down the spine of the machine – 'is the finest automatic weapon that the Almighty could have provided to the British. Just be glad we have it and not the Germans.' He nodded for assurance.

The crowd raised their eyebrows in unison.

'But you can't shoot straight with it,' replied one officer. 'The sight is set to the right by five-eighths of an inch.'

Another said, 'It's very limiting. You can only swivel to the left and right. It can't go up and down. Whereas with the Bren gun, it can be pointed in any direction you like.'

And yet another, 'Yeah and your gun is water-cooled, so you have to carry a jerrycan of water around with you.'

It became obvious to Raj that they weren't fans of the Vickers, and so he decided to see if he could convert them. 'Let's go to the range, shall we?'

Reluctantly, the group, together with Colonel Evans, who was fascinated by Raj's assertion, made their way to the firing range.

'All right, I need three volunteers now,' Raj said as he pointed out the most sceptical looking of the group to join him at the machine gun. 'Good, now load the gun with a belt of ammunition, please.' Once this was done, Raj cleared his throat and sat upon the ground. He fired the gun in a long explosive burst. 'Now.' Raj patted his hands together, wiping away the dirt. 'Can someone please go and fetch the target?'

A corporal in the back ran and unpinned the target, and with wide eyes brought it back for the group to see. 'That's bloody amazing!'

Every single bullet had hit the bullseye in a close cluster.

Colonel Evans pushed past the crew to take a closer look. 'I have never seen that done before. Impressive, Lieutenant,' he said.

'All right, but what about what Davis said? It doesn't move up and down,' a gunner yelled above the crowd as he crossed his arms.

'Good point,' Raj said with a furrow of his brow. He turned to the gun and quickly began dismantling the weapon.

The soldiers looked at one another, confused by Raj's actions. With intermittent orders shouted out for various parts, Raj began to reassemble the gun. Once he reattached the barrel and the trigger, he stood up. He loaded it with a belt of ammunition again and pointed it back out at the pinned targets in the field. Again, he unleashed a rain of bullets, but this time he moved the gun up, down, left and right.

'Bloody hell!' he heard the gunner gasp.

'Lieutenant Kohli.' Colonel Evans's jaw was agape. 'Never in all my years ... How in the world did you ... Where did you learn to do this?'

Raj smiled. 'Just now. This was a concern, and so I decided to see if there was a solution.'

The colonel shook his head. 'Unbelievable.' He then dismissed the class.

***

A month passed, and Raj successfully brought all who had witnessed him use the gun to believe that the Vickers was the most superior weapon. When he did have spare time, which was very limited, he ventured out to explore more of Tel Aviv and Jerusalem. However, Raj couldn't help but feel guilty for enjoying himself, while he knew that his regiment was far from any sort of relaxation.

One August day, Raj was summoned to Colonel Evans's office. They exchanged salutes.

'Sir? You wanted to see me?'

'Yes, I thought you'd like to know that I've put in a request for the entire British army to be instructed on how to use the Vickers in the manner you modelled.'

Raj bowed. 'What an honour, sir.'

'And now that you have accomplished your goal of superb instructing, you will be pleased to know that you are being sent back to your battalion with the Punjab Regiment.'

Raj raised his eyebrows. 'Oh, thank you, sir. Thank you.'

'Yes, quite right. But you can't return before…' The colonel lifted a small wooden box from his desk, opening it to reveal two silver metal pips. He took them out and began to pin them on each of Raj's shoulders. 'Captain Kohli,' he said with pride, 'let me be the first to congratulate you on a well-deserved promotion.' He gave his hand to shake.

Raj, stunned, saluted Colonel Evans, who stood up straight and offered a long salute back.

***

A few days later, Raj rejoined his battalion in Haifa. He received a tumultuous welcome upon his arrival, with almost everyone standing and clapping as he walked by.

'Welcome back, old chap! And a captain, no less.' Major Boulter hugged Raj. 'We're going to need to drink to your return.'

Raj agreed and continued down the line, greeting the officers. He noticed that some were no longer there, but he was afraid to ask about them.

Major Boulter, apparently noticing Raj's query written all over his face, said, 'Yes. We lost a good many since you were last with us.'

Raj stared at the floor for a moment to make sure he didn't lose his composure, then continued on his way.

He stopped by Havildar Major Ahmed. 'How is Mohammed Raffa?' he asked.

'Salaam, Sahib. He transferred to a hospital not far away. He is recovering well, from what I hear.' Ahmed smiled sadly.

There was talk of what was coming next for the battalion. The Italian Army had surrendered, but the Germans showed no indication that they would. The Allies knew that, as they got closer to the German homeland, the fighting would, in all likelihood, increase in ferocity. But until they received their new orders, the officers and men of the 3/1st Punjab Regiment took full advantage of the downtime to recharge their batteries and hone their fighting skills.

***

A few days after Raj's arrival at his unit, Major Boulter was sent on an assignment to brigade headquarters, and Colonel Dalton approached Raj in his tent.

'I'm sending you back to Jhelum,' he informed him. 'The regimental centre there needs an officer of company commanding rank, and as you're the new kid on the block, so to speak, I'm sending you back.'

Raj stepped backward, his heart pounding. 'But I only just returned here, sir.'

Colonel Dalton took in a large breath. 'I understand that. But my hands are tied. To be honest, I'm not a fan of this decision, but there isn't much I can do.'

Suddenly, Raj remembered a directive that was issued recently. 'Sir, it's my understanding that all company commanders must hold the rank of major, which I'm not.'

Dalton nodded. 'Yes, that is correct.'

Raj watched his face for a moment, trying to see if he understood what he was implying. 'Sir, that would mean I couldn't go. Unless I'm promoted, which forgive me – would be ridiculous. I'm not a major, I am not qualified to go.'

Raj wanted to feel some sort of relief, but Dalton's composure hadn't changed. The colonel sighed deeply. 'I'm sorry to do this, Kohli. Really, it doesn't bring me any pleasure, which sounds odd with what I'm about to say next … I will have to promote you.'

Raj blinked rapidly, trying to comprehend what was happening. 'Sir—'

Dalton shook his head. 'There's nothing I can do.'

Raj thought for a second. 'You could demote me,' he said to the utter astonishment of Colonel Dalton.

'Captain, do you understand what you're saying?'

'Yes, sir, I do. If you demoted me, then you couldn't send me to Jhelum.'

'Why would you want me to do that?' the colonel asked, obviously baffled by Raj's thinking.

'Sir, the reason you shouldn't promote me to major is because I don't have enough battle experience.'

'That is correct, Captain.'

'In which case, sir, demote me.' Colonel Dalton closed his eyes in disbelief. Raj's eyes widened, 'If I were a lieutenant would I have to be sent back?'

'No, a lieutenant cannot be sent.'

'Then demote me to lieutenant and send someone more qualified,' Raj replied without skipping a beat.

The colonel guffawed. 'Are you mad?'

'Sir, if that's the only way for me to remain here, then yes.' Raj nodded.

Colonel Dalton shifted in his stance. 'Are you sure you understand what you're saying, Kohli?'

'Fully,' replied Raj, sensing that the colonel was about to relent.

'I'm just not sure what to say, Captain. There aren't many men who would beg to be demoted. I wasn't prepared for that, I must say.' The colonel remained silent for what seemed like forever to Raj. Finally, with a loud sigh he continued, 'After your behaviour at Gabr el Abidi, I should have guessed it. You want to stay with your men, and I admire that. But to be willingly demoted so as to do that, my – that takes incredible devotion.' He extended his hand.

Raj took it. 'Thank you, sir. You don't know how relieved I am to stay.'

The following week, the orders came through and a fellow officer came up to Raj with the news. 'Well, old chap,' he said, 'seems like you're no longer a captain.'

Raj smiled. 'Are you on your way to see the colonel?'

The officer nodded.

'Please do me a favour.' Raj reached up and unpinned his pips. 'Give these to him.'

The officer obliged, confused.

The news of Raj's demotion floated about the camp, and quickly his men were becoming outraged. The colonel, afraid of a mutiny, requested Raj to see him.

'Kohli, this is getting out of hand.'

'I'm sorry, sir. I've tried to tell them, but they don't believe it's true,' Raj said as he watched the colonel pace the length of his tent.

'I'm going to have to ask you to speak to them again and really squash this. You're aware that rebellions have occurred in other battalions? That men have turned on their own commanders and it has resulted in the execution of their officers. I cannot have that happen here,' Dalton said.

'Yes, sir,' Raj replied. 'I will speak with them tonight.'

After coming up with a plan, Raj pulled aside Major Boulter, who had come back from his assignment.

'You've been demoted to lieutenant?' shouted Major Boulter.

'Listen, it was by my request,' Raj began to further explain the reason why, and slowly Boulter calmed down. 'I need you to come with me to speak with the men. I believe having a British officer whom they trust endorse what I'm saying will really convince them I'm telling them the truth.'

Major Boulter agreed and, by Raj's side, walked into the mess tent where the men were enjoying their dinner. They sat amongst the other ranks and ate with them. After the meal was over, Raj decided it was time to make his impassioned plea.

'I had two alternatives,' he said. 'One was to go back to Jhelum, as requested by the regimental centre, or to remain here.'

The sepoys and havildars stopped chewing to listen.

Raj continued, 'I could have gone back to Jhelum as a captain, miserable knowing that I no longer had you under my command, or stay here and take a demotion. There are captains here that are senior to me and need to be promoted first. In the end, there really wasn't an alternative. I wanted to remain here with you. We are all Punjabis. We stick together. If I am blessed to do so, I will get my opportunity to lead you all as a company commander. I promise you, above all, that the decision to take a reduction in rank was my idea and my idea alone.' Raj finished and looked to Boulter to add to his statement.

'Men, Lieutenant Kohli is only relaying the truth to you. I've seen it with my own eyes – he would do anything to stay within this regiment.'

Major Boulter's words echoed out amongst the crowd as the silence grew. It was only interrupted when a jawan stood up.

'Lieutenant Kohli, we will stand by your side no matter what. Don't worry, we know you will be a captain again very soon. We are sure of that.'

'And a major soon after!' shouted another jawan to a burst of applause.

Lieutenant Kohli was promoted to captain three months later.

# CHAPTER THIRTEEN

## *Gibraltar, 1943*

The *Leinster* began its Mediterranean voyage. Bright, sunny, cloudless, hot days were followed by clear nights, calm waters and a peasant moon.

The staff of the hospital ship took advantage of the empty days by enjoying some sunbathing, which eventually always resulted in a nap (or two) on deck.

Norah was thinking about how it was yet another perfectly sunny day at sea as she made her way up to the deck, accompanied by the book of John Keats' poems. She looked out upon the calm sea, seeing nothing but stretches of bright blue water that shimmered back at her. This peace and calmness weighed heavily on Norah. She knew there was a war going on – she just didn't feel a part of it. She remembered the newsreels that played at the movies back home, showing the horror of war, and all she could think about was when would the war start *for her*? Her country had injected fervour into recruiting everyday people to fight for the good cause, deeming it an honour to serve. She signed up to be a heroine, to do her part for her country and the world, to be of service. She felt a restlessness within her. All she seemed to be doing for the moment was sunbathing day in and day out. It didn't feel right.

She took intermittent breaks from reading to fan herself with its cover, all the while subconsciously fixing her tropical hat, fearful that too much sun would cause her skin to burn. As she indulged in an internal debate about whether or not to go inside to find shelter from the heat, Ruth, plopped into a chair next to her.

'Norah,' said Ruth, taking Norah's hat from her as she examined it. 'How interesting. Have you written the names of the ports we've been to around the rim?'

Norah laughed, 'Yes, but don't think of it as clever, it's just so that when I'm an old maid, I won't forget where I've been.' The fear of sunburn ever looming, she grabbed her hat and tugged it on tightly.

So far, it was adorned with only a few names: *Scotland, June 1943 – Gibraltar.* Norah planned on completely filling the rim with all the exotic places she'd adventure to while on the ship. She wanted to properly remember all the details of where she'd been so as to easily recount to her friends and family when she got back home. She was anxious and excited as she thought about the stories she'd have to tell.

'Hopefully, you won't have too many places to write.' Ruth gestured to the calm turquoise sea that stretched on for miles and miles before them. 'You know, when Mikey and I volunteered for the war, we foolishly thought it would be romantic. We could serve on a ship together. Sail around the world together. Little did we know that he'd be sent off to serve on the *St David* as an orderly and me on this very-different-than-his ship.' Ruth lay back in her wicker chair, gently pulled her sunglasses up over her eyes, delicately crossed her hands, and let out a deep sigh. 'Might as well enjoy this bout of boring … I just wish they'd get on with it and finish this damn war. I want to get home, see my gruff husband and start having children. You know, Norah, the mundane things of life.'

Norah agreed. 'What I would give to just have another Sunday roast with my father, brothers and sisters again.' With a slight laugh, her mind drifted to one of those weekly lunches where fond chaos always ensued due to the sheer number of those taking part in the meal: Norah and her sister Muriel giggling about their brother John's rumoured fascination with a young woman, Emily, who lived a few doors down; her father's booming voice rising above all other sounds as he lovingly lectured their youngest sister Betty about life; all of which tended to be interrupted by the second youngest, Peter, who painstakingly detailed the cricket match he had heard that afternoon on the radio; the orchestra of clinking bowls and serving trays as they passed the food back and forth between one another – roast lamb in all its glorious juices, peas, roast potatoes and gravy…

'Mikey always said I was a wonderful cook – better than his mother, he said.' Ruth raised her eyebrows before sharing a scandalous secret. 'You know, he wants to have children as soon as we return home. "We aren't going to wait on that, Ruthie," he would always say.' She let out a laugh. 'Mikey, he never had patience for anything.'

'With a schedule like that, I guess you won't be going back to St Mary's after the war then, will you?' Norah asked.

'No, probably not. Probably go up to his village in Yorkshire and pop out babies, one after another.'

They both laughed and Norah patted Ruth on her back. It was fun to joke with Ruth, and the levity momentarily helped take her mind off the uncertainty that lay ahead.

'At least you have someone.' Norah folded her book shut and began to fan herself again. 'I am insistently reminded by my sister Muriel, in her letters to me, that I don't have a husband.'

'I thought you had someone.' Ruth looked puzzled.

'Who? Cecil? No, that relationship's over.' Norah shifted her hat. 'We grew too far apart from each other when I left Kidlington for London.'

'No, the professor, silly.' Ruth rolled her eyes.

Norah let out a nervous laugh. 'Oh, Norman? I had quite forgotten about him, Ruthie.' She extravagantly swatted her hand, brushing the thought away, as if it was too ridiculous to bring attention to.

It wasn't ridiculous, however, and Norah knew it. How could she forget about him? She was reading the book he had gifted her, after all. The book that routinely occupied the top of her nightstand. His memory lingered fondly and seeped into her dreams every night. She often found herself imagining a future with Professor Norman, a future filled with poems, fantastical evenings with his friends, who were as brilliant as he was – a very comfortable future.

She shook away the thought as she took a deep breath. I think he likes me more than I like him anyhow, she thought. Norah hesitated for a minute, her thoughts drifting back to the last time they saw each other. They were in the café, *their* café. The way he touched her hand gently, his piercing green eyes staring into hers as he tried to persuade her. 'Don't go,' he had said. 'War is awful, it will change you forever.' Norah didn't disagree as she played out his words in her head. She hadn't seen much damage yet, but she knew it was only a matter of time.

'Come on, let's go and get a cuppa, Ruthie!'

And with that, they both walked arm in arm across the deck and down to the canteen, where they were greeted by Robert, the cook.

Robert was always a delight to be around. He took it upon himself to care for everyone on board as if he had known them his whole life, as if they were all just long-lost cousins. He was often found with a spatula in one hand attending to a hot pan of greasy sausages, with the other hand ceremoniously tipping a bottle of brandy to his lips for indulgent swigs, all the while joyously belting out yet another traditional Celtic song. Along with an extremely strong Scottish accent, his words always seemed to get lost or at least stuck in his unkempt bushy red beard. This made for an amusing game that the medical staff would partake in, each taking turns guessing what Robert could possibly be saying.

'Gud aftahnun, laydies!' his voice boomed at the sight of them walking down the stairs. 'Whe ken eh gaytcha?' he said as he wiped his hands on his apron.

'Good afternoon, Robert.' Norah smiled. 'Just a cup of tea, please.'

He hurried off to the kitchen and returned quickly with a piping hot kettle and a basket of biscuits.

As Robert excitedly poured Ruth and Norah their afternoon tea, he started to tell them what he had overheard a few minutes ago from the captain. 'Yer'd neyvar gahs, baht wi'd gawtin eh mehsauge frruhm te Eymericun' sheep! Envightin' te Lyenester tew eh pertay unn berd tear sheep!'

Norah and Ruth were at a real loss with this round, and it was a nearby doctor who came to their rescue and translated for them: 'An American ship has invited us aboard. Turns out they're having a party.'

'Das whe eh sehd!' Robert took the kettle and his excitement with him as he poured tea for a table on the other side of the canteen, no doubt sharing the same news.

Norah and Ruth giggled as they imagined what an American party might entail, and were caught up in the excitement when Matron Edge walked by and Ruth stopped her to ask, 'Matron, did you hear about the American party?'

The matron sighed. 'Ah, yes, on the *Seminole*. The radioman told me. Are you sisters going to join in the American fun?'

Ruth's eyes were wide with enthusiasm. 'We're allowed, are we not?'

The matron crossed her arms. 'I suppose a little fun here and there wouldn't spoil anything. Just do be careful, I've heard Americans' – she hesitated, searching for the correct words – 'take their partying very seriously … and liberally.'

Unsure of what the matron meant, but eager to find out, Ruth and Norah hurriedly went to their respective cabins to get ready for such a soirée.

***

In anticipation of the night, Norah put on a little more powder and blush than she was accustomed to. She wore her royal-blue cotton dress patterned with different coloured roses. It was Norman's favourite; he had said she looked breathtakingly beautiful whenever she wore it.

'Thank you,' Norah said and smiled as a handsome American lieutenant took her hand to help her on board the *Seminole*. He nodded in response and Norah felt her face flush. So, this is what Americans look like, she thought.

Ruth must have seen Norah's obvious interest and elbowed her, whispering, 'Maybe that pesky husband Muriel's been bothering you about is lingering among this group.'

Norah snorted and covered her mouth, afraid she'd laugh too loudly.

They were herded with the rest of the crowd to the main event, which was taking place below deck, in the lounge. A Bing Crosby record, amplified by the ship's radio system, roared loudly among the partygoers. Orderlies, nurses, doctors, patients, sailors – American and British alike – commingled. They indulged in dances, games and, of course, alcohol. Exorbitant amounts of whisky, brandy and wine flowed freely. A young fresh-faced sailor danced from one person to the next, with the sole purpose of topping off glasses. Unfortunately, though, as the night went on and the more drunk he got, the more careless he was with his pouring – aggravating an American captain when he mixed his brandy with Italian red wine.

Ruth and Norah wandered around the room arm in arm, nervous to fend for themselves if they happened to get separated. Ruth had finished her second glass of red wine brandy when she accidentally bumped into a fellow who was in the middle of playing poker, allowing the British orderly who was sitting next to him to see his cards.

'My goodness! Please forgive me.' Ruth was embarrassed and covered her face.

'Don't worry, I'm sure this isn't the first time he's seen my cards anyhow.' He extinguished his cigar and handed his cards to the British orderly, which caused a chorus of groans from others at the table. 'See if your luck will change now.' He patted him on the back.

He stood up and tapped his glass. 'Need a refill anyway. Can I get you gals anything?'

He was tall – very tall – and muscular. Norah noted his strong jaw, short blonde hair and deep blue eyes.

'I'm all right.' Ruth giggled. 'But Sister Eggleton needs a fresh glass.' She pushed Norah forward, almost causing a collision between them.

Norah jabbed Ruth in the side, at which Ruth elbowed her back playfully.

'Sister? You two related?' he gestured.

Taken aback by his accent, it took Norah a moment to decipher what he had asked. She had heard American accents before, in films, but not like his. His dialect was slower, drawling.

'No, we're not,' Norah replied.

'Now, didn't I hear you right? You said you were sisters.' He looked from Ruth to Norah and back again.

Ruth shook her head and smiled, 'No, we're *sisters*, not sisters.'

This did not help the man at all. He scratched his head. 'Hold on a minute, does sisters mean something else in Brit talk?'

Norah piped in, 'Sister is the equivalent to what you call a nurse.'

He stood up straight. 'Well, how about that…' He paused for a moment, his face contemplating something very serious. 'Now, does everyone call you sister?'

Norah and Ruth both nodded, their smiles growing wider.

'Even the men … soldiers?'

'Yes, everyone.' Norah was amused at what could be so confusing.

'You see, sister in American' – he pointed to himself – 'means something else entirely. And it would cause complete and most likely uncomfortable confusion if I were to call you sister. I'll keep to nurse, if that's all right with you.' He winked and took the last sip from his glass.

Ruth giggled. 'Well, whatever you call her, she unfortunately is still without a drink.'

Norah blushed and thought to herself how Ruthie was becoming quite the courageous one, but quickly chose to forgive her since it was probably the brandy talking. This was *not* the way Norah would choose to go about finding a husband.

'Would you care for one?' He pointed at Norah.

Breaking from her thoughts she asked, 'Pardon me?' She smoothed her dress.

'A drink.' He leaned in to whisper in Norah's ear. 'See, I'm not a mind reader, but I think your sister here is trying to get you to have a drink with me.'

Norah knew she must have turned a dark shade of pink. 'Well, Sister Ruth has had one too many herself.' She gestured to a now distracted Ruth, who was dancing with an American. She laughed loudly, and Norah couldn't help but feel a little self-conscious.

Ruth is having fun – I should too. What harm could it do, she thought. And with that, she took his hand and made her way to the makeshift bar.

They pushed through the sea of partygoers, who seemed to sway collectively from one side of the lounge to the other. Norah was unsure if it was due to the alcohol or the rocking of the boat. Maybe a combination of the two.

The American caught his breath as he laughed. 'My, does a drink always get you this excited? There are other ways to get a drink, you know, than yanking a man's arm out of its socket.' He massaged his shoulder.

Norah chuckled. 'My apologies! I hope I didn't hurt it too badly, Doctor…?' She was hoping he was at least a doctor of some sort.

'James. Major James Ryan. I'm a surgeon on this here boat.'

Norah's mouth began to curve into a smile. 'It's a pleasure to meet you, Major.'

'The pleasure is all mine.'

They stood there for a moment, not bothered by anything around them, staring into each other's eyes. Norah could swear his eyes had grown brighter.

James grabbed a bottle of whisky from behind the box that served as a counter, and two glasses. He handed her a glass and poured a generous portion.

Norah cleared her throat and took a sip. 'Major, may I ask where you're from? Your accent is so unique.'

'Is that right?' He smirked. 'Well, I'm from the great state of Kentucky.'

'Oh.' Norah reciprocated his smile. 'Does that make you a southerner?'

'Only the finest the US of A has to offer.' He winked.

'And, Major, may I also ask how you spend your time on the ship? No doubt gambling at poker?' She raised her eyebrows at him.

'Please, call me James. Actually, when I'm not in the theatre—'

'The theatre?' Norah almost choked on her drink. 'You have a theatre? On this ship?'

James smiled, bewildered at Norah's excitement. 'Yes, I would like to believe you folks do too.'

'No! We don't have such a luxury.' Norah set down her glass, 'Can you show it to me?'

James nodded. 'If that would please you, I guess I could give you a tour.'

Norah grabbed his hand again, this time waiting for him to lead her through the crowd. As they passed through, Norah spotted Ruth animatedly dancing with yet another sailor, apparently having the time of her life.

They walked down a dark, long and narrow hallway, where the sounds of the party grew fainter with each step. The clack of their shoes echoed off the steel walls.

Norah's excitement was battling with nervousness. Is it all right for me to be alone with this major, she wondered. Oh, what would the matron think if she knew?

She calmed her worries and resolutely concluded that there were no wrong intentions between her and the major – she only wanted to see the theatre.

The hallway led to a small door. The handle creaked as James turned it and swung the steel door open. He ducked as he entered. Norah could barely contain her excitement as she stepped through to see … an operating room. A common, old operating room. Complete with an operating table and medical equipment.

James must have seen the excitement drain from Norah's face. 'You look as thrilled as my patients do before I cut into them.'

Norah politely smiled. 'I'm sorry.' She let out a slight laugh. 'It must be the silly language differences again.'

'I thought we had the same language?'

'I'm afraid not when it comes to certain terminology.'

James leaned against the surgical table. 'Is that right? Now would that terminology happen to be … *theatre*?'

Norah nodded. 'I'm afraid so.' She walked around the room as she continued. 'Your theatre is our operating room.'

'We seem to be getting ourselves into a lot of these situations, aren't we?'

'Yes, I suppose we are. You know, it was George Bernard Shaw who once said that the British and the Americans were separated by a common language.'

'Did he now?' James stood and moved over to Norah. There were just a few inches in between them. 'I reckon we can remedy the separation.'

His eyes looked familiar … Norman?

Norah backed away.

'Excuse me, it's a bit stuffy in this … theatre … need of fresh air.' She hurriedly left the room, almost tripping over the door frame. She didn't stop until she found her way outside to the deck.

Brushing away an errant tear, she shook her head, disappointed that she had acted so childishly in front of James.

I must look positively mad, she thought and let out a deep breath. It must be the alcohol … I'm not used to it. She looked out into the starry sky.

'Aren't you cold up here, nurse?'

Norah turned to face James, who had walked up to where she was standing. It was late, darkness had fallen and the only light by which she could distinguish anything of him came from the stars above her. The lights on the ship had been extinguished as it lay at anchor, just off the coast of Bizerte.

'Yes, doctor,' she replied, being rather formal. 'It is getting rather chilly, I must admit.'

He flicked the cigarette he was smoking into the sea, took off his jacket and placed it around Norah's shoulders. She smiled her thanks.

'I just gave you a promotion,' he added with a smile.

'How very nice of you,' replied a timid Norah, and with that, she went back to leaning on the railings of the ship, letting the cool breeze float through her short, dark hair. It was refreshing.

She closed her eyes and let her mind wander back to Kidlington for a few seconds before those thoughts were interrupted by James again.

'I hope I'm not disturbing you, Norah.'

At first, she wanted to tell him that she would rather be left alone to her thoughts, then felt that doing so would be rude. So, she forced herself to smile. After all, he had given her his jacket and it had helped warm her somewhat.

'No, James, you're not disturbing me.'

James could perhaps see through her concealment and figured the flirtatious session had regrettably found its end. 'I'm going to have to leave soon. I'm on duty in a few hours. I have to be awake, otherwise people will wonder what I've been up to.'

'Oh, I fully understand.'

He let out a slight laugh. 'Until now, the only person I've operated on was one of the crew, who slipped on the wet deck and broke his leg.'

Norah was hoping that the darkness would be her ally and hide her forlorn face.

At that precise moment, a Royal Navy sailor walked by a little worse for wear, and Norah attracted his attention.

He stopped and faced her. The slight rocking of the ship adding to his unsteadiness. 'Yes, sister?' he asked slowly and then, seeing the American service jacket on her, became very confused. 'Nurse Eggleton, why are you wearing an American uniform? Did you change armies?'

'No, ensign, this kind American doctor gave me his jacket as it's rather chilly up here.' The ensign continued to rock, and Norah continued, 'Is the boat from the *Leinster* here?'

'Yes, sister. That's where I'm going, if you care to follow me.' His speech was slightly slurred.

Norah let out a slight laugh. 'I'm not quite sure that's a good idea. How about we go together?'

'As you please, sister.'

'Well, I'll keep you from falling into the sea.'

'That would be most helpful.'

With that, Norah smiled at James and handed him his jacket. She turned to leave and then turned back to face the American surgeon. 'Thanks a lot for everything, especially your jacket. I hope to see you at the next party.'

James smiled and nodded. 'I look forward to it.' He gave Norah a pleasant salute and walked back inside, his jacket folded over his right arm.

# CHAPTER FOURTEEN

## *Off the coast of Sicily, 1943*

Norah kept her mind occupied, afraid that if she didn't, she'd think of her unbecoming behaviour towards the American surgeon. She was spared dwelling on the embarrassment during her morning tea in the canteen, when the matron interrupted with an announcement. The *Leinster* was being ordered to Palermo to pick up the wounded.

'It's about time.' Ruth raised her teacup in readiness.

The matron eyed Ruth, who slowly lowered her cup. 'Yes, well, some of you see it as delayed, but I must warn you…' She cleared her throat as she hesitantly continued, choosing her words carefully, 'I must warn you, these battles are savage. There will be hundreds, if not thousands of casualties.' The room went quiet and became sombre. 'None of you are old enough to have been involved in the Great War and seen the devastation up close and in person. Unfortunately, I am and I have. Regardless of what you might think, you are not and will not be prepared for what you will see. At first, I expect you to be horrified, and I'm sure in some cases, shaken by what you will witness. Each one of us will react differently. Some may become emotional, while others may become physically sick.

I expect that of you, and I'm sorry to say this, but I also expect you to adapt quickly and remain professional. Those men will need us. They will need us to treat them and, in some cases' – she took a deep breath and then let it out slowly – 'we will be the last people they see on this earth. I was given a similar talking to before I saw my first lot of wounded in the Great War, and I remember thinking to myself, "I can handle this, this is what I've trained for, this is what I signed up for." But let me tell you – no, no you have not. You will not be ready for what you will see and hear. But what I do know, is that each and every one of you is a professional and you will do your duty. May God bless you all.'

Everyone stopped enjoying their tea and sat in silence. Norah watched as several women bowed their heads to silently pray, compelling her to say one of her own: 'Dear Lord, I pray for the strength to manage my emotions while serving. Please guide me in my duty. Amen.'

Norah's tea grew cold and she pushed it aside, as feelings of inadequacy began to steep and brew in her mind. She hoped she would be prepared. She *had* to be prepared.

***

Norah and Ruth held each other's hands as they went up on deck to watch the coastline of Sicily grow nearer. They didn't exchange words. They wouldn't know how to, even if they wanted. Their hearts beat faster with every second they got closer. A couple of landing crafts began their slow journey towards the *Leinster* and towards the fuel doors, which had been opened.

It wasn't until they anchored that the horrors of the war became clearly visible.

The earth stopped turning, the wind died down, the sun hid behind the clouds as there was a collective gasp from the medical staff. The matron's words jumped to life as the stretchers were brought on deck. One by one, each stretcher was transported with the greatest sense of urgency. As fast as they were tended to, there were more rushed on board. A never-ending stream of severely wounded men. Blood. Dirt. Screams. Chaos … There was no end in sight.

With each stretcher, a young soldier. With each soldier, wounds that would bring any one with haemophobia to their knees. Some with mutilated legs or torn-off arms, heads covered with bandages that were unable to staunch the amount of blood that oozed incessantly from the wound. Deep red trickled from the bodies to the floor, and soon little rivers and lakes of blood gathered along the deck. A slippery mess, it made staying upright almost impossible for the medical staff who darted from one patient to the next. The screams were unbearable. One British soldier in excruciating agony, who couldn't have been older than nineteen, clawed at the air where his legs used to be.

The sea of screams clashed with the barked orders coming from the doctors and nurses. Norah stood motionless, overwhelmed. The sounds were becoming indistinguishable. She watched as some men lay there connecting with the world to come. They would never see their homes again. They would never see their parents or brothers or sisters again. All the dreams and plans they had made before they left home would remain just that, dreams never to be realized.

Then suddenly, Norah sprang into action. There was no more time to stand and cry, no time to weep for the wounded, no time to hold each other, as the true horror of war hit her between the eyes. She had to save as many of these men as possible. One second could make all the difference.

'Here, sister,' spat a gruff British soldier. 'This one's a German. Let the bugger die.' He tossed the stretcher on the ground, making the German gasp for air and reach for his chest.

Norah bent down over him to evaluate his wound, her hands hovering over him. His chest had been ripped open by what looked like a giant metal claw. Each and every vital organ had been violated. His eyes were fixed on the sky, his breathing fast and heavy, his fists clenched in agony. A steady stream of tears silently rolled down his dirtied face. Norah locked eyes with him.

She quickly grabbed the trouser leg of the man who had brought him on board. Almost falling face-first from Norah's intervention, he stopped and turned. Norah slowly stood up. Her five-foot-one frame equal to the man's six-foot-something frame in every respect.

'Corporal,' the volume of her voice caused others around them to turn, 'correct me if I am wrong, but I believe we are in a war fighting against the very belief you just presented me. It does not matter if he is German. He is a human. And for that reason, we will treat him. He has a family just like you do. And if I ever hear words like that again, I will have the greatest delight in having you court-martialled.'

The corporal was stunned, unable to form any words in reply.

'Did you hear me, Corporal?' she shouted at him.

'Y—yes, sis—sister,' he stuttered and saluted, before hastily darting off with his tail between his legs.

The German now had his eyes fixed on Norah. A slight smile appeared on his white lips and using all his energy, he gently blinked. She knew it was his way of saying thank you.

'Orderly!' Norah shouted to anyone who would hear. 'Orderly,' she shouted again, and this time a man came running. 'Help me here, please. I need some morphine, quickly.' The orderly did as he was told.

He returned swiftly with the tube of morphine.

'Orderly, once I'm done here, please take him to an operating room immediately. Is that clear?'

He nodded and waited for Norah to finish administering the drug. Norah hoped it was the morphine that caused the German to fall limp and asleep, afraid to believe that the real cause was the severity of his pain. Another orderly was corralled, and the German was evacuated to an operating room.

Norah stood up and began to scan the deck, eager to see where she could be of service next. She stopped when she spotted a man lying under the stairs, unattended. Norah tiptoed around the stretchers and pushed past the buzzing staff to reach him.

He appeared to be in his early thirties, though it was difficult for Norah to ascertain this due to his injury and the look of serenity on his weathered face. What used to be a green woollen military blanket covering his torso was now drenched in blood. Norah lifted the blanket and silently prayed that his wound would be treatable. Her eyes closed when she saw the gash from which his lower intestines splayed and twisted outside his body. A victim to a shell, no doubt. He wore the uniform of a sergeant in the US army. His deep blue eyes were greying over. The life left in him was seeping out. His eyes were fixed on some point in the not-too-distant future. In contrast to the severity of his wound, he appeared to be at peace. Norah struggled to compose herself. She took several deep breaths before she felt comfortable enough to address him.

'Sergeant,' she said quietly, her head not far from his ear, 'sergeant, you're on board a hospital ship now. We are going to do everything we can for you.'

His eyes didn't move, still transfixed on something only he could see. Norah gently unbuttoned his uniform to see if he was wearing a chain that would tell her his name. The least she could do was have the chaplain come pray over him. She unbuttoned the top two buttons and a bit of his silver chain sparkled. She pulled it out gradually from under his shirt. Norah was surprised when, tangled with the dog tag chain, she found a delicate gold chain with a modest Star of David.

She gently moved the star to read his name on his tag: David Apfel.

She squeezed his hand gently, and a brief smile rippled across his lips. She sat down next to him and noticed an officer who performed the duties of chaplain – though not ordained – walking amongst the wounded. She waited for him to come closer, and when he did, she called him over.

Norah pointed to the soldier. 'Sir, he's Jewish.'

The officer nodded and knelt by his side.

*I lift my eyes to the mountains – from where will my help come?*
*My help will come from the Lord, maker of heaven and earth.*
*He will not let your foot falter; your guardian does not slumber.*
*Indeed, the Guardian of Israel neither slumbers nor sleeps.*
*The Lord is your guardian; the Lord is your protective shade at your right hand.*
*The sun will not harm you by day, nor the moon by night.*
*The Lord will guard you from all evil; He will guard your soul.*
*The Lord will guard your going and your coming from now and for all time.*

After the prayer was done, she sat beside the wounded sergeant. She knew there were dozens of other soldiers in need of attention, but she felt compelled to stay just a few more minutes with him.

Norah was about to leave him and walk over to another stretcher when she felt a tug on her apron. She turned, her heart beating quicker, as the sergeant, with an outstretched arm, held tightly on to her. Norah smiled sadly, falling back to her knees. She put her hand on his.

Silence.

Seconds later, his grasp weakened, and his arm fell limp by his side. Norah took a deep breath and slowly exhaled. She gently closed his eyelids and pulled the blanket over his head.

'Be at peace, David Apfel.'

Norah wasn't afforded the luxury of sitting there any longer as the wounded kept piling in.

'Sister Eggleton!' she heard someone call from across the deck. She looked up to see the matron. She walked over to Norah. 'Norah,' she repeated, 'weren't you an operating room nurse at St Mary's?' Her eyes were filled with exhaustion, and an obvious struggle to hold it together painted her face.

'Yes, matron, I was.'

'I thought as much. They need your help in the operating room. They are running out of qualified staff.'

'Yes, matron,' replied Norah as she hurriedly stood up and made her way downstairs to where she was needed. The corridors were crowded with the wounded lying on stretchers, waiting their turn to be operated on, and by the scurrying medical staff now working on adrenaline.

'Over here, sister,' a doctor, in his operating garb, called to her from the last operating room on the right.

Norah hurried and tied a mask on. She entered the room and couldn't help but let out a gasp at the state of the operating table and floor. Everything, once spotless, was now covered in blood.

Norah took her place next to the doctor, trying to prepare herself for whatever was needed of her.

'Welcome to hell,' he whispered.

***

Hours, maybe days later, she emerged and walked upstairs on to the deck, which had now been cleared. A tear slid down her cheek as her gaze fell upon the body bags that lay organized in rows across the entire deck of the ship.

So, *this* was war.

# CHAPTER FIFTEEN

## *Off the coast of Sicily, 1943*

As dawn began to break, the *Leinster* was ordered to depart and pull back ten miles to what was known as the safe zone, the zone where hospital ships were to go to avoid being bombed – the rules of the war.

Everyone was so engrossed in their jobs that no one realized they had set sail again, and only the slight rocking of the boat served as a reminder. As the sun rose higher in the early morning sky, waves of emotion – of loss and helplessness – pounded the staff aboard.

Ruth helped Norah change the bandages on an unconscious and feverish American infantryman. He had taken a bullet straight to his abdomen.

The speaker clicked on with an announcement: 'A service for the deceased will begin shortly on deck. If you can, please join us as we lay them to rest.'

'Ruth,' Norah began, 'do you think you could continue changing his dressings for a moment?'

Ruth solemnly nodded. 'Of course.'

Norah wiped her hands on her apron and walked up to the deck as her stomach fluttered. She felt a deep sense of responsibility to the Jewish-American soldier. He didn't have anyone on board; out of respect for him – and his mother, his sister, his girlfriend, his wife, or whoever was back at home – she would go.

The officiant diligently moved from one body to the next to pray over. Even though he was an Anglican, he was fully conversant with the prayers and rituals of different religions, and based on the markings chalked on the bags, he would pray accordingly. Each body, regardless of nationality, and whether they were ally or enemy, was afforded the same treatment.

Once the prayers were finished, orderlies carefully and respectfully tipped the bodies, one by one, over the side and into the sea.

The officiant noticed Norah and walked over to her side. 'Thank you for coming, sister,' he said in his Yorkshire brogue, a twinkle in his eye. He then reached for her hand, opening it with his fingers, and placed an object within before tightly shutting it. 'I think it's better with you than with the fish.'

He tipped his hat and walked off, leaving Norah there with her fist closed. She slowly opened her hand to see its contents. Sparkling up at her was the Star of David chain. Her hand closed around it again, and she placed it in her pocket, silently saying goodbye.

***

The *Leinster* set sail for Malta, where the wounded were offloaded, and after a day's rest it returned to Sicily for more wounded. It was never-ending. Norah's days and nights blended into each other on their trips between Palermo and Bizerte, as she was tasked with evaluating the casualties.

Later that year, the news came that the Italian army had surrendered, and the *Leinster* would no longer be heading to

Palermo. Instead, she would be picking up the wounded at Salerno and Anzio in Italy proper.

Mussolini had been hanged, but the Germans had vowed to continue fighting. Everyone had the feeling that as the fighting got closer to Germany, it would become even more intense, which meant the casualty rate would increase.

And indeed, it did.

***

The ship was now part of a small fleet of hospital ships in the Bay of Naples: the *St Andrew*, the *St David*, the *St Julian*, and the only non-saint, the *Leinster*.

It was January 1944, and the weather was damp. The skies were grey, and those medical staff who didn't smoke cigarettes began to. Intermittently, snow squalls came flying through. The sounds of war grew louder, and the sickly-sweet smell of cordite hung in the air as they sailed closer to the shore. As instructed, all four hospital ships had their lights on, lit up like Christmas trees with large red crosses. And although it was dark, they were clearly visible from miles away in the air and on land. A clear marker: HOSPITAL SHIP – DO NOT BOMB.

The ship rocked violently.

People and material were thrown about, and Norah, who was administering morphine, was thankful when the needle missed the patient and now stood at sharp attention in the cot.

The matron was helping a patient who had fallen out of his bed. An officer swiftly came to her side and whispered something in her ear. Her face filled with horror until she remembered where she was and quickly composed herself. She looked around the room and nodded to the officer, who left for the deck as rapidly as he had come.

She stood at the front of the room and cleared her throat. 'I have just been informed that the *St David* has been hit.' Audible gasps echoed around the room as she continued, 'Please remain calm and continue with your work. I will give you further information as I receive it.'

'Hit? Who in their right mind would hit a hospital ship for God's sake?' spat out a doctor who was ripping off his bloodstained gloves.

Suddenly, the sound of whirring planes was heard, followed by a monstrous boom that left the ship shuddering. Everyone's eyes looked up as it dawned on them – the German Luftwaffe was flying overhead.

The same officer as before reappeared at the matron's side, whispering something again, and horror quickly flickered across her face once more. With a nod, the officer shot back upstairs.

The matron cleared her throat once more. 'Those who are readily available, please make your way up to the deck.' Curious faces lined the room, prompting her to share more: 'The *St David* is sinking.'

Nothing else needed to be said as a swarm of nurses, doctors, and any patient able to walk hurried upstairs.

Their faces fell in defeat. Flames leapt into the night sky as the *St David* creaked and moaned from its affliction, surrendering to the sea.

Norah panicked. She knew some of the crew on board that ship. She knew Ruth's husband was an orderly there.

She didn't know what to do. But do something she must.

Norah could hear screaming from the water below her.

'Let's do something!' she shouted to the other nurses around her.

And as if on cue, there was a splash, and she saw in the glow of the sinking ship, one of the hospital orderlies holding a life ring jump into the water. Soon, there were several splashes as most people standing on the deck began to follow the orderly's lead. Norah untied her apron, closed her eyes, held her breath and leapt into the dark sea. The cold Mediterranean waters sent an alarming chill up her body as she was first completely submerged before she swam to the surface and gasped for air. Her breath was the only thing she could see in the darkness, but as her eyes came focussed, she found herself surrounded by debris and the dead.

The shrieks and splashes from the survivors anxious to be rescued punctured the cold night air. Every available life ring was thrown haphazardly into the water by the crew, and those who could, hysterically swam to them. The captain of the *Leinster* directed the searchlight down on the water. It was only then that the full extent of the loss of humanity became clear. Norah desperately swam from body to body. Survivors splashed frantically, trying to stay afloat, causing a disaster of turbulence in the water. Wave after wave rose above Norah's head, and each time she was shocked by the biting cold that washed over her.

A little further away, Norah heard shouts crying out in the dark. She grabbed a life ring close to her, and with the help of the searchlight, swam out towards the sound. She finally reached a man floating in a pool of blood.

'Take this,' she shouted as she threw the life ring around him and began to pull him back towards the *Leinster*. Still in shock, he continued to flail about. Norah's muscles ached, her body longed to give up, but she fought with every fibre of her being to get him to safety. Her teeth chattered uncontrollably, and her breathing became quick and sudden.

Finally, she made it to the fuel doors, where sailors stood at the ready to pull survivors aboard.

'Sister,' a sailor shouted in his strong cockney accent, 'you've done your job, come back inside! The cold will be the death of you. We can't afford to lose nurses.'

She pretended she didn't hear him and began to swim again, out into the chaos, thinking: Mikey is out there.

The *St David* had now completely sunk. Planks of wood, books, medical gowns, papers and other sorts of debris slowly bubbled to the surface. Norah pushed past them, desperate to find Mikey.

Exhaustion battled with her, but she refused to allow her body to dictate her actions. The sea had gone quiet, and most of the survivors had been rescued or were swimming to safety. Norah wasn't sure if it was mainly from adrenaline or from the icy waters, but her whole body was consumed with violent shivering. Her lips were purple, and her teeth continued to chatter. Sadly, she knew she could no longer stay in the water, or she herself could become a casualty. She mustered up the last of her strength and began to swim for the *Leinster*.

She reached the fuel door and was unceremoniously pulled on board by a couple of sailors.

'You'd better get inside and get warm, sister,' said the same sailor who had tried to warn her before, while another wrapped a blanket around her and led her to the top deck and into the lounge, where he poured her a large glass of brandy.

'Thank you,' she managed to say through her chattering teeth.

As she sipped the brandy, she looked around the lounge. Others were in the same state as her – shivering and holding on to their brandy glasses as if it held fire itself.

'Come, sister, I'll take you to your room to get into dry clothes.' Matron Edge took Norah by the elbow and led her downstairs to her cabin.

Once there, Norah pleaded with her body to help get her into the only dry clothes she could find. Stings and sharp pains prodded her muscles as she pulled her uniform over her head. One final wince, and she began to button her dress.

'Sister, I know you are close with Sister Ruth as you both came from St Mary's, so I feel it is important to tell you that her husband died.'

Norah shot a quick, panicked look at the matron. 'How do you know that?'

Taken aback and stumbling over her words, the matron replied, 'He … he wasn't among the … sur—survivors.'

'Matron, just because he wasn't found doesn't mean he isn't still alive,' Norah snapped, tired of hearing bad news. She longed to be hopeful.

'But they did. They found his body in the water.'

Norah covered her mouth and closed her eyes. Her knees gave way as she sat back on the bed. A sharp pain ran up her body.

'How is she?' Norah asked.

'Who, Sister Norah—'

'Ruth.' Norah's eyes shot to the matron. 'Does she know?'

Matron Edge nodded.

'Where is she?'

'In her cabin. But—'

'I must go and see her. I need to make sure she's all right.'

'I know the two of you are very close, so I expect you to go and check on her. But – and I know this sounds cruel – we do need you back up on deck,' she said, finding her authority.

Norah paused and weighed her response. She wanted to scream at the top of her lungs. It took an extraordinary amount of restraint not to.

'Yes, matron. As soon as I make sure she's okay, I'll come upstairs.' She clenched her jaw.

'Thank you.'

Matron Edge left the room. Norah raised her head and walked over to another cabin a few doors down. She stood outside the door, hoping that maybe it was all some sick, cruel joke. Norah found her when quiet sobbing could be heard from the other side of the door.

She knocked almost inaudibly on the steel door. 'Ruth, are you in there?' There was no answer, only more soft sobs.

I wouldn't answer either, if it were me, Norah thought as she opened the door.

In the dim light of the cabin, she saw her dear friend lying on her bunk, her head buried in a pillow. Norah knelt quietly by the side of the bunk and placed her hand on Ruth's back. Ruth lifted her head slightly in acknowledgement, with her face still in the pillow. Norah stroked her hair softly. Her heart ached as she listened to Ruth cry in anguish, as she was drained of tears.

Norah prayed that sleep would come upon Ruth, so that at least in her dreams she wouldn't have to suffer. The matron's orders plagued her as she sat there all night, but as Ruth continued to weep, she knew she was doing the right thing.

Norah was awoken by the sun as it peeked through the small cabin window. Ruth's back gently moved up and down, her breathing steady as she slept.

It was now in the daylight that Norah realized she had reached into the wrong pile for her uniform. She sat on the floor of the cabin, dressed in the blood of unknown warriors – some who had survived, some who had not.

Her eyes closed as she reached into her pocket. Her fingers slid along a delicate chain until they met with the prodding edges of metal and closed upon the Star of David.

# CHAPTER SIXTEEN

## *Taranto, 1944*

On 19 March, the battalion boarded troopships at Alexandria to make their way over to Italy. The sea was calm and the skies blue, though there was a definite chill in the air. Raj looked back at the receding African coastline. His sojourn in Palestine seemed like an eternity ago.

As Raj looked at the men lining the sides of the boat, peering over and into the sea, he thought of the soldiers who weren't there with them – the ones they had lost in the fighting, who had been buried in foreign territory. They would never see home again, their remains occupying small pieces of land on a strange continent, but for them that piece of land would always be India.

The journey was slow, and two days later, the distant coastline of Italy came into view – and with that came concern and trepidation. How many more men would they have to lose until the fight was over? Raj's eyes were fixed on the horizon, over the rolling hills, at what looked like small wisps of smoke rising into the sky. In reality, he knew they weren't small wisps at all. Up close, they were large billowing flames engulfing someone's home. Someone's farm. Someone's village. Someone's life.

The ship docked at Taranto, a coastal town that probably looked magnificent in peace time, but now was just another port like all the rest. No welcoming throngs, just a gangplank to walk down. On the other end of the cement dock, the men fell into formation. Colonel Dalton informed the group that they would be heading towards the Adriatic coast to relieve the Canadian troops who had been engaged in brutal combat.

The battalion knew that the toughest part of the war lay ahead. The Germans had thrown everything into protecting Italy and wouldn't back down easily. The 3/1st Punjab Regiment was going to be held in reserve, while the rest of the division engaged the enemy. While in reserve, the men spent every day training in mountain warfare and hand-to-hand-combat. They knew they would have to fight for every inch of land.

All their waiting was over when, in May, as the Italian countryside burst into colour despite being battered, artillery duels intensified. Raj and his men worked tirelessly, patrolling the enemy lines in search of any weak spots. To their dismay, there were none.

'You and these men go over here.' Raj dragged a pointed finger to a marked spot on a map as he ordered Havildar Major Ahmed. 'We'll come from this end. Once in your position, signal to us what you find.'

Havildar Major Ahmed nodded and went off to inform his men of their orders. Raj folded the map and tucked it into his uniform pocket. He instructed his men to follow him as they moved east of the German lines and up, to penetrate any open pockets and infiltrate their camp. As they moved stealthily around under the cover of night, Raj knew their position was given away when a bullet flew past his head.

'Heads down!' Raj shouted, and his men took cover behind the rubble that lay around them.

The Germans opened fire and bullets ricocheted off the wreckage. For a few moments, the consistent pattering of bullets continued towards them before the enemy changed its target.

Raj peeked through his binoculars to see the German gunners pointed west. Havildar Major Ahmed and his men!

He turned to his company and gestured for them to move forward.

The sepoy closest to him shook nervously, his gun rattled in his hand. 'No, sir,' he replied in Urdu. 'They are still shooting.'

'They've stopped. Now, move forward, sepoy.'

The young sepoy sat frozen under cover, as the other men watched with great interest. Growing in agitation, Raj stood up and waved his hands above his head.

'See, they've stopped. Now *move*. That's an order,' Raj commanded.

The sepoy, along with the rest of the company, hesitantly stood up with guns at the ready. They moved to relieve Havildar Major Ahmed and his men, causing casualties on both sides, bringing their dead back with them to camp.

***

Instead of resting, Raj went in search of comfort – which he would find in a strong cup of hot tea. As he walked to the canteen, he came across some of his Muslim men lying on the ground next to their tent, singing loudly.

'Is that alcohol?' Raj asked when he spotted Jawan Adalat Khan's enamel mug filled with a deep red liquid.

'This?' slurred the jawan, thrusting his mug towards Raj. 'No, Sahib, this is Italian tea.' He hesitated a moment before pushing himself to stand against the wall.

'Italian tea? Is that right?' Raj smiled. 'I've never heard of it. Is it as good as the tea you get in the mess?' he teased.

'No, sir.' Adalat Khan hiccupped as he saluted. 'But sometimes, it's good for a change.' He winked.

'Oh, I agree,' replied Raj, trying not to break into uncontrollable laughter.

'Would you like some, sir?' Adalat asked eagerly. 'They have more over there.' He pointed his mug in one direction only to squint, scratch his head and twist his body to point in the other, spilling some of the mug's contents. The red liquid splashed on to the dirt floor and clumped into a dark red spot. 'Or there.'

Raj shook his head. 'No, Adalat Khan. You enjoy your Italian tea, and I will stick to our wonderful Indian tea.'

'Ah, yes. Here's to doodh waali chai,' he cheered and promptly fell to the ground with a thud.

Raj couldn't help but let out a laugh then, and after making sure Adalat was fine, continued on his way to the canteen.

***

After Raj had finished his cup of tea, he retired to his tent, knowing his new tent-mate was to arrive that afternoon. He was anxious to find out who would occupy half the space he had so been accustomed to calling his own.

He reached under his cot for a copy of *National Geographic*, which he had stashed away for just such an occasion. He rarely had time to relax, but now seemed as good a time as any to help ease the anticipation. He thumbed through the pages until he came upon an article on Africa. He was halfway through reading 'Big Cats of the Sahara', when he heard the tent flap make way for a rather imposing fellow.

The stranger shared an unmistakable resemblance to the Hollywood actor Errol Flynn. Tall and muscular, with dark hair that was slicked back, bright green eyes and a perfectly thin and trimmed moustache.

Uncanny, thought Raj.

The stranger scanned the room intently, taking his time to check the inventory of his new living quarters. Two cots on opposite sides. One rusty and clouded square of mirror that could only occupy the image of one cheek and possibly the faintest sliver of a side of chin. Hanging by a sole nail in the central pole of the tent, it lightly swayed back and forth to the movement of jeeps that drove past intermittently. After taking in the approximate square footage of the dirt floor, the stranger finally noticed the other occupant of the tent.

'Kohli, I presume.'

The stranger smoothed the green wool blanket on his cot before delegating his kit bag to a corner on the floor, and walked over to Raj with his hand outstretched.

Unsure of what to make of him, Raj got up from his cot, and after placing the magazine face-down, shook his hand firmly.

'Raj Kohli,' he said, introducing himself.

'Ronald Roach,' the man replied, with an open smile that eased Raj a bit.

Raj sat back on his cot while Ron began to empty the contents of his bag, seemingly taking an inventory of it as well. Razor on top of towel at end of cot. Extra pair of socks by razor on top of towel at end of cot. Toothbrush by pair of socks by razor on top of towel at end of cot.

'Has anyone ever told you that you look like Errol Flynn?' Raj began.

Ron shook his head. 'No, that's a new one for me. I usually get mistaken for Cary Grant.' A smile appeared.

Raj lay back on his cot and picked up his magazine. 'Where have you come from?'

'I was being held in reserve, old chap. I understand you guys are going through officers quicker than they can find replacements.' As Ron chatted, Raj noticed his meticulous unpacking of his belongings. Bar of soap by toothbrush by pair of socks by razor on top of towel at end of cot. 'What's going on here? Is this battalion of the Punjab Regiment bad luck?'

Raj peered over the top of his magazine, pausing for a moment before answering. 'It's a dangerous place, the battlefront. The Germans are no longer firing blanks.'

Ron laughed. 'I guess I'll need to keep a watch out for you guys.'

'Please do,' replied Raj. 'We need all the help we can get.'

Finished with unpacking, Ron sat on his cot, bouncing once or twice to test the quality and condition of the coils that were to hold up his large frame.

'*National Geographic*?' Ron scoffed. 'Do you like geography and that sort of nonsense?'

Raj hesitated for a second. He wasn't quite sure whether the man who was to be his tent-mate was likeable. 'Love it,' replied Raj. 'How about you?'

'No, sir. I love music, the classics, poetry – stuff like that. Did poorly in school in geography. I couldn't understand how knowing exactly where another continent was positioned would help me in life.'

'What did you read in university?'

'Didn't go, old chap. I was in the civil services when I got called up. They looked at me and said, "You're officer material," so here I am. In Italy. In June. And about to share a tent with a fellow officer who read geography at university.'

'Oh no, I didn't read geography in university. I just happen to love it.'

Ron scrunched his nose. Obviously, the thought of loving such a thing was ridiculous to him. 'Pray tell, old chap. What *did* you read at university?'

'Chemistry.'

'Chemistry!' Ron repeated nearly at the top of his voice. 'Did I hear you properly? *Chemistry*, old chap?'

'Yes, you did,' Raj replied, and decided that he wasn't going to like his new tent-mate.

'Cambridge?' asked Ron, expecting an affirmative answer.

'I was, at first, but then transferred to King's College, London.'

Ron jumped off his cot in one quick move and came over to Raj's side of the tent.

'Well, I'll be damned,' he said with a broad smile, which made him look more and more like the swashbuckling Errol Flynn. 'I've always wanted to share a tent with a genius, and I've finally managed that. Thank you!'

Both men laughed. Raj changed his mind and decided he might like his new tent-mate. He enjoyed a person who was both quick-witted and dapper. And going by the way Ron took care of his appearance as an officer, he was someone to admire. Boots polished, though they wouldn't stay that way for very long, hair combed and greased down enough to weather a strong thunderstorm, a crease in his trousers sharp enough to cut one's finger on, and above all, well mannered.

In Raj's opinion, there were far too many officers who shouldn't be officers in the first place. Their demeanour, especially when eating in the officer's mess hall, made him cringe on many an occasion, though he was careful not to show his disdain. He was much more comfortable eating with the enlisted men out in the open, but that was not always acceptable.

'I believe you said you like the classics?'

'I do.' Ron was now sitting on Raj's cot. 'By the way, call me Ron, my parents do. What do they call you?'

'Your parents? Well, I'm not sure what they call me, but mine call me Raj.'

Ron let out a loud laugh. Raj was now certain he would like his new tent-mate.

As water welled up in his eyes from laughter, Ron walked back to his cot and lit up a pipe. 'You know what, old chap? This is very funny.'

'What's funny?' asked Raj.

Ronald pointed the end of his pipe at Raj and continued. 'Well, if I were to close my eyes' – which he did – 'I could swear you sound like an Englishman.' He enthusiastically opened his eyes again. 'In fact, not only do you sound English, but your mannerisms are very upper-class English as well.' He waved his pipe in Raj's direction. Confused, Raj wasn't sure if he was paying him a compliment. Ron continued after taking a long puff on his nearly extinguished pipe. 'What I'm trying to say is that you behave more British than the British.'

Raj decided Ron only meant well and was indeed trying to pay a compliment. He smiled in appreciation. 'Do you really think so?'

'Old chap, not only do I think so, but in honour of that, you will no longer be Raj to me.' He stood up taller and pushed out his chest, as he bowed shallowly in Raj's direction. 'Tommy! That's right, I shall call you Tommy.'

'I'm honoured,' replied Raj, reciprocating the shallow bow.

'Come on, let's go,' Ron said as he threw his arm around Raj, 'and get a whisky!' He led him towards the mess hall.

The hall was empty, except for one or two orderlies – who were brewing tea, no doubt, for their superior officers.

Setting down his glass of another round of whisky, Ron squinted at Raj and asked, 'Now, do you enjoy classical music?'

'What sort of classical music?' Raj inquired as he set down his empty glass. Ron took the liberty of refilling it generously.

'*Really* classical music,' replied Ron, expecting Raj to profess his ignorance.

'Beethoven?'

'Opera, old chap.'

'Verdi?'

'Yes, and Puccini.'

'Puccini! I love Puccini. *La bohème*?'

'Only with Gigli singing.'

'I saw him in Covent Garden a few years ago.'

'As did I, old chap.'

'Maybe you were there the same night I was.'

'Possibly.'

Raj smiled, enjoying the banter. 'I think, in fact, that Errol Flynn was there that night. At least that's what I heard the guy sitting next to me say.'

'Argh!' Ron shook his finger at Raj. 'But does Errol worship opera as I do?'

Raj shrugged and took another sip from his glass.

'Oi!' Ron shouted to the orderlies, who flinched at such a boisterous sound in a rather quiet tent. He gestured for them to come over. Raj was puzzled at his new-found friend's actions and chose to be amused by his strange behaviour.

The orderlies came over, bowing, and Ron waved for them to stop doing so. 'Could you please find a gramophone and bring it in here, please?' Ron took a swig of his glass as he added, 'Along with a *decent* classical record.'

The two orderlies stood there looking at one another and Raj laughed, grabbing his bench to keep from falling.

'Now what is so funny?' Ron asked, perplexed.

Raj, gathering his composure, smiled at a very confused Ron. 'You gave them orders.'

'Yes. Correct me if I'm wrong, but I thought that was required of a major,' Ron said, crossing his arms.

'Yes, it is in fact something a major should do. However, I'm afraid you did so in English and these men only speak Urdu.' Raj stifled another laugh.

Ron released his arms and smiled, 'I see. Well, could you ask them in Urdu to fulfil my request then, and apologize on my behalf for acting like such a raving lunatic?'

Raj bowed and turned to the orderlies and explained everything to them. The taller of the two smiled and let out a laugh before bowing deeply and scurrying out of the hall.

A short moment later, he returned – almost buckling under the weight of a gramophone. The other orderly helped him bring it over to the table, where Raj and Ron waited. Wiping his brow, the taller orderly placed a record on the device with other additional records at its base and bowed deeply one more time after accomplishing the task. Ron, hesitant to say anything now, reciprocated with a quick nod.

The unmistakable sound of classical music, opera to be exact, crackled from the horn. Raj let the familiar strains fill his mind.

'Gigli,' Ron said.

'*Rigoletto*,' Raj said.

Ron smiled. 'So, you do know opera.'

'Some,' Raj replied. 'My headmaster at Bishop Cotton School lived and breathed opera. For some reason, he took me under his wing and decided I was worthy enough to unofficially tutor in music. From him, I learned to appreciate it all. My knowledge is probably not as vast as yours, though.'

'Let's test it, shall we?' With that, Ron walked over to the gramophone, removed the 78, put it back in its sleeve and extracted another. It began a little scratchy at first, but the music was familiar enough.

'*La bohème*,' Raj answered, feeling very pleased with himself. His headmaster would have been proud.

'Very good, Tommy,' Ron replied. 'And for the bonus round – who is the tenor?'

'Gigli again,' Raj said, and Ron seemed duly impressed.

'It's wonderful to share quarters with an officer who loves classical music. Until now, they have all been heathens.' Ron pulled a cigarette from his shirt pocket and lit it up, and they both listened to the record in silence.

***

Over the next few weeks, the camaraderie between Ron and Raj grew, based upon a mutual love of single malt Scotch whisky, a similar sense of humour, and above all, opera. Invariably, Ron, who was a company commander, and Raj, who was a platoon commander in a different company, went out on patrol at differing times of the day and night.

A ritual began between them, where they would meet in the officers' mess hall before the first person went out on patrol, and enjoy a single malt. At the end of the drink, both Ron and Raj took turns ending the conversation by mentioning an aria from an opera. The goal was to try to stump the other. They needed something to look forward to, and this always did the trick.

'Là ci darem la mano,' Ron said as he took the last sip from his glass.

Raj's eyebrows drew together. 'Haven't got a bloody clue.'

'Oh, Tommy. *Don Giovanni*,' Ron relented, giving the next clue.

'Mozart,' said Raj.

'I'm surprised you didn't know it.'

'Not fond of Mozart.'

Ron shook his head. 'Until next time, old chap.'

He slapped Raj on the back and left for his patrol.

While Ron was on patrol, Raj took it upon himself to scour the makeshift record library, which was sparse to say the least – just one bookcase filled with books that the men had brought with them. Raj wanted to find something, anything, that could stump Ron. It wasn't an easy task, and after seeing how dedicated Raj was to this endeavour, some of the officers, whose knowledge of opera was immensely limited, tried to help.

'Sorry, Tommy.' His new nickname had caught on and spread like wildfire. 'I thought *Wuthering Heights* had been turned into an opera.'

Raj smiled, not wishing to insult the officer.

'How about Charles Dickens? Were any of his books turned into opera?'

'No,' replied Raj, appreciative of his intentions. 'But many of Shakespeare's plays were.'

'I have his complete works in my tent. Shall I go and get it?' asked a young lieutenant. Without waiting for a reply, he bolted, only to return a few seconds later with a large book in his hands. 'How about *Hamlet*?'

'Don't know about *Hamlet*, but definitely *Macbeth*.'

That was enough to cause a frantic search through the play for an appropriate passage that might be the subject of an aria. There were many false alarms, until Colonel Dalton walked into the tent. Everyone jumped to attention.

'What are you chaps up to?' he asked with a beer in his hand.

They all looked around at each other, wondering how it might sound to tell the truth.

'Trying to stump Major Roach, sir, with an aria from an obscure opera like *Macbeth*,' piped in the same young lieutenant as before.

'Perfidi, all'anglo contro me v'unite,' replied the colonel, taking a rather large gulp from his glass.

'Sir?'

'You asked for an aria from *Macbeth* and I just gave you one.'

The officers looked at each other in amazement.

'Sir, our apologies. We weren't aware you knew much about opera.' Raj smiled.

'What made you think that, Tommy? Just because I don't join you chaps in your drinking games?' Colonel Dalton put his beer down on the floor, adjusted his trousers, took in a deep breath and belted out the aria with extreme emotion.

The officers stood with their mouths agape until Raj broke the silence with applause. The others joined in enthusiastically.

Colonel Dalton curled the ends of his handlebar moustache and picked up his glass. 'Anyone care to fetch me another?'

The young lieutenants in the room fell over themselves to attend to his request.

The following day, just before Raj went out on patrol, both he and Ron went to the officers' mess hall for their drink. Raj was ready and excited to finally stump the un-stumpable Ron. The others from the library had gathered around the two, eager to see Raj finally beat Ron at his own game.

Raj raised his glass and eyebrows to the crowd before looking at Ron, 'Perfidi, all'anglo contro me v'unite?'

Ron looked quietly at his glass for a moment, raised it to his lips and then said, '*Macbeth*.'

Raj set his glass down while the jaws of those around them hung open in surprise.

Ron smiled widely and all of a sudden let out a burst of laughter. 'I have a confession to make.' He wiped his eyes with his sleeve. 'My orderly was in the library last night and heard the conversation!'

Everyone joined in Ron's laughter.

He turned to Raj. 'Good one, Tommy. I would never have guessed it. Cheers!'

Ron and Raj clinked glasses and downed the rest of what was left.

***

Other than a stray thunderstorm, the weather in Central Italy in July is nothing short of miserably hot, though a breeze from the northwest keeps the humidity low. The men of the 25th Indian Brigade – which now consisted of the 3/1st Punjab Regiment, the 1st King's Own Battalion, and a regiment of the Garhwalis – spent a few days catching up with sleep and engaging in sightseeing, even though much of the surrounding cities and villages had been reduced to rubble. Montone stood on a hill with a commanding view over the Tiber River valley and was the 25th Indian Brigade's next target.

Raj sat on the edge of his cot and listened to the distant sound of an artillery barrage.

'So, what do you think?' he asked his friend Major Charles Boulter.

'Think of what, Tommy?' he replied, lighting his pipe for the tenth time. 'This damn tobacco is awful. Can't anyone tell the Italians how to make good tobacco?'

'Tomorrow's action.' Raj paused for a second. 'I would be lying if I said I wasn't nervous to lead.'

Major Boulter laughed. 'Really? Did you forget about Gabr el Abidi?' He puffed hard on his pipe and then quickly threw it on the ground in disgust.

Raj was pensive for a second, reflecting on that operation, where he had lost a few men, all in a matter of minutes. He felt the need to clarify even further. 'Well, that was a one-off charge. Not a full-blown operation like tomorrow's.'

Major Boulter bent over and picked up his pipe. He banged it against the tent's pole until the unlit tobacco fell on the floor, where he stepped on it, squashing it into the dirt. 'Tommy, any time you have bullets flying at you, you've been in action. I will be leading the company; you will be under my command. Just listen and learn, and we will all be the better for it.' He shook his pipe aggressively, agitated that it refused to cooperate. He finally gave up, got off the cot he was sitting on, opened the tent flap and chucked the pipe out into the Italian summer.

A short moment later, Ron Roach entered the tent holding the damaged pipe. 'Major, I'm pretty sure it works better if you keep it in your hand while you smoke.'

Major Boulter grumbled and took it from him. 'See you two tomorrow morning for breakfast, no doubt.' He stopped for a second and looked back at the two officers, his demeanour becoming anxious as he pulled at the collar of his uniform. 'From now on, I wouldn't assume the Germans will yield to us. The fighting will be intense, and unfortunately' – he paused – 'more troops will be killed than will return.' He nodded sombrely and left.

Both officers exchanged concerned glances as Ron lay back to light and finish his cigarette.

***

The next day, 5 July, the camp was unnervingly quiet. The only sound was the clanking of forks and knives against plates as they ate their breakfast, which turned into clicking and clacking as the soldiers cleaned and checked their weapons, making sure they were in working order. They were to move out at 8 p.m. – not quite sundown, but close enough. With each passing hour, the stress level among the officers and the enlisted alike became more and more palpable.

The officers busied themselves in giving out orders and some prayed with the battalion. As Raj kneeled next to the praying Muslim men, he said a silent prayer of his own. Though not overly religious, he allowed himself to seek reassurance in the Almighty, that all the men he would lead would return alive.

After spending about an hour with his men, he walked back to his tent, where Ron was sitting on the edge of his cot, a cigarette hanging precariously out of the left corner of his mouth. He was polishing his boots.

Raj chuckled at the sight of him. 'What the hell are you doing that for, Ron?'

Ron looked up at Raj and grinned. 'Hell,' he said, the cigarette still managing its balancing act. 'If I'm going to die, I might as well die wearing shiny boots.' He continued polishing them vigorously.

Raj laughed on. 'I hope you don't expect me to polish mine.'

'Why not? I want you to join me, old chap.' He picked up a tin of Kiwi polish and a bristled brush and threw them at Raj.

Raj moved out of the way and watched them land on top of his cot. 'I hope no one else comes in. They'll think we're daft,' he said as he opened the tin, dabbed on the black gunk with a rag and made round strokes with it against his boots.

Ronald's cigarette by now had fallen in the dirt, where it met its fate under his slipper. 'I think you should go out there, Tommy, and tell all the officers we are having a shoe-shining contest.'

Raj wasn't sure if he was joking, but thought it a great idea. Without saying another word, Raj left. A few minutes later, he returned with some other junior officers, all carrying their boots and tins of polish. There was nothing like polishing boots to distract the worried minds of officers.

Soon the tent was filled with officers sitting on the two cots, or the juniors on the floor, but they were all doing the same thing. Polishing boots. A few minutes later, the level of mirth had grown and must have attracted the attention of the commanding officer, Colonel Dalton, who appeared at the entrance to the tent with his boots.

'Any more room in here?' he asked. A chorus assured him there was.

A captain jumped off Raj's cot and offered his place to the colonel, who declined it in favour of a small space on the floor in the middle of the tent.

Suddenly, the room's mood transitioned into one of silence and reflection. Memories of their families and villages flooded their minds. They exchanged last wishes in case they had not done so the night before.

The clock kept ticking. The sun had already begun its descent, throwing long shadows across the tents.

Then, it was time.

They each found their places, readying for the assault. 8 p.m., they had been reminded by their commanders.

'We will start our walk along the road towards Umbertide. May God be with you,' Major Boulter announced to the group.

The silence now matched the darkness, and there was no more laughter, no more jokes, no more shoe-shining contests. Those boots were now on their respective owners' feet. Belts were buckled, and the officers had their sidearms on their waists. The enlisted had their rifles loaded and at the ready. Heartbeats grew rapid and sweat glistened on foreheads. And then the order came. They were moving out.

They walked cautiously along the roadside, not knowing what obstacles they might encounter. Prior attempts to take the town, which commanded a view of the entire valley, had been unsuccessful. The countryside was hilly, with deep ravines filled with jagged rocks, and the silence of its fields was no longer peaceful.

Major Boulter's company, with Raj leading a platoon, made their way slowly down the path. No one dared to even sniffle or cough, afraid of revealing their positions to the Germans. Complete silence was the key to success. To survival.

Then suddenly, it was shattered.

The barking of a dog erupted from one of the small farmhouses above them. Everyone froze. Hearts raced, guns were kept at the ready, but there was no sound from the Germans ahead of them. The dog continued to bark, keeping everyone on edge.

Raj crept up the line to Boulter. 'Sir, should I kill the dog?' he whispered.

Major Boulter shook his head. 'And how were you going to do that?'

Raj pointed to the bayonet in his belt.

'Where's your gun, Captain?' asked Major Boulter, furrowing his brows.

'I don't have one, sir.'

'What? Still doing that, are we?' The dog continued to bark as loudly as possible. Major Boulter blinked. 'We'll deal with this later, Tommy. But answer a question for me, please. Do you really think you could crawl all the way to the farmhouse and kill the dog with your bayonet without alerting the Germans?' Major Boulter shook his head. 'No, Captain Kohli. Now, get back in line.' He gritted his teeth.

'Damn dog,' Raj whispered as he got back in line, next to his second in command, Jemadar Bachan Singh.

'Damn dog,' the jemadar repeated.

A little while later, the order came down the line and the troops began an excruciatingly slow march along the sides of the road. The dog continued its incessant yapping. The jemadar repeated the words 'damn dog' under his breath and giggled quietly to himself.

The road began to wind uphill, and eventually, because of the stress on the soldiers, coupled with the climb, the order was given to hold off the attack until just after sunrise.

Suddenly, without warning, a mortar round exploded in front of them, causing those closest to be thrown backwards. The troops ran for cover wherever they could find any, as machine-gun bullets began to rip through them.

'Head for the cemetery!' Major Boulter shouted above the blasts and the unleashed bullets.

Raj led his men to duck behind the cement headstones, from where they took turns to pop up and fire back.

Raj crawled up to Major Boulter, who took cover behind a lone standing brick wall. 'Sir, you should've let me kill that dog, sir,' he fumed. His eyes glared and he clenched his jaw.

Major Boulter ignored his enraged friend, but Raj wasn't done.

He pointed back to his platoon who hid amongst the tombstones. 'I have lost many men, sir. Many men. You told me to follow you and everything would be okay.' His voice cracked.

Without waiting for an answer, Raj crawled back to his men. They were ordered to retreat below the hill. Raj examined the group, counting to see who was there. Raj's eyes fell upon the jemadar's face. Streaked with dirt, sweat, and caked with blood, he was barely recognizable.

'Where's Adalat Khan?' Raj asked of his men.

No one answered.

'Bachan Singh, where's Adalat Khan?'

And each time, as he asked, his blood pressure rose.

The jemadar put a hand on Raj's shoulder and shook his head – his way of asking him to stop. Raj took in a few deep breaths.

Morning soon arrived, and with it came the knowledge of which men they had lost. Forty-one enlisted men, five from Raj's platoon.

Once they returned to camp, there was doodh waali chai waiting for them.

'Where is Adalat Khan's mug?' Raj asked in Urdu.

Those around stopped what they were doing. The clinking of cups came to a halt.

'Is anybody listening to me?' Raj shouted out. 'Where is Adalat Khan's mug?'

A few moments passed as Raj furiously stared at the group for some sort of response. Finally, another jawan approached with a bow.

'Here it is, sir.' He handed Raj a white enamel mug that had seen better days.

'Thank you,' Raj replied, and without uttering another word walked up to the kitchen, and in a loud voice shouted: 'I want some Italian tea!'

Upon hearing his words, those around followed suit and quietly lined up for their fill of Italian tea.

# CHAPTER SEVENTEEN

## *Perugia, 1944*

Very early on the morning of 29 July, after Raj had returned from an all-night patrol in which he and his troops had managed to penetrate the German lines and capture some enemy soldiers, he crashed on his cot, much to the amusement of Ron, who at that moment was getting ready to lead his company out on a mission.

He had not been asleep for very long before he woke up with a start. Someone was shaking him. He tried to open his eyes, but his strength had been drained. He had been living on adrenaline for hours and had no idea what time it was. With all the effort he could muster, he managed to get his eyes open. The sunlight was bright, and he had to shield his eyes to avoid an immediate headache. He groaned as he remembered the last time he had felt this bad, which had been after a night at a decrepit bar in Cairo.

That was many months ago.

Slowly, the fuzzy image standing by the side of his bed came into focus. It was Raj's orderly. 'Captain Sahib, the colonel wants to see you,' he said in Urdu.

'Now?' asked Raj, rather taken aback.

'Yes, Sahib,' he replied, saluting as he left the tent.

Raj swung his feet on to the floor and made a very poor attempt to return his salute, as his right hand only managed to make it up to his chest before packing in.

'I wonder what the old man wants with you?' Raj heard Ron ask from a canvas chair at the opening of the tent. 'The sun's out you know.'

Raj nodded in agreement. His head began to pound. 'What time is it?' he asked.

'Nine in the morning,' replied Ron.

'Nine in the morning!' shot back Raj, the words rattling around in his head. 'I've only had about two hours sleep.'

Ron laughed. 'Well, go on. See what he wants and then you can crash again, Tommy. You know the old man doesn't like to be kept waiting.'

Reluctantly, Raj got up. But before he took another step, he had to make sure he was dressed. He was. Raj leaned forward gingerly and grabbed his cap off the nail above the mirror. He took a deep breath.

'Well, here goes,' he said, putting one foot in front of the next, making sure he didn't fall over.

So far, so good. He punched open the tent flap and the sunlight made him shield his eyes again.

'Good luck, old chap! I probably won't be here when you get back, but I can't wait to hear what he has to say to you.'

Ron's laughter followed Raj, and he had to think for a moment to remember where the colonel's tent was. A few seconds later, Raj recalled the location and began his unsteady walk towards it.

The camp was quiet, not many soldiers were sitting and talking. Only a jeep drove slowly by, or that's how it seemed to him, as he continued on his way, determined to make it without collapsing in the mud. Raj knocked on an empty chair outside Colonel Dalton's tent, which had been put there specifically for that purpose.

Almost immediately, he heard the colonel's voice bellow, 'Is that you, Kohli?'

'Yes, sir,' he replied, straightening his uniform as much as possible. After all, he had slept in it. He opened the flap and smartly saluted. Thank God that was instinctive, Raj thought to himself.

Colonel Dalton smiled at his feeble attempt. 'Sit down, Kohli,' he said, gesturing to a chair across the makeshift desk from him. Raj sat down, took off his cap and again tried to straighten his uniform. Colonel Dalton leaned forward, and Raj thought that whatever he had called him in for couldn't be that bad. 'Rough night?'

Raj wasn't sure if that was a question or a statement. He nodded.

'I guess our intelligence let us down again,' said the colonel, lighting a cigarette.

Raj was surprised he didn't have one already lit – he wasn't known to be without one. Raj nodded again.

'Well, there were far more Germans than we had been led to believe. In fact, we were up against what turned out to be a Panzer battalion,' Raj added.

'The Fifth, and I see we brought back a couple of prisoners.'

'Yes, sir, my company took those prisoners.' Raj felt proud of the men under his command. They were the best that humanity could offer. He trusted them with his life, and they trusted Raj with theirs.

'But that's not why I asked you to come here, Kohli.'

'No, sir?'

'No, Captain,' he replied. 'In fact, it's for a rather more serious matter.'

Raj felt a lump in his throat. He was now wide awake. Raj's brain quickly went over the engagement of the night before to see if he had made a mistake, but none came to mind. Raj was about to ask him, when Colonel Dalton continued.

'I understand you weren't carrying a weapon last night. Or, for that matter, on any of your engagements with the enemy.'

Raj immediately felt a sense of relief. 'No sir, I wasn't,' he replied, feeling more confident.

'Why not?' Colonel Dalton sounded incredulous.

'Well, sir, the way I look at things, I don't need one.'

The colonel raised his eyebrows.

Raj continued. 'If anyone started shooting at me, I have over a hundred well-trained men to fire back.'

Colonel Dalton leaned back in his chair a little more. Raj wasn't sure of the look on his face. It appeared to be a combination of a smile and a look of astonishment. He had to help him out.

'I never do, sir.'

'Never?' the colonel repeated.

'No, sir, never.'

'Not even a sidearm?'

'Not even a pistol, sir.'

It was obvious that Colonel Dalton had never had such a talk before with anyone, and why would he? Everyone, except Raj, carried a weapon. It made sense. They were in a war, and that's what one does in a war – carry a weapon.

'Captain,' began Colonel Dalton after a few seconds of reflection. 'I'm really curious to know your logic.'

'Sir, there is no logic in war, is there?'

The colonel furrowed his brow.

'My job is to lead my men. A weapon would be one more thing to worry about.'

'You're right. War isn't bloody logical. But that doesn't mean you can't be. You need to carry a weapon, Captain.'

Raj thought for a second. 'I have a stick, sir.' He realized how ridiculous his response sounded.

Raj watched the colonel's face intently as his brain desperately tried to find the right words. Finally, the colonel opened the top right-hand drawer of his desk. He reached in and pulled out an automatic pistol, already in its holster. Without a word, he placed it on the desk and pushed it towards Raj.

And there it lay for a few seconds.

Raj knew the colonel wanted him to dutifully reach over and take it, but he wasn't going to unless he was ordered. Colonel Dalton finally broke the silence. He extinguished his cigarette on the floor and let a sly smile escape his lips.

'Captain Kohli, from now on, whenever you go into action you will, and I emphasize *will*, strap this weapon on. Is that clear?'

'Yes, sir,' Raj answered.

And so, he reached across the desk and placed the pistol on his lap. The colonel picked a cigarette out of the nearly empty pack, put it between his lips and lit it, even though there was already one burning in the ashtray. 'Aren't you tired, Captain?'

Raj jumped up, saluted him and walked out of his tent without another word.

He was elated. Yes, he would carry the weapon as ordered, but he had only been instructed to carry it, not use it.

When Raj reached his tent, Ron wasn't there. Raj collapsed on his cot with a solitary thought in his mind. 'This is Italy. How did I ever end up here?'

Deep sleep overtook him. The sounds of war subsided in his mind and his thoughts turned to home and his dear, dear mother.

***

In summer, the hourly shelling by the Germans intensified as the Indians began their slow slog up into the depths of Italy. Most of the time, the Germans were way off target, but that didn't mean that the soldiers of the 25th Indian Brigade could take things lightly. Some, though, did become stupidly confident and a game began, which involved bets with small sums of money as to where a particular shell would land.

No one, however, could have predicted that a shell would land on a house right in the middle of the camp.

A shriek was heard, followed by a boisterous explosion.

'What in the devil?' Raj heard Ron say as he sat up on his cot.

Then, all of a sudden, echoing screams to take cover were heard from all over camp. Ron and Raj quickly evacuated their tent. Shell after shell began to rain down on them. The whole regiment lunged for cover. Every place, whether man-made or natural, that could provide some sort of protection was used. Unfortunately, some didn't turn out to be up to the task.

'Bloody bastards!' Ron's nostrils flared.

Raj looked out at the middle of the camp and the house that served as the colonel's headquarters. It had stood untouched a few moments ago, and now was no more. Raj began to run out from his cover towards the explosion, but Ron grabbed his arm and stopped him.

'Tommy!' he shouted, 'there is nothing you can do.'

Raj looked back at Ron, who pleaded with him to stay under cover. As much as Raj felt compelled to go and search for the colonel, he knew Ron was right. There was no way anyone could have survived an attack of that magnitude.

They held their position and gave orders to secure the scene. As the raid continued, Raj kept his eyes locked on the pile of rubble that used to be the house, watching for the slightest movement. Raj internally screamed for some sort of life to make itself known. But no such movement came.

Memories of his encounters with the colonel came flooding in. The first time Raj saw battle, Colonel Dalton's toast to Raj's good fortune at being transferred to the Middle East Training Centre in Palestine – though he did not want him to go – and more recently:

upon the sunny shores of Italy, it was the colonel who had called Raj into his office and handed him back the pips he had been given when he was demoted.

'Here you go, Kohli,' he had said to Raj, grinning for the first time without the aid of alcohol. 'Congratulations. You're a captain once more.'

Raj had taken the pips and was about to leave the tent without another word when the colonel stopped him for a second. 'I am glad that you're a captain once more. No doubt you will be a major soon.' With that, Colonel Dalton had stood up, walked around from his side of the desk and held out his hand. 'May I?'

Raj had given him the pips and Colonel Dalton had fixed them on Raj's uniform. Then he'd taken a step back and saluted smartly.

***

In August and September, the battalion was pulled back from the front and engaged in vigorous patrolling along the coastline. They were introduced to their new commander, Colonel Clifford. He was their third colonel in as many years.

As quickly as October came, it also came to be known for the worst memories in battle, and more importantly, as the month with the most severe weather. Rain became a daily occurrence, and even though the Indians were used to the monsoons, they looked upon the ankle-deep mud as a hindrance. Tanks were useless, and mules carrying ammunition up to the front invariably got bogged down, so ultimately the ammunition had to be carried by men.

It was 2 a.m. on 10 October, and an assault had been planned on Roncofreddo. The rains continued. Raj was assigned to C Company, commanded by Major Ronald Roach. This was the first time that Raj had been attached to Ron's company. But they weren't about to break tradition, and so off to the officers' mess hall they went.

'Habanera?' asked Ron, a larger than normal amount of Glenfiddich in his glass.

Raj, who had by now become somewhat of a junior expert in opera, replied immediately, '*Carmen*.'

'You've become very good, Tommy.' Ron tapped his glass.

Raj noticed that Ron appeared more uneasy than usual.

'Shall we continue drinks when we return then?'

'I look forward to it,' Raj replied, slapping Ron on the back, hoping his playful mood would lighten Ron's.

'Come on, let's go.' Ron sat up and hesitantly turned to Raj. 'By the way,' he began, 'I know we have become good chums, but since this is the first time we are going into combat together, will you do me a favour and follow my orders?'

Raj nodded. 'Of course.'

Ron tried to return the smile but failed. 'It's just that I want everything to go smoothly. No hiccups.'

Raj understood that his friend was feeling an enormous amount of pressure – this was, after all, one of the most important attacks he had to lead out thus far.

Ron winked at Raj. 'I need to keep you alive. No other bugger here knows as much as we do about opera.'

Pleased that Ron was easing up a bit, Raj replied, 'Not true. I heard Colonel Clifford is an excellent baritone.' Raj smiled.

'That's too much competition. I like to win most of the time.'

And with that, the two friends walked out of the mess hall and prepared themselves for battle.

The skies were dark, and the ground ahead of them was covered by a low fog. The ankle-deep mud had now turned into halfway-up-the-leg mud. Combat boots made things worse, becoming traps that made every step more difficult. Everyone had to lift their feet as high as possible to navigate, until they came across planks of wood that had been laid down by the engineers. Torches shone in the dark. Orders were barked so that they could be heard over the pouring rain. Raj smiled for a second, because it reminded him of when he was a child lying in bed, listening to the monsoon rains beating down on the tin roof of his parents' home.

'Do you have anything to add, Captain Kohli?' asked Major Roach, taking a glance at his wristwatch. It was time for the company to move out.

'No, sir. Your orders are perfectly clear. Let's move out.' Raj was jolted back to reality by Ron's question. Backpacks were loaded, rifles and machine guns were armed, bayonets were fixed, torches were extinguished. The chaplain gave his blessing, and the soldiers began to follow their officers into the darkness one by one.

'This is much worse than the rains back home,' bemoaned one soldier, who had been corralled into carrying ammunition on his back. 'At least back home we could sit on our cots and eat mangoes!' That was always the bright side of the monsoon season – its arrival brought with it the king of fruit.

His pronouncement was met with laughter. A much-needed diversion from the gruelling job. Happy memories of mango pulp and juice running down smiling faces. Raj once said that the best clothing to wear when eating a mango was a bathing suit, and he was right.

'That's right. What I wouldn't give for an Alfonso or a Langra,' added another unhappy warrior.

But whether he thought it or not, the back and forth had the desired effect of lifting their spirits and made the weary trudge through the muddy fields and gullies much more bearable. Soon, each soldier shouted out the name of his favourite type of mango – there are, after all, about 500 varieties – but as each one was drowned out by the name of the next, the miles evaporated.

They were entering enemy territory, and instinctively the men's conversations came to a halt. The slightest sound could give away their position.

The few hours of distracted light-heartedness were now disrupted by the sights and sounds surrounding them. The smells of cordite and decaying corpses of slain Germans hung heavily in the air. Allied dead had been covered by tarpaulin to protect against inclement weather. The Germans weren't afforded the same courtesy – as one wise sergeant major had said upon seeing the body of his best friend from his village: 'They deserve nothing but the worst that God can give them. If it weren't for them, Jehangir would be alive and we would be home with our wives and children. So, let them rot in the rain.' The British officers didn't intervene and privately agreed with his sentiments.

Minute by minute, mile by mile, the weary company marched in silence towards the sounds of the front line.

The sounds grew louder, and soon the artillery shells from the allied positions began their shrieking journey over their heads and slammed into the German positions called in by the forward post.

The plan was simple. The Royal Artillery men, who were positioned a mile away on a hill, were to carry out a bombardment of the German positions for thirty minutes, ending exactly at 0100 hours. Then and only then would the infantrymen of the 25th Indian Brigade, which included the C Company of the 3/1st Punjab Regiment, attack on foot. The hope was that the Germans, who now stood just a few yards away, would be so rattled by the shelling that they wouldn't expect a follow-up attack right in their camp.

***

Each shell had been marked with the name of a dead soldier by the artillery men. 'There you go, you Kraut bastard!' shouted Lance Corporal James Rattigan, a proud member of the Royal Artillery.

Shell after shell screamed through the dark night and without fail, whenever the shell made a direct hit, cheers went up amongst the ranks. Each direct hit brought them that much closer to the end of the war. Everyone was tired of the years of fighting. The quicker it came to an end, the better it would be for all.

'Good job, mate!' shouted James Rattigan's sergeant as he watched a shell with the name of one of his friends on it score a direct hit on a German tank.

The pace of the artillery shells grew as every direct hit on a German position brought cheers from those manning the twenty-five pounders and the infantrymen of the 3/1st Punjab Regiment, who were quietly waiting for the pounding to end and for orders to be given to move forward.

Major Ronald Roach moved silently to a forward position after he had conferred with his platoon commanders, of whom Raj was one.

Once he reached the front, staying low, he was greeted by Havildar Major Ahmed. 'Sir, what are you doing here? Go back a little bit, please,' he said in his best English.

Ron, who took it upon himself, after the incident in the mess hall, to learn the rudiments of Urdu so he could converse with the soldiers, replied, 'I here with you, okay?'

Havildar Major Ahmed, smiled at the effort his commander had put in addressing him in his native language.

'My English better than your Urdu,' he replied and then for good measure added, 'sir.'

The others around them smiled and decided to add their little bits of English, and then, sensing that the mood was changing, Havildar Major Ahmed, in the most authoritative tone he could muster, said, 'That's enough. The major is trying to bond with us. We must appreciate that and not think of it as funny.'

The rest stopped and looked down at the ground embarrassed. Ron did not understand what the havildar had said to the men, but felt that he had come to his defence. He patted him on the back and smiled.

'Okay, Havildar Major, we need to begin moving up in a few minutes.'

'Has the signal been given that shelling stops, sir?'

'No,' replied Ron matter-of-factly, 'but I believe it's to end at 0100 hours and it is now 0058. Close enough.'

'Sir, no. These artillery buggers will keep right on. We wait until 0100, okay, sir?'

The rest of the men in the forward position nodded.

'Okay, we will wait the extra two minutes, but I'm just going up a little way to take a look through my binoculars.' Before Havildar Major Ahmed could stop him, Ron ran up a little way out of the tall grass, away from their hiding place.

It was at that very moment that the one thing most infantrymen live in fear of happened.

An errant shell fired by the Royal Artillery, whose trajectory had been badly miscalculated, landed with devastating results near the forward troops.

Everyone stood frozen. Raj grabbed the signalman. 'Tell them to stop. They just hit us. Tell them to stop,' he demanded. The signalman relayed the message, but before the barrage stopped, Raj took it upon himself to run up to the front where Major Roach was positioned.

Even though he knew the answer, he looked around in the torrential rain and mud, desperate to find his friend.

'Where is your commander?' Raj asked loud enough to hear over the rain.

No one answered.

Havildar Major Ahmed walked up to Raj and took him by his elbow. 'Let's go, sir,' he said softly, but Raj refused to budge.

The rain fell harder.

Raj's eyes fell upon a body covered by a blanket in the mud.

'I have to see him,' Raj replied, his voice cracking.

'No, sir,' replied Ahmed. 'There is no need.'

Raj stood up straight, his eyes not leaving the body on the ground.

'Major Sahib died very bravely. He did not need to be up here with us. It was his choice.'

But Raj still refused to leave.

'I have to see him,' he repeated.

'Sir,' he said quietly, 'Major Sahib's body needs to go back to battalion headquarters. Muzaffar Shah and Mohammed Suri will carry his body back on a stretcher.'

Raj's face was devoid of any emotion. 'It is my duty to lead the company now.'

Havildar Major Ahmed paused for a second before he continued, 'You know, it's dark and those two could lose themselves in a barrel. Why don't you accompany them back?' He smiled sadly and let go of Raj's elbow.

Raj didn't reply as he watched his best friend lifted on to the stretcher.

The rain swallowed Raj's tears.

# CHAPTER EIGHTEEN

## *Naples, 1944*

At the beginning of the year, the fighting had intensified in all the Italian sectors. In late October, the fighting had moved up towards Rome. The casualty intake was becoming overwhelming, and the staff of the hospital ships were given the task of setting up a base hospital in Naples.

They began to set up their mission at an existing local hospital. The medical staff, who had been cooped up on the ship for a year, were excited to stretch their legs within the vast hospital grounds. Its garden presented a promise of life as it could be: one with flowers, trees and rose bushes. Norah would often visit it, hoping to see the faintest sign of life in bloom, but realized she wouldn't until early March. Spring was far away, but her curiosity and her yearning heart drew her out every chance she got.

Norah was happy to be off the ship. All the ship's occupants were in dire need of some change. After watching what had happened to the *St David*, those aboard the *Leinster* lived daily, minute by minute, with the ever-present awareness that they too might be targeted by the German Luftwaffe. So, when Matron

Edge announced they were to dock and set up a team on land, an audible sigh of relief rang out.

Norah was more excited for the change on Ruth's behalf. Since Mikey's death, she hadn't been her normal bubbly self; she had become less talkative and would burst into tears at a moment's notice. Norah felt that Ruth needed some room to breathe, to finally be free from living on the thing that served as a daily reminder of Mikey's death. This change would be for the betterment of her health.

Unfortunately, the magic of the garden rapidly fell away once inside. The sights and sounds of the hospital were a gruesome reminder of the carnage being visited on both sides.

The nurses were each assigned to different wards, and because of her experience both at the Radcliffe and St Mary's as an operating-room nurse, Norah was assigned to the surgical ward along with Ruth and Beth. The ward had twenty-four beds and not a single one was ever found empty. A new patient would come in, undergo surgery, and depending on the severity of their wound, would either recover or pass away. No sooner had the sheets been stripped and replaced, than a new wounded soldier would show up to occupy the space. Thus, the never-ending cycle of the surgical ward continued.

In bed twenty-two lay a Sikh officer who had both his legs amputated below the knee after they were torn to shreds by a landmine. The surgery took four hours and was beset with many complications. Despite his circumstances, the Sikh officer was never seen without a smile.

It was the third day since he had arrived, and Norah was doing her rounds and administering morphine.

'Good day, Sister Eggleton.' Captain Grewal Singh smiled up at her.

'Good day, Captain. How are we today?' She surveyed his chart for the latest dose.

'Never been better,' he answered, his grin unwavering.

'I hope it only gets better and better,' Norah replied, reciprocating his smile. 'I see Sister Gibbard dressed your wound not too long ago, so I'm just going to go ahead and give you some morphine.' She affixed a new morphine tube to his shirt collar.

'Thank you, sister.' He bowed his head. 'The only thing that could be better than this is if I were back home in India.'

'Yes, home would be nice, wouldn't it?' Norah thought of Kidlington often.

'Have you ever been to India, sister?' He lifted his head.

'Never, but who's to say I won't in the future, when this is all done?'

He nodded. 'You must go and try the food. The best in the world. Especially Punjabi food. Have you ever tried it?'

Norah shook her head. 'I'm afraid I haven't. And if I'm telling the truth, I'm not sure if I would like it. Isn't it rather spicy with all that chilli?'

'It can be, yes,' Captain Grewal Singh replied, 'but it can be made mild as well for those who can't handle the heat.'

Norah smiled as she updated his chart.

'Captain?'

'Yes, sister?'

Norah hesitated for a second, not quite sure what the best way was to ask the question on her mind. 'Your chart here says you stepped on a landmine?'

'Yes, a stupid mistake.'

'Stupid?'

'Yes. See, I was supposed to locate and diffuse the landmine, but it became obvious to me that I would not be able to defuse it in time. It was in such a place that my men would die. So I did the only thing I could think of and stepped on it.' He burst out into laughter.

Taken aback by his story and his laughter, she said, 'I thought you said it was a stupid mistake, Captain?'

'Yes, sister, it was. I should've made one of my men step on it instead of me.' He roared with laughter again.

She smirked. 'Sounds awfully brave to me.' She patted his hand. 'Is there anything I can do for you, Captain?'

'No, sister,' he replied calmly, a sign of resignation in his tone for the first time. 'There's nothing more to be done for me.'

Norah knew what he meant but decided it would be best to brush it off. 'You're a very brave man, Captain.' She squeezed his arm.

Captain Grewal Singh barely smiled as he mouthed the words, 'Thank you.'

She would have sat and talked with him all day if she could, but there were other patients she had to attend to. Before her shift was over, she made it a priority to say goodnight to the captain. 'I'll see you tomorrow, bright and early.'

'Until then,' he replied, as he bowed his head and brought folded hands to his heart, his smile ever glowing.

The next day, Norah arrived for her shift after a good restful sleep. She had gone to the hospital library to read up on India, and thought she'd surprise Captain Grewal Singh with her new knowledge.

However, when she entered her ward and looked for the captain, she saw another officer asleep in his bed. She quietly scanned each bed again. Perhaps she was looking at the wrong bed, or perhaps they had moved him to a different ward.

Norah grabbed the elbow of the closest sister to her. 'Sister Anne,' she began, 'Captain Grewal Singh … Where is he?'

Anne opened her mouth, preparing to tell Norah, but she shut it again.

'Was he transferred to another bed? To another ward?' Norah's eyes searched Anne's for an answer, praying it wasn't what she feared it was.

'He smiled until the very last moment, Norah.' Anne made to hold Norah's hands, but Norah retracted them.

She knew his prognosis wasn't good, but he had seemed to be doing well.

'I know you had grown rather fond of him. I made sure to sit with him until he passed.' Anne waved Ruth over – she had just walked into the ward.

'Norah, dear. I'm so sorry. Anne brought me over once he passed.' Ruth took Norah's hand. 'He was a brave man, and you did so much for him.'

'Maybe I could have done more.' Norah gently pulled away.

'You know that's not true,' Anne replied. 'Unfortunately, this is just how it goes.'

'He had such a pleasant demeanour about him,' Ruth piped in.

Norah nodded slowly. 'He was an extremely brave man.'

Her eyes glazed over. She had thought that being around death every day, she would have grown immune to it by now. However, the pace of her heart and the lump in her throat proved otherwise. The thoughts of her career choice began to plague her – she began to wonder if she had done the right thing becoming a nurse. It was becoming harder and harder to refrain from showing emotion. If she were to become a concert pianist, showing emotion would enhance her art, but for a nurse, it was taboo.

She turned her back to Ruth and Anne, and as she wiped away a single tear, she silently vowed to not allow herself to get emotionally attached to her patients again. She would not, she decided, allow this war to hurt her. Here on out, she was to see to their injuries. Nothing more. Nothing less.

***

Over the course of the next few months, Norah spent time with patients only to treat them or administer medication. Without compromising a warm bedside manner, she refused any personal small talk or extra time devoted to getting to know those in the ward. She would know their rank, name, and how best to treat their injuries.

Work became monotonous, filled with long shifts and very little time off. With the persuasion of Anne and some other nurses, the matron granted an afternoon off, as long as their shift was covered by another sister.

'We girls are going into town to walk around the shops. Won't you join us, Norah?' Ruth stood over Norah as she read in her bed. 'It will be a lot more fun than staying inside on such a gorgeous day, reading.' She pinched Norah's book closed as she read the title, '*The Poetical Works of John Keats*. Yes, I'm certain a lot more fun.' She laughed.

Norah, encouraged to see a smiling Ruth once again, sat up. 'Why not? Would be nice to explore the town and see the history.'

Ruth took Norah's arm as they walked into town, accompanied by a few other sisters: Anne, Margaret and Katharine. They strolled by the shops on Via Toledo, as shop owners used all their tricks to persuade them to enter.

'Pretty girls need pretty things, eh? Come see our leather bags, eh?' One shop owner waved them over while twenty or so handbags dangled on his arm.

'You're hungry, come try some of our homemade pasta!' shouted another man in a sauce-stained apron.

'Because I like you so much, bella, I give you this bracelet for free. Just come pick which one you want!'

The sisters all giggled and pulled each other tighter as they linked arms down the alleys. They enjoyed some pastries in the warm Italian sun, and sat on benches to people-watch but found they were the ones who were being watched. Men walked by and flashed flirty smiles, yelling sweet Italian nothings. After the fifth dramatic marriage proposal, the sisters decided to continue on their stroll down Via San Carlo.

Across the street, Norah looked up to see several large white columns perched on grey brick arches that stood over the street. Ornate scenes of art and musical characters frozen in gold plates were set into the wall. Gold angels with horns and trumpets framed a chiselled sign that read: REAL TEATRO DI S. CARLO.

'Oh, my.' Norah covered her mouth with her hand.

'What is it, Norah?' Anne asked.

Norah's heart thumped with excitement. 'This is one of the most famous opera houses in the world.' Her eyes affixed on the monument, she took in as much of the sight as humanly possible.

'It's very beautiful. Why don't we go inside then?' Ruth said, placing a hand on her forehead to shield her eyes from the sun as she looked up at the theatre.

'I'm not even sure that's possible. The doors might be closed. It was bombed by our troops. Probably isn't in working condition.' It saddened Norah. What a tragic fate for such a historical structure.

'Well, let's just try to see if anybody is home,' Ruth exclaimed as she skipped across the street.

The rest of the ladies followed as they burst into laughter.

'You can't just go in there!' Anne chuckled.

Now standing at the entrance, Ruth looked back at them and winked as she pushed the door open. Norah's jaw dropped.

'Ruth, don't go in there!' Norah, equal parts amazed and horrified by Ruth's daring, slid through the door, catching up to Ruth to drag her out.

Ruth snickered as she walked further into the foyer and pushed through the doors to the auditorium, their footsteps echoing off the marbled floor. 'Aren't you just a bit curious to see what it looks like inside?'

'I would assume it's a devastated mess.' Norah peeked from behind her, praying that nobody was around.

Ruth's smile grew bigger as she placed her hand on the door's handle. 'We could just find out for ourselves…'

Norah's eyes widened as she watched Ruth pull open the door and disappear inside.

'Ruth! You're going to get us in trouble,' Norah hissed after her.

Norah stood nibbling at her bottom lip while pacing back and forth, waiting for Ruth to reappear. She did not. Realizing Ruth probably wouldn't come back anytime soon unless she went after her, Norah took a deep breath and squinted her eyes as she slowly pulled the auditorium doors open.

It was dark. The only light available shone on a lonely piano sitting stage left. As Norah's eyes adjusted, she could make out several rows of seats and aisles. She started down one of the aisles as she whispered, 'Not funny, Ruthie, let's go.' Her words bounced off the walls.

Suddenly, lights flickered on to illuminate all of the auditorium. Norah stood frozen at the front, debating whether she should duck and hide behind the first row or just make a run for it. However, she was captured by the majestic beauty that stood before her. Rows upon rows of bright velvety red chairs. Lavishly ornamented balconies with gold trimmings. The ceiling was covered in a painting that recalled the style of the late Baroque period, depicting a scene of heaven with hues of turquoise, orange, gold, white and red.

'Hello, there,' a man's voice with a refined Italian accent echoed from the back. 'May I help you?'

Norah squirmed. 'I'm so sorry, I didn't mean to just barge in here. I was looking for my friend.'

'Ah, I thought you might be the singer I am supposed to audition today.' He walked closer, and as he did, Norah saw he was a man in his early to late fifties, wearing a fashionable buttoned-up shirt and jacket with sharply creased trousers, held up by a shiny leather belt that matched his equally shiny leather shoes.

'No, I'm afraid not,' Norah replied. She felt her heart slowing down.

'She plays piano, though!' Ruth's voice rang out.

Norah and the man both quickly looked around, trying to locate where that voice came from.

'Over here!' Ruth shouted again, and Norah's face flushed when she spotted her waving wildly from the royal box.

'Ruth, maybe you should get down from there,' Norah said as she gritted her teeth, her pulse picking up once again and her face becoming hot.

'Oh, but it's so beautiful!' Ruth said, taking in the view.

Norah stood in horror. How silly of Ruth and how embarrassing! Now they were really going to be in trouble.

The man turned and lifted his chin to take a look at who was shouting. He was silent for a moment before cracking into a laugh and waving back. 'It *is* quite the view up there.' He turned to Norah and said, 'She's not wrong about that.'

Norah apologized again. 'We will leave immediately, forgive us.'

He shook his head. 'Your friend, she's right?'

Norah cocked her head. 'I'm sorry, I don't think I understand.'

He walked closer as he pointed to the stage. 'You play piano?'

Norah blushed. 'Oh, erm, I do, yes, but—'

'Please, play something,' he replied, lifting his chin in the piano's direction.

'I really couldn't—'

'You must. Don't make me call the polizia on you.' He smiled.

Norah looked to Ruth, who was nodding emphatically, and then looked to the piano. It was such a long time since she had last played – perhaps before she had started at St Mary's.

The man walked down the aisle and sat in a seat in the middle row. Norah shook her head as she reasoned with herself. It would be such a story to say I've played at *the* Teatro Di San Carlo, she thought. She gathered her courage and took the steps up to the stage. The sounds of her shoes tapping on the wood floor echoed throughout the auditorium. The wooden piano bench screeched as she slid it out. She sat herself down and pulled up the cover. Her fingers hovered over the keys before she gently touched them, reminding herself what the touch of them felt like – cold and smooth. She slowly tapped one with her right index finger twice. The key bounced, as a sharp *ding, ding* sounded out in response. She remembered each key. She could only hope they remembered her.

She gently pressed the keys to play the first notes of Doppler's *Fantasy on "Rigoletto"*. At first, she pressed one key slowly, and then another, and then another as the notes' reverberations overlapped, until finally, her fingers' memory flooded back in. Her mind was transported back in time to sitting at the piano at Sir Athelstane and Lady Baines' home. The awful war disappeared into history. Peace overflowed in her heart and soul. Norah was once again home, playing as she looked out the window on a warm summer's evening…

Her fingers stopped and the piece came to an end.

She sat still with her eyes closed, and feared opening them for she knew that if she were to do so, she'd no longer be home. She was safely tucked away in Kidlington, listening to the delighted squeals of her brothers and sisters playing, while deeply inhaling the intoxicating perfume of the roses from the garden that danced sweetly in through the window. She didn't want it to end.

The sound of clapping broke her concentration. Her eyes slowly blinked open; her memory slowly drained away. She was back in Italy now, in a time of war. She softly closed the key cover, turned to bow her head towards her audience, and began her walk down the stairs off stage.

'Thank you for letting me play,' Norah said to the man as he walked over.

'Brava, my lady. Brava!' He placed his hands in his pockets. 'After that, I have no choice but to forgive your country for bombing this place.'

Norah let out a laugh. 'I wouldn't go that far.' She looked up to see Ruth walking down the aisle towards them. 'Now, we've overstayed our welcome. We will get out of your way.'

'Please,' the man put up a hand. 'I am the manager here, mi chiamo Pierumberto.'

'Nice to meet you.' Norah smiled.

'You must come again to play, for an audience on the bigger side next time, eh?'

Norah blushed. 'Oh, thank you, but I couldn't.'

'My lady, but you could!' He held her hands in his. 'Such talent in these ... I insist you come play anytime you desire.'

Norah bit her lip as she thought how wonderful it would be to practise once again. 'I'll compromise with you,' she began. 'I will come and play, but not for an audience. I'll play just for fun and for you.'

He bowed his head slightly. 'I will be delighted,' he said as he kissed Norah on both cheeks. 'Anytime you want,' he assured her.

'Thank you.' Norah said goodbye as she and Ruth made their journey back outside.

'Looks like me being mischievous paid off,' said Ruth as her mouth curved into a smile.

Norah grinned as she put her arm around Ruth. 'I guess you're right.'

# CHAPTER NINETEEN

## *Roncofreddo, 1944*

The chaplain, who not much earlier had trotted out his well-worn prayer for their safety, now resorted to his other well-worn prayer for the dead. As he prayed in Latin, his voice faltered and cracked.

The stretcher was laid down once the prayer had ended, and the medical officer went over to the body and removed the dog tags. He was about to stand up when he paused for a moment and reached over to the body's left wrist and removed his watch. He stood up with the dog tags in one hand and the watch in the other.

'Here, sir,' he said sombrely. 'I think Major Roach would have liked you to have these.'

Raj didn't reply. He was afraid he wouldn't be able to keep his composure if he were to open his mouth. He took the watch and gripped it tightly in his fist as he looked down at the grey blanket that covered the body of his best friend. He wasn't sure how long he stood there after the stretcher had been picked up again and moved to a different location. He didn't want to move. He was afraid that if he did, time would begin to move again, that it would mean that Ron was really gone. If he stayed frozen, maybe time would too.

'Would you like to talk?' he heard the chaplain's voice next to him.

Raj swallowed, the lump in his throat growing.

'Well, son, if you did, I would welcome it.' The chaplain put his hand on Raj's back before he left, no doubt to continue in his rounds to console those who had returned, and to pray for those who had not.

Raj stumbled back to his tent and opened the flap door. He stepped into the darkness, welcoming it. The only light leaking in was from the campfire outside. He stood in the middle of the tent with a blank mind. Nothing felt real. A jeep drove past outside, and he reached out to steady the mirror that hung from the nail on the pole, catching a glimpse of his eye. He held it there, unsure of who he was looking at. The man in the mirror looked worn, lost. A fire raged within his stomach and was building. He no longer wanted to look at the reflection and instead of letting go of the mirror to let it fall back into place on its string, he lifted it and threw it with all his might at the ground. A resounding shatter as it smashed into tiny little pieces upon the dirt floor. Raj followed the trail of fragments with his eyes as they led up to the cot on the other side of the room. Toothbrush by pair of socks by razor on top of towel at end of cot.

He walked over and picked up the razor, which was immaculately clean, and a teardrop landed on the silver handle. Then another one and another one, until Raj collapsed on the floor at the end of Ron's cot, his sobs becoming uncontrollable.

'It's not fair,' Raj's weak voice whispered. 'It's not fair.'

It wasn't fair. Raj looked forward to being friends outside of war. There weren't many friends he had in London, and Ron would have fixed that. It wasn't fair.

***

The 3/1st Punjab Regiment was relieved and went into reserve near Forli. It was the end of November, and the Italian countryside, which hadn't been obliterated, had begun to show signs of the oncoming winter. Trees were losing what little leaves they had, and the grass dried and browned. The skies darkened with thick clouds and the occasional snowflake floated serenely down to earth. Ordinarily, it would have been a blissful, postcard-like scene. But it was nearly December in 1944, and Italy was in the midst of hosting a war.

Occasionally, the sun would come out and dance among the clouds as the temperatures rose, but as soon as the sun set behind Faenza, the Indian soldiers resorted to gloves, jackets and mugs of hot, sweet tea.

Raj, who had been going around to check in on his men, who were stationed on the outskirts of camp to keep watch, jumped out of his jeep when he saw one of his men directing traffic. It was pouring with a mixture of heavy wet snow and rain. It was cold and miserable. He approached the young soldier, who waved a lorry by. The soldier saluted and Raj returned the salute.

'How long have you been out here, Corporal?' he asked the shivering and soaked man in Urdu.

'About two hours, sir,' he replied.

'Two hours,' shouted Raj. 'In this weather!' He looked around, and having set his eyes on a military policeman sitting under a makeshift awning, he beckoned him over. 'Why is he doing your job, Lieutenant?'

'Sir,' replied the military policeman, his eyes not meeting Raj's, 'we are short of men.'

Raj looked the man up and down. It was obvious that he had commanded the corporal to do his job. He took a deep breath. 'I'll tell you what, Lieutenant. Get one of your own men. Do not take any of my men again. They are fighting men, not policemen. Is that understood?'

The lieutenant raised his head and nodded in silence.

'Come with me, Corporal,' said Raj, grabbing the man by his sleeve. 'Get in.'

The corporal looked back at the military police officer and hesitated.

Raj noticed his apprehension. 'Corporal,' he continued in a softer voice, 'you belong to the Punjab Regiment, not the RMPs.'

The corporal smiled and got into the backseat of the jeep as the driver put it into gear.

'Where to, sir?' asked the driver.

'To the officers' mess. This man needs a mug of hot tea before he catches his death.' Raj looked back to gauge the reaction from this lower-rank soldier, convinced he'd be beyond honoured to be given such a privilege.

'Excuse me, sir,' the Corporal began meekly. 'I hope I'm not overstepping my bounds, sir, but what sort of tea do they have there?'

'Tea, regular tea, corporal.' Raj's eyebrows furrowed, unsure of what other kind of tea he could have possibly meant.

The corporal wrung his hands. 'Sir, is it all right if you drop me off at my mess instead? I would like a mug of doodh waali chai.'

'Doodh waali chai?' Raj asked in Urdu. 'Milk tea?' he repeated in English.

'Yes, sir.' The corporal smiled. 'It's much better than the English tea you officers drink.'

Raj let out a laugh. 'Soldiers' tea?'

'Yes, sir,' replied the corporal excitedly, 'that's all we drink in my village.'

'And in mine, too.' Raj stopped mid-sentence. 'You know what, Corporal, I think we all deserve a little bit of home right now. Do you think they would mind if I joined you?'

The corporal's mouth hung open and he blinked. 'I don't know what the colonel would say, sir. You officers aren't supposed to fraternize with us lower ranks—'

'Hogwash,' interrupted Raj and turned his attention to his driver, who was enjoying the conversation. 'To the other mess tent, please.' And the driver quickly nodded.

As they pulled up to the mess tent, the corporal jumped out first and ran to open the tent flap. Raj pulled off his cap and ducked as he entered. The noise in the tent dissipated all of a sudden, as the men already occupying the mess watched Raj step in. Coming to their senses, the men rose to their feet and came to attention.

'At ease.' Raj smiled. He looked around at the men standing in no particular order. These were the men he commanded in battle. They were other Indians. They were his brothers. He felt at home with these men, and not with his fellow officers who spoke with posh accents and had an air of superiority.

A senior corporal pulled a chair to the front of the table. 'Sir,' he said in Urdu, 'please sit here.'

Raj didn't move, 'Corporal, if it's all right, let me sit on the bench with you.'

He walked over to the closest bench. The men rushed to make room for him. As soon as he sat down, the regular chatter returned.

The corporal whom Raj had rescued from the rain brought over a steaming cup of tea. Raj frowned at the delicate teacup with a floral design that was placed in front of him and turned to the corporal. 'No mugs?' he asked.

The corporal stammered. 'Sir,' he finally answered, 'we thought this would be more to your liking.'

'Arre yaar,' replied Raj in all seriousness, 'do you think I will be able to get the full effect of the chai in something as small as a thimble? Surely there must be a spare mug around here somewhere.'

One was produced and placed in front of Raj, filled with the best thing to happen to milk in history. There was a moment of silence as Raj raised the mug and eyed it tenderly. He knew the extra mugs used to not be extra at all – they had once belonged to those who met their fate in the war.

He took a sip and closed his eyes. As the sweet milky tea touched his tongue, sweet memories of home flooded his mind.

'This is so much better than what we get in the officers' mess.' Raj smiled. 'The English don't know good tea from bad because they drink it in little cups.'

'With their little finger stuck in the air,' added a soldier, feeling emboldened.

Laughter broke out, Raj the first among them.

The tea was excellent, but the camaraderie between the men of all ranks was what made it taste even better. Raj knew that these men, all volunteers, would soon be joining him in battle, and that the mug of tea they were enjoying could well be their last. With each sip, the war which was raging outside the tent kept disappearing into the distance. If only the remaining days of the war could pass in peace…

***

The sounds of war were all around them. The battles were now raging to the east of Bologna, and the never-ending streams of dead and wounded served as a reminder that the Germans were not giving up. The fighting was so intense that even the thought of the upcoming Christmas season brought no cheer to the troops. It wouldn't be long before the battalion would be called back into action. It was when Raj was promoted to major that they were finally, at the beginning of December, given the task of capturing two ridges which lay three miles southwest of Faenza.

At 9 a.m. sharp on 8 December, the four company commanders were called to Colonel Clifford's tent. Their mood was buoyant, unlike the weather, which still persisted in bringing a mist of rain intermingled with spits of snow. Annoying, in Raj's mind. He'd much rather the weather decided between the two. As Raj walked to the colonel's tent, his ears locked on the distant sound of German artillery somewhere near Faenza, muffled by the dense layer of fog.

Other than the thick silence, they were each greeted by Colonel Clifford with a firm handshake and a smile. The tent was cold. Raj's toes prickled, going numb from the lack of heat. He watched as some officers huddled around somebody's idea of a heater: an enamel plate filled with dirt combined with kerosene and then set on fire. It was a poor attempt at heating, and did more psychological than physical good. Occasionally, the flames would subside. Then, the closest officer would give it a good stir and the plate would erupt into flames once again.

'Gentlemen,' began Colonel Clifford, 'we have just received orders that tonight the Allied forces in this region will begin the final push to Faenza and then on to Bologna, which we hope will break the back of the German army and put an end to this horrible war.' He looked at each one of his company commanders in turn, probably to judge their mood. 'We here, at the 3/1st Punjab Regiment, have been given the honour of leading the assault. And we start tonight.'

The room went silent. Only the sound of the wispy subsiding flames on the plate could be heard.

The colonel pointed to a large, topographical map lying open on his desk. He pointed to an area and continued, 'Here are our objectives, Colombara Ridge and Qarrada Ridge. Major Carey, you will lead A Company into action, followed an hour later by B Company, commanded by Major Kohli.' He then turned to Raj.

'Kohli, this is going to be your first opportunity to command a company in such an action.'

Raj's eyes fell on the encircled words: Colombara Ridge.

He wasn't supposed to be commanding a company in the action that night. But since the original major commanding B Company had been injured two days earlier in a traffic accident and had to be evacuated, the job fell to him.

Colonel Clifford continued, 'Once you have reached your objectives, you are to hold your positions until daylight. At that time, D Company – commanded by Captain Keogh – will occupy the area in the valley and prevent any German counter-attack.' He paused for a second. 'Any questions?'

Looks were exchanged around the room. Raj knew what they were thinking, he was thinking it too: Tonight, more men will die. It might be some of those in this very room.

'All right, gentlemen. I would suggest you return to your tents and get as much rest as possible before the night's operation. The artillery will open the front at exactly 2200 hours to soften up the German positions east of Qarrada and Colombara, and once that has been completed, our operation will begin. Good luck everyone, and God be with you.' The colonel concluded his talk, and the company commanders saluted and left in silence.

Outside the tent, the quietness was immediately cut by the screaming of German artillery shells flying in the distance.

'Shut up!' Raj shouted at the sky.

He opened the flap to his tent, fell upon his cot and closed his eyes. For a moment, he regretted his decision to leave university.

He had seen enough of his battalion die. Not all the men he would lead into battle tonight would make it home. They were young, they had their entire lives in front of them, yet some would have theirs stolen tonight. They would not return to their families and villages scattered across the plains of the Punjab. In need of a distraction, he picked up the book he was reading: *War and Peace*.

But after re-reading the same sentence for the tenth time, he decided to try and sleep.

***

Raj awoke to his orderly, Sepoy Mohammad Salam, tapping on the tent door.

'Sahib, it's time.'

At 2200 hours, under a cloudy and rainy night sky, Raj led his company, one comprised mostly of Muslim soldiers, towards Colombara Ridge. Major Carey, commanding A Company, attacked Qarrada Ridge first, and after intense fighting secured their objective. They were then immediately subjected to a fierce German counter-attack by infantry supported by three tanks, which caused A Company to withdraw.

At midnight, B Company began their attack. Raj led his men slowly down a steep hillside from where they were to begin their assault on the ridge.

Moving as quietly as they could, they lifted branches and crawled past brush, to eliminate any chance of giving their position away to the Germans below. Once the final jawan had slid down the last bit of the hill, rocks began to dislodge from within the dirt and tumble down upon the path with a series of loud thuds. Raj signalled for everyone to freeze.

He closed his eyes, trying to focus on sounds coming from up ahead. The pulse in his ears thumped rapidly.

'Hier drüben! Hier drüben!'

Raj's eyes opened.

'Take cover,' Raj signalled silently, just as bullets began pelting the ground around them.

The rugged terrain only offered the occasional boulder to hide behind. Raj was thankful that the lack of moonlight provided additional cover. They stayed there, pinned down by incessant fire. Finally, Raj summoned the signalman Lance Naik Sarwar Shah.

'Send a signal to headquarters demanding that the artillery give us cover, otherwise we will be here all night,' he whispered.

Lance Naik Shah nodded and at once began transmitting the message.

'What was the answer?' Raj asked.

'None, sir. There was no answer.'

'No answer?' Raj said incredulously, trying not to shout. 'Keep trying.'

'Yes, sir,' he replied and picked up the handset again. But no sooner had he done so than Raj heard the crack of an artillery shell as it whizzed over their heads. Followed by another and then another.

Raj enthusiastically slapped Shah's back, 'Yes! Tell HQ that the shells are landing perfectly.'

Lance Naik Shah relayed the message, and the allied shells continued showering down on to the German positions until the slope going up to the ridge, and the entire valley, was in their line of fire.

Once the German guns were silenced, Raj signalled his company to follow him, and with his stick in hand and sidearm still in its holster, he led them – crawling at times – through the brush.

Suddenly, Raj put up a hand, ordering his men to stop. Ahead of them, in striking distance, were the German lines. He waited until the Nazi officer facing him had turned around, and then gave the order to charge.

The Germans had not expected an attack on their flank, and not knowing how many troops they were facing, turned their fire towards them. It took three hours of intense fighting, ending in hand-to-hand combat, to inflict heavy casualties on the Germans, and not once did Raj draw his weapon. After many Germans lay dead, he continued leading his men in their climb up to the house on top of Colombara Ridge.

'Signal the base that we have reached our objective,' Raj instructed Lance Naik Shah once they secured their position on top of the ridge inside the three-storey house.

Lance Naik Shah wagged his head and picked up the receiver to send the message. Raj waited for the signalman to dictate HQ's response, but instead, he watched as his eyebrows drew together.

'What is it, Lance Naik?' Raj asked, concerned.

'Sahib, all I hear is … music.'

'Music?' Raj replied sceptically and grabbed the receiver from Shah's hands. He pressed it to his ear, and out of the crackling static came the sound of trumpets. Raj's own brows drew together as he recognized the composition: Jeremiah Clarke's trumpet voluntary. Raj pulled the receiver down and examined it. 'Well, send the signal again.'

'Yes, sir.'

Again, the same piece of music broke through the sizzle and pop of the signal. A shiver ran down Raj's spine. Something was wrong.

Raj was about to ask for the signal to be resent, but before he could, a series of screaming shells blew into the house, causing an explosion that made the house rock.

'Get out of here!' Raj shouted to his men. But unfortunately, the order came too late.

He watched Lance Naik Shah's body cut in half by a shell which then whizzed past his left ear and exploded on the back wall.

The house collapsed.

Suddenly, the world went silent and fell away. An overwhelming sense of peace, and then suddenly … Raj couldn't breathe. He gasped for air and awoke to a loud, high-pitched ringing. He struggled to free his body from the debris that covered it.

Dust floated and hung in the air. His vision blurred and then came into focus on the outline of a severed arm a few feet away from him. Raj's breathing quickened, and his heart pounded as it threatened to explode. His eyes fixed upon a still body which lay on the floor next to him. Over the ringing in his ear, he heard German voices and followed the sound with his eyes until he saw German soldiers running alongside a tank. They were headed in his direction.

The sound of the tank's diesel engine grew louder, and he watched the dust settle in its headlights as it moved closer. Raj reached for his pistol, but his hand fell upon an empty holster.

Quickly, he spotted a machine gun lying next to the lifeless body of one of his men. Raj reached out and took the gun into his possession. With fire in his eyes, Raj gripped the gun tightly and stormed into the open. In front of him stood the German tank with its hatch open, the gun still hot and smoking.

The six Nazis who were racing into the burned-out building froze in their tracks, obviously surprised that anybody had survived their attack. Raj lifted the gun, and as his finger reached the trigger his mouth fell open and an unrelenting roar burst forth. His finger felt as if it would break off from how hard he pressed upon the trigger, but he would not let go. Long bursts of bullets flew, and one by one the Germans were cut down. And as he yelled, he felt a release from the pain, anguish and sadness he had held on to for far too long. 'This is for Ron. This is for Colonel Dalton. This is for Adalat Khan!' he screamed, dedicating every bullet that pierced a German to his slain comrades. It felt good to see these monsters fall to their knees and scream for help as all signs of life fled their eyes.

The Nazis inside the tank frantically attempted to close the hatch and swing the gun around to face him. But Raj, fuelled by fury and purpose, ran up to the top of the turret and fired a continuous burst into the tank itself. Bullets ricocheted against the metal, causing explosions of light to illuminate the inside of the chamber. The screams of the dying Germans echoed within.

Raj continued until the last of the screams had subsided and watched the hollow-bodied Nazis slump over. Sweat and blood dripped down his neck and face, and on to his uniform. As he slid down the body of the tank, he felt his legs go wobbly and suddenly fail him. He collapsed.

The blood from his head now soaked the soil around him. As if in a dream, he saw his second-in-command, Subedar Ali Khan, kneeling over him, his shouts sounding as if they were miles away. His mind grew peaceful, and he watched as his mother waved to him from afar.

The world dissolved into darkness.

***

Raj awoke with a massive headache, and with closed eyes, immediately put his hand up to his head. He didn't understand when instead of touching his forehead his fingers landed upon soft fabric. His head began to pound. He opened his eyes and his sight blurred, blocked by tears. The pain in his head became excruciating, the sound of blood whooshing and pulsing became louder and louder. He squinted in the bright sunlight to see if he could recognize anyone around. He turned his head to the left and was met immediately with a sharp stab of pain that rang through his head. His hearing sounded blocked on his left side. He thought about popping his ear to relieve the pressure but was intimidated by the possibility of another stab of pain.

He tilted his head to the right, trying to understand where he was. Flaps of a tent surrounded a large enclosed area filled with various cots, which were occupied by bandaged soldiers. That would mean he was injured too, then. What had happened? Coming into focus was the image of a nurse not too far away.

'Sister, sister,' he called out weakly.

The nurse turned away from what she was doing and walked over to Raj.

In a gruff American accent, she barked back, 'I'm not your sister.'

Raj felt stupid. 'I'm sorry, how should I address you?'

'I'm a nursing officer. Or you can call me nurse.'

Unsure of what to make of her reply, Raj decided to get to the point. 'Nurse, may I please be issued something to manage the pain?' He winced as the movement of his jaw created a stinging sensation on the left side of his face.

Without a response, she left and returned with a tube of morphine.

'Thank you, nurse.' Raj smiled as the pain reliever took its effect and he fell into a deep sleep.

He was awoken hours later, when he felt a pull on his bandages.

'Close call, Major,' said an American doctor, who stood over him. He was examining his injury as he handed the bloodied bandages to a nurse.

Raj cleared his throat. 'Where is the piece of shrapnel that hit my head, doctor? I was hoping to keep it as a memento.'

His question was met with troubled and puzzled looks on both the nurse's and doctor's faces. For a moment, he wondered if he had said something wrong and was about to ask again when the doctor hesitantly replied.

'Sorry, Major, we don't have a piece of shrapnel to give you.'

He let out a sigh. 'I see,' he replied, disappointed. He wanted to see what had caused the damage.

Both the doctor and nurse remained calm as they continued their examination.

'Major,' said the doctor sternly, after a couple of moments of silence. 'We certainly would have given you the piece of shrapnel, if there had been one.' He glanced at the nurse, who had begun to wash the left side of Raj's face and remove large clots of blood. He continued, 'Major, do you know the extent of your injuries?'

Raj eyed the doctor, who looked grave but composed. 'I'm coming to the conclusion that I don't.'

'Okay, let me tell you then. You were not hit by a piece of shrapnel. A whole damn tank shell flew by your head, so close that it took your entire left ear off.' He stopped to gauge Raj's reaction.

After a second or two, within which the gravity of his injury finally hit home, Raj sat up abruptly and shouted, 'No ear? I don't have an ear?' He reached for the left side of his face and hoped the doctor was wrong. But he was right. His fingers fluttered about, trying to find it.

His outburst surprised both the attending nurse and doctor who, calmly, once Raj had finished his shouting, appealed to his better side.

'Look around you, Major.' He put a hand on Raj's shoulder. 'The captain across from you will never see again. The major next to him will never walk again. How about those other officers? You, Major, you just lost an ear. You won't be able to hear out the left side again. A small price to pay. You will be able to see and walk and live your life as normally as possible.' He hesitated a moment, hoping what he had said would have the desired effect on Raj.

Raj didn't need to look at the other officers in the beds around him. He knew they were in worse conditions than he, by far. He sat back down and pulled the covers up, embarrassed. Under his breath, he apologized to the doctor and nurse.

The nursing officer, having finished bandaging Raj's head, smiled sadly and squeezed his hand. Raj lay his head back down on the pillow and fought the urge to reach up again – perhaps the next time he'd find an ear?

The following morning, Raj managed to open his eyes without suffering searing pain. His attention turned to a senior American officer, accompanied by a junior officer, who walked over to each injured soldier gifting them something which the wounded accepted with great excitement. Raj could feel his nerves jitter. What was it they were giving out?

The American general leaned over Raj.

'You're a damn lucky young man,' he began. 'I understand you nearly had your head blown off while leading a charge against the Krauts!' Without waiting for an answer, the general saluted Raj, which he clumsily returned.

'Here you are, Major,' the general said in all seriousness as he turned to the junior officer for a medal which he pinned on to the blanket that covered Raj. 'We need a hell of a lot more men like you, Major.'

Raj's mind fell short of finding words in response. He looked at the purple ribbon that held a heart-shaped ornament. A medal of honour of some sort.

'Thank you, General,' he said.

The general, oblivious to Raj's accent, continued down the line of beds. As he did so, the attending nurse walked over to Raj's bed.

She leaned over and meekly said, 'Sorry, Major. The medal is only for American servicemen. I will have to remove it.'

Raj watched the shade of purple in the heart darken in the nurse's shadow as she unpinned the medal. She smiled sadly in exchange and continued on her rounds to each bed.

***

Christmas wasn't far away, and Raj continued his treatment at the American hospital. Once it had been determined that his injury was no longer life-threatening, he was transferred to a British-run hospital in Barletta.

On Christmas Day, a small choir made up of hospital staff visited the wards and sang familiar carols, and a very inebriated Father Christmas in a moth-eaten costume handed out presents, which no doubt came from unclaimed Red Cross packages. Dinner was served to everyone, including the staff, who ate with the wounded in the wards. Raj loved the roast duck, but he was feeling very homesick for England when in walked an orderly pushing a cart upon which there was a giant Christmas pudding, already in flames, surrounded by Christmas crackers.

He wondered what Colin might be doing. Perhaps he had joined the war as well. And if he had, was he still alive?

Dinner was washed down with loads of bitter, or for those who didn't care for beer – port, sherry or Italian wine. Raj smiled as he remembered the Italian tea episode with Adalat Khan. Another swig of bitter was in order.

The Italian countryside was now in the nasty grip of winter. Snow fell constantly and the skies were forever grey and gloomy. The sparse trees which dotted the landscape were covered in a continual blanket of angelic snow, giving a false impression that all was peaceful or that, at least, it was far away from the sights and sounds of the war. Further north, the fighting was beginning to end – the German army was now in full retreat.

Raj invariably lay in bed and watched, disinterestedly, the comings and goings in the ward. A small team of orderlies came and stood by his bedside.

'You're leaving here in a few, Major.'

Raj was exuberant at the prospect of being shipped back to London. His heart began to race and the negligible smile on his face grew wider as each second went by. He offered to get out of bed by himself but was encouraged to lie back.

'No, Major,' he was told sternly by the corporal.

Raj lay down. 'Am I being flown back to London from here?' he asked.

The four orderlies looked at each other. The corporal finally answered, 'No, Major. You're on your way to Naples.'

'Naples?' asked Raj, loud enough for the other patients to turn in his direction. 'Why not back to London? I'd prefer to go there.'

'Look here, Major,' replied the corporal rather irreverently, 'if you were to go to Blighty, I would insist I accompany you. Unfortunately, that's not the case. To Naples you go.'

Not the news Raj had expected. But he knew the army well enough to know that orders such as these were to be obeyed. Despondently, he lay back down and let the orderlies do what they had been sent to do – that is, transport him to the railway station.

There was nothing left for him in Italy. He had had enough of that country. He wanted to return home, to the sight of welcoming faces. But he had no choice. He was lifted on to a stretcher and into the back of a ten-ton lorry, together with some other wounded, and was driven down to the railway station.

There, he got on to the train on the night of 31 December 1944.

# CHAPTER TWENTY

## *Mussoorie, 1944*

'A telegram has arrived from the war office!'

The house went silent. A knife dropped in the kitchen.

'What's wrong? Why a telegram?' shouted Kundun, wiping her hands before running out of the kitchen.

'Bring the telegram here,' ordered Raj's father, Mohan Singh, who was relaxing on the veranda before lunch was to be served. Ramesh handed the envelope to Mohan Singh, who then waved his hand to dismiss the servant. By then, Kundun had reached the veranda and watched as her husband opened the envelope, read the telegram, then folded it and returned it to the envelope. He placed it on a nearby table and closed his eyes again, all without saying a word.

Kundun couldn't believe his behaviour. She had to know what it said. She was convinced it was about Raj. However, Mohan Singh, seeing that she was about to ask the obvious question, decided to pre-empt her.

'He is fine.'

'Who is fine?'

'Raj is fine.'

'That's not possible! One does not get a telegram from the war office to tell you that your son is fine.'

'No,' replied Mohan Singh, who was trying to convey a sense of calm by his attitude, but failing.

'No?' repeated Kundun. 'No what?'

'No, you don't get letters or telegrams telling you your son is fine. But he is.'

Kundun began to panic. She snatched up the envelope from the table, but it was no use. Kundun was illiterate and couldn't read, and neither could any of the servants. It was obvious that Mohan Singh felt there wasn't any need to elaborate and kept his eyes closed.

'Is lunch ready?' he asked, nonchalantly.

Without saying a word, Kundun stormed out of the room, telegram in hand. She had to know what it really said.

'Ramesh!' she shouted at the top of her lungs. Ramesh, who stood only a few feet away from her, jumped at hearing his name called out so loudly.

'Memsahib?' he said.

'Ramesh,' continued Kundun, 'how do you know this telegram was from the war office? You can't read or write Hindi, let alone English.'

'The postman told me.'

Kundun suddenly had a bright idea.

'Run,' she said, pushing Ramesh towards the door. 'Run and ask the postman to come here at once.'

Without another second wasted, Ramesh complied and returned a couple of minutes later with the bewildered postman, who had never set foot in that house before. He had been told that the lady of the house wished to confer with him. He folded his hands in a namaste, but Kundun, who was now a nervous wreck, didn't acknowledge his greeting and instead thrust the envelope in his face.

'Read this,' she commanded, and obediently he took the envelope, extracted the telegram and read it to himself at first.

'Well?' asked a stressed-out Kundun.

'Mr Mohan Singh Kohli stop this message is to inform you that your son Major Rajendra Shamsher Singh Kohli has been severely wounded in action stop.'

'Now, in Punjabi please.'

The postman dutifully complied. But before he had translated the last word, Kundun had snatched the paper from him, and in a very visible fury, raced out of the room and confronted her husband, who still sat with his eyes closed, waiting patiently for his lunch. He felt her presence.

'He is still alive, isn't he? That means he's fine.'

Kundun was lost for words. Not because she didn't know how to respond, but at his utter callousness. Instead of searching for the appropriate words, she threw the envelope at him and stormed out, uttering a stream of colourful invectives. She stopped before reaching the door to the kitchen, though, and turned.

The postman still stood frozen to the spot where he had read and translated the telegram to Kundun.

'Give him some tea,' she instructed Shanti as she dug into the pockets of her salwar kameez and found a few coins, which she gladly gave him. He was both surprised and very appreciative.

'As for making lunch,' continued Kundun to the staff, 'he can make his own damn lunch!' Kundun emphasized the word 'he' with the jab of her index finger in the direction of her husband, who kept his eyes closed, waiting patiently for his food.

'I'm sure Raj is fine. He's a very brave man,' interjected Shanti, trying to calm the tense situation. 'You will see, he will come home.'

Each and every day, until a letter arrived from Raj about four weeks later confirming that he was indeed alive, Kundun kept her distance from her husband and only talked to him when she had to, which was rarely. The letter from Raj was addressed to his father, but the postman had been instructed to deliver it directly to her – and in anticipation of receiving another tip, he did. He then proceeded to read it aloud and translate it to the relief of the entire household, with the notable exception of Mohan Singh, who was at work that day.

'Sahib has terrible handwriting,' uttered the postman, hoping his extra effort would indeed be worthy of an extra tip. His ploy worked, much to his delight. Shanti hugged her employer, and then the entire staff of the establishment returned to their normal existence, as did Kundun – but only after she had taken the letter and thrown it in the fire.

'Memsahib, but what about sahib? Shouldn't he read it?' Shanti asked.

Kundun turned on her heel and walked to the kitchen. 'Let him suffer for a while.'

# *Part Three*

# CHAPTER TWENTY-ONE

## *Naples, 1945*

While all of Naples remained hungover from their New Year's Eve celebrations, a train rolled into the sleepy little station. Silence hung frozen in the cold winter air as the city slept off what had been a wild night filled with boisterous celebration, of live music in the piazzas and choral chanting from the drunken masses. The train screeched on its brakes, alerting everyone of its presence, making the locals groan and turn over in their beds.

A long puff of steam billowed out from the train's underbelly, a sigh of relief as it finally made it to its destination. This particular train had lugged hundreds of wounded soldiers across the heart of Italy to Naples in order to be treated at the 69th British General Hospital.

Among its cargo and contents lay a very discontented Raj. He thought about his fellow officers and troops whom he had to leave behind. He rubbed the left side of his head gently to ease the persistent, throbbing pain. His thoughts became exceedingly bitter as he travelled further and further away from his battalion. He sighed when they pulled into the station and he saw a small army of hospital orderlies and commandeered Italians swarm near its doors, ready to unload the wounded.

Each was lifted on to a stretcher and transported to one of the ambulances waiting there. All at snail's pace, at least that's what an impatient Raj thought. The train was comparatively warmer than the crisp winter air that lingered right outside. Raj was not looking forward to the cold. Winter in Italy varies from the extreme cold of the Alps to bearable in places like Forli, and Raj had thought, wrongly, that Naples being even further south would be immune to the winter weather. When the stretcher-bearers came for him, he had a sullen look on his face.

'Welcome to not-so-sunny Naples, Major,' said a soldier with a strong cockney accent and a sly smile on his unshaven face.

'Today might not be sunny, mate, but I'd rather be here than in cold northern England,' replied another as he crouched down at the ready.

'Give me London, any day,' mumbled Raj as he was lifted rather callously and plonked on to a stretcher.

'Careful, Corporal,' shouted a captain, whose job was to make sure that the transfer of patients to the hospital was carried out proficiently. 'You don't have to be so rough. These men are all severely wounded.' He moved on down the line.

Raj rolled his eyes at 'severely'. He didn't feel severely wounded. The only thing that he thought was severely wounded was his pride. He was sure he'd be returned to his company after receiving treatment at the field hospital in Barletta, but was taken by surprise when they notified him that he was to be shipped off to a hospital in southern Italy for further treatment. As he surveyed the lot he was grouped with, he couldn't help but feel like a fraud. He only saw himself as a severely sad excuse for what it meant to be wounded – to be boarded on to a train, dragged away from all the fighting and brought to a hospital in Naples, all because of a mere head wound. And this solemn ceremony of unloading felt over-the-top and utterly unnecessary. He didn't deserve this treatment – he would never let himself think otherwise. He was left without an ear, *an ear* for goodness' sake! Others weren't afforded the same luck, as they were left without limbs or worse.

'Cor blimey. You give these uni chaps an army rank and think they're generals,' said Corporal One out of the corner of his mouth.

'Are we hurting you, Major?' Corporal Two laughed as he asked Raj.

'No, Corporal. You're doing fine.' Raj crossed his arms, irritably anticipating the rest of the journey in the ambulance with those two.

'I bet he's never seen a gun fired in battle…' Corporal One hesitated for a second before he continued, 'I bet you have. Right, Major?'

'Unfortunately, yes, Corporal. A few too many.'

'Can I ask what's wrong with you?' Corporal One motioned to Raj's bandaged head and then added 'sir' for good measure.

'My ear was blown off,' Raj said, his eagerness for the privacy of the closed-door ambulance growing.

'Blimey! Ear blown off! By what?' Corporal Two waited wide-eyed for the answer, adjusting his hat, which slid forward and covered his eyes as he leaned closer in anticipation.

'A tank shell, Corporal.'

'A tank shell!' responded Corporal One, nearly dropping the stretcher.

'Careful, Corporal. I told you that once before.'

Wary of the captain's admonishment, Corporal One leaned in closer to whisper something to Raj.

Raj let out a deep breath. 'Corporal, it would seem as I am left without a physical ear on my left side, I am also left without the functionality of that ear.'

'Oh!' Corporal One shifted the weight of the stretcher so he could whisper into Raj's right side and excitedly repeated, 'A whole blooming tank shell, Major?'

'Yes, Corporal, a whole blooming tank shell,' whispered back Raj as he closed his eyes, aware of the anger that was bubbling up inside.

'Bloody hell! I would reckon that must've hurt!'

Raj pinched the bridge of his nose as a headache started to make its appearance.

'A whole tank shell! Have you seen the size of them?' whispered Corporal One to Corporal Two.

They continued in this manner the whole way to the ambulance, Corporal One loudly whispering to Corporal Two and so forth.

'If that was you, you'd be crying all the way back to your mum!'

'Oi, no I wouldn't!' Corporal One let go of one side of the stretcher to take a playful swing at Corporal Two, the stretcher sharply dipping as he did so. That made Corporal One catch it on top of his knee, as all the while they continued with their bickering.

If the journey were any longer, Raj would have had a bout of motion sickness, but thankfully they made it to the ambulance and Raj was hoisted up and settled between two other stretchers.

'Good luck, Major! Hope those Germans get hell fer doing what they did to you!'

After an hour or so of sustained bumps – the roads were awful, having put up with tanks and a bomb or two – the ambulances arrived at the base hospital. Raj, together with the others in the first ambulance, was hurriedly offloaded. The stretchers lay side by side on the veranda. The ambulance then left in a hurry back to the railway station, to ferry back more wounded. Raj lay there for about half an hour or so before a nursing officer came by and checked on him.

She surveyed him from head to toe. 'Do you speak English?'

'Yes,' replied Raj, and she let out a breath of relief.

'Are you warm enough, Major?' she asked.

'Yes, sister,' Raj replied and then turned his head around to look at the other stretchers surrounding him. 'Sister, is there some reason why I was brought to Naples instead of being sent to London?'

She laughed. 'Major, unfortunately I don't get to make those sorts of decisions. That was made in the hospital you came from.'

'My wound isn't as severe as others though,' he said under his breath, but loud enough for her to hear.

'For your sake, Major, I hope you're right. But in the meantime, I'm going to have a couple of orderlies carry you to a bed in a ward.' She then turned to some men who were standing around waiting for orders. 'Corporal, can you and another please transport the major to the surgical ward.'

The corporal nodded and waved over another for help.

'Sister,' Raj said quietly, 'would it help at all if I got off the stretcher and walked to the ward?'

She looked a little puzzled. 'Can you?' she asked.

'Yes, sister,' he replied with a smile. 'I have a mere head wound. My feet are just fine.'

'Well,' she replied, 'if you are able to ... that would indeed be of great help. I wasn't sure if you would be steady on your feet, because a head wound can have that effect.'

Raj sat up, and after pushing forward with effort, he made it to his feet, 'Now which way to the ward...' And suddenly Raj felt woozy and his knees started to buckle.

'Whoa, Major,' said the corporal as he ran to his side, catching him before he could fall. 'Easy does it.'

The nurse was about to order him to lie down, but Raj held up a finger and deliberately straightened his uniform. He paused for a short moment, and then began to walk towards the building with the aid of the corporal.

As they walked to the ward, which proved to be more of a challenge than Raj would have liked to admit, he noticed how cold and dreary the place was. Similar to a cathedral, if the cathedral's goal was to be as sterile and unwelcoming as possible. It felt hollowed out, with high ceilings and tiled floors that amplified the smallest of sounds. The meekest cough from one side of the hall could be heard clear as day on the other side. It was quiet, it being only about 8 a.m., and the only light and heat came in from the windows high up.

Raj could see dust swirling in the light's path. Sisters quietly tiptoed from one bed to the next, trying to not wake any patients. The ward, which looked more like a generous hallway than anything else, was lined with two rows of beds. Hardly any of them were unoccupied, and each occupant was wrapped in more white bandages than the next. Raj's eyes fell upon a bed that was being gently stripped of its sheets by two sisters, the shape of its last occupant still imprinted in it. Obviously, its guest wouldn't be returning any time soon. Raj's feelings of inadequacy quickly reappeared.

'Do I have to stay here, Corporal?' he asked quietly.

'Afraid so, Major. I'm too far down the totem pole to make decisions like that.' He pointed to an empty bed at the far end of the ward. 'Here you go, Major. Let me direct you to your new home away from home – bed fifteen in the surgical ward.'

Raj relented and allowed the corporal to guide him to his bed, which was between a wall and a sleeping serviceman who, by the looks of it, had his right leg amputated.

Without another word, Raj sat on the bed and took off his boots, determined to not let the corporal perform that chore. Then he settled back and pulled the blanket up to his neck in an unsuccessful attempt to escape the cold.

The corporal tipped his hat and quietly left, no doubt to bring in another new inhabitant to the space.

Raj lay there for a few minutes, going over the events that had transpired at the front. He was angry for allowing himself to be injured – it could mean that the war had ended for him. He dearly wanted to return to his unit. He replayed the moment over and over in his head, or at least what he could remember. Perhaps if he had taken a moment longer to secure the perimeter of the house … Perhaps if he had called for the victory signal outside of the house instead of the inside … Perhaps if he had ordered his men to stay hidden in the field surrounding the house, extinguishing any possibilities of them being killed and of him being…

'Why the hell am I stuck in this dreadful place?' he grumbled to himself.

'Oh, Major, dreadful is a bit harsh, don't you think? This is a beautiful part of the country.'

Raj opened his eyes slowly, embarrassed that what he had just said had been overheard by someone else. Standing next to him was a sister, who was dutifully writing up a chart to hang on the edge of his bed.

'Not so sure I enjoy being here, sister. I'd much rather be back with my company, that's all.'

'Oh, is that all? Well, I was going to offer you some nice southern Italian food for lunch, but now I'll just order someone to come shoot at you while we strain some ice-cold water over your head – you know, to make it feel like you're back in the battlefield that you're so fond of. How does that sound, hmm?' Her eyebrows were raised.

Raj wasn't sure what to say, but he felt that he must say something. 'I apologize, sister,' he finally mustered. 'I guess I should keep my feelings to myself.'

'Good idea, Major. Here you go, a pill and a glass of water. Drink up.'

Raj looked at her, unsure if he had earned the privilege to ask what kind of pill she was giving him.

'Chop-chop. Who knows, you might wake up after taking this to find you're back in paradise.' Her tone was growing more and more sarcastic.

Raj didn't put up any more resistance and took the pill and glass of water and gulped it down.

'Sleep well, Major,' said the nurse as she took the glass and walked back to the end of the ward.

Raj fell asleep before she had reached her station.

# CHAPTER TWENTY-TWO

## *Naples, 2 January 1945*

The next day, Norah reported for duty to the surgical ward.

'Good morning, Beth. Time for you to go to bed and my turn to deal with the lot.'

'Right you are, Norah,' replied Beth, yawning on cue. 'How was your day off?'

Norah was about to reply when Beth interrupted her. 'Don't need to tell me, love. I bet you went down to the opera house again.'

Norah smiled. 'I'm sorry, but I just love it there.'

'We all know that.' She hugged Norah tight. 'I can only speak for myself, but we are kind of envious of you, love.'

Norah pulled away, 'Envious? Of me? Whatever for?'

'The way you play that piano … it's the most beautiful thing I've ever heard, it is.' Beth nodded emphatically.

Norah couldn't help but smile. 'Thank you, it's all a bit of fun.'

Ruth came over to join the conversation before she, too, headed to bed. 'It's true, Norah. You should have been a pianist, you would have gone very far.'

Norah waved her hand, swatting away the idea. 'Thank you, but I am exactly where fate would have me.'

Beth scoffed. 'Fate would put you here in a surgical ward in Naples, dear?'

Norah chuckled and shrugged. 'Anyway, back to work. Anyone new?'

'Just that Indian at the end of the ward. Ruth said he's a real trip.' Beth elbowed Ruth, encouraging her to continue the story.

'He's been asleep most of the day. We keep him that way, Norah, so he doesn't complain more than he needs to.' Ruth nodded to where he was sleeping.

'I'm sorry to hear that. Wish me good luck then.'

'Well.' Beth leaned in to whisper to the both of them. 'You know how these Indians are. They become officers and they think they can boss us around.'

Norah's face flushed. She hadn't dealt with many Indians, but she couldn't imagine Beth's comment to be warranted. The only Indian she really encountered was Captain Grewal Singh, and it hadn't been long since he died. The sting of his passing was still fresh.

A few moments of uncomfortable silence passed before Norah let herself respond, 'I'm not sure I agree with your sentiments. The only other Indian we had here was the captain, and if you remember he was an utter delight to be around and laughed until the minute he died. Didn't he?' Norah directed her question pointedly at Beth.

Beth shifted her weight and smoothed her uniform. 'Yes, dear, you're quite right. He was a wonderful Indian.'

'A wonderful *person*,' Norah corrected, 'and a very brave one at that.'

Beth soberly nodded. 'Come on, Ruth. Time for us to go nighty-nighty, then.' She cleared her throat, 'I hope this Indian is a delight too, and not the troublemaking kind.'

Norah responded with a tight-lipped smile as she watched Beth and Ruth walk out of the ward. With a shake of the head, she started her shift.

Beth's reaction added to the rough morning Norah was already experiencing. Each day proved to be harder to deal with than the next. Each day brought another serviceman whose life would be forever changed, and rarely for the better. The worst cases she dealt with in London paled in comparison to what the war had presented. As the days wore on, she ended her shift by reminding herself of Captain Grewal Singh and swore she wouldn't let it all get to her. She would often lie awake at night, staring at the ceiling, reprimanding herself for being so sensitive.

Today was just another day. Or at least that's what she thought.

As usual, she went around to each bed, to either ask how the patients were doing or administer morphine and other medications to manage pain. She walked slowly along the beds, routinely checking the charts to make sure protocol was carried out properly. After the warning from Ruth and Beth, she took her time before checking on the Indian major. If there was any truth to what they had said, she did not have the patience to deal with any difficult or unnecessary behaviour. She made up her mind that she would take a quick look at his chart, make sure he was situated suitably, and then leave as quickly as possible. Maybe give him another sleeping pill and be on her way.

She reached his bed. He was still fast asleep. She was gentle with her steps in order not to wake him. Maybe she wouldn't have to deal with his attitude if he wasn't aware of her presence.

Norah delicately picked up the chart which hung at the end of his bed and looked at his name: *Major Rajendra S.S. Kohli*.

SS, she thought to herself. Steamship? She had a quiet laugh at his expense and continued to read the rest of his information. Oh my, she thought when she read of his injury, ear severed. So close to his head ... What a lucky man!

She looked up from the chart to check which ear had been severed, and as she did, he began to stir. Her heart began to pick up pace. She held her breath and stood as still as possible, hoping he wouldn't wake up. He stretched a little as his eyes fluttered open. They locked eyes and Norah noticed their deep grey colour and how they lit up when he saw her. His eyes began to slowly close again, no doubt the effect of the sleeping pill Ruth had given him hours ago. They shut completely, his head falling limp again, allowing Norah to exhale. She stood at the end of his bed, studying his face, which looked so peaceful.

'These Indians are damn brave men.'

Norah was startled by the captain who was in the next bed. 'This one decided to attack a German tank all by himself.' He gestured towards Raj.

Norah turned her attention to the captain. 'Oh, my goodness.' She looked back towards the Indian major, curious. He was young, at least younger than her, and was boyishly handsome, with a rigid jawline. She cleared her throat as she turned back to the captain. 'How thoroughly immature.' She straightened her uniform and walked over to check if he was ready for another dose of morphine.

The captain let out a laugh. 'I fought with several Indian units. I'm glad they're on our side, especially these Punjabi guys. They're animals!'

Norah looked at him rather quizzically.

He expanded: 'I was stationed in India a while back, sister. I've seen these guys from the Punjab fight. They fight to the last man. They don't give up. And by the looks of it, this major is the same way. Could have used his help. Maybe I wouldn't have received this souvenir if he was fighting by my side.' He motioned to his legs, the right one ending at his knee.

Norah smiled, at a loss for an appropriate reply. She unpinned the used morphine tube from his shirt collar. 'I will be back with a fresh tube in a minute.'

She glanced back at the Indian major once more before walking to the nurses' station.

***

When Raj awoke, he felt very groggy. He had forgotten where he was for a moment, but as his eyes slowly opened, his memory and a feeling of bitterness came flooding back in. He had no idea how long he had slept. He craned his neck to take a look at the window above him, hoping he'd find his answer, but it was of no help. All he saw was sunlight pouring in. He was convinced he couldn't have dozed off for more than a few hours. His stomach was growling, and he soon remembered he hadn't had anything to eat since arriving in Naples. He had also remembered that the nurse had talked about a nice southern Italian lunch.

In search of relief for his hunger, he looked around for a nurse. He blinked his eyes. The grogginess did not seem like it was going to give up its hold over him anytime soon. It felt very much like being drunk – but without all the fun parts. He very carefully turned his head to the right, and even that slight bit of motion made the room spin.

What kind of drugs did these sisters give me, he wondered.

Through his blurry vision, he spotted what he presumed to be a nursing officer at the end of the ward.

'Sister,' he feebly called out, and in doing so realized how thirsty he was. His mouth was parched, forcing him to cough when he spoke, and as he did, he winced at what felt like thorns scraping along the inside of his throat.

Norah turned around to see which patient had called for her. Upon seeing it was the Indian major, she hesitated. She braced herself for the encounter by filling up a glass of water and searched for a sleeping pill. Pill and glass in hand, she began to walk towards him.

As she walked over to him, he noticed the glass of water she was holding. He instinctively sat up straight, preparing to gulp the whole thing down. When she reached his bed, he stretched out his arms and hastily grabbed the glass, guzzling every last drop. His eyes closed as he thanked God for such relief.

'Are you finished?' Norah seized the empty glass from his clutches, understanding now why Ruth and Beth had kept him asleep. She couldn't believe how rude he was, snatching the glass from her grasp, almost making her spill the whole thing on herself with no 'thank you' attached.

Raj lay back in bed, trying to catch his breath.

'Well, I guess I need to refill the glass? Unless you can take pills without the aid of water.' She placed the sleeping pill on the table next to him and waited impatiently for his response.

Raj looked at where she had placed the pill and eyed it for a second. 'Sister, I don't think I'm in need of any more sleep, just more water and something to eat.' He peered up to ask her if it was possible to have a large portion of whatever the meal option was but was caught off guard.

She was beautiful. Her piercingly bright blue eyes drew him in. He felt dizzy – and this time not from the effects of the pill. Her skin was so delicate, with a dewy complexion. Her short, dark brown hair styled with ringlets was pinned perfectly in place. She was stunning, and for the first time in a long while, Raj felt the joy of life flooding back into him.

'Sister…' He felt a smile form on his face.

'Yes, Major?' Norah said, noticing the way he was looking at her. She shifted her weight, her face beginning to feel hot.

'What day is it, sister?'

'Tuesday, January the second, Major. Happy New Year.' Norah instinctively brushed her hair behind her ear, and Raj thought he detected a slight flush on her face.

'Yes, sister.' Raj wondered if she was feeling the same way as him. 'I have a feeling it's going to be a very happy new year.'

She blushed. He knew he wasn't mistaken now. She cleared her throat and a rather forced stern look appeared on her face. Raj feared that he may have overstepped his bounds.

'I'm going to have a barber come in and shave the hair around your left ear so it can be dressed.'

Norah reminded herself of her vow: Do your duty – nothing more, nothing less.

He nodded his consent and convinced himself that he was the only one of the two who had felt the way he did. Must be these bloody pills, he thought, his smile slowly fading.

Without another word, Norah turned and left.

Her façade of sternness faded as she walked away. She felt off balance and touched her hand to her forehead, deciding that the uneasiness she felt was merely a symptom of a lack of rest. Nothing more.

# CHAPTER TWENTY-THREE

## *Naples, 1945*

Even though he thoroughly enjoyed the Italian food he was served, with the exception of the pasta which he never really cared for, he couldn't help but feel disappointed when an orderly came to deliver it to him.

The sister must want nothing to do with me, he thought.

He felt childish and stupid for how he had acted earlier. With every bite, he dwelled more and more on the interaction with the sister, and his bitter demeanour returned. He cursed the pills, convinced they were the reason he had felt out of character.

A few minutes later, an Italian barber – a slender man of somewhat diminished height, with slicked black hair courtesy of a bottle of hair dye, a thin moustache of the same unnatural colour, and breath that stank to high heaven of garlic – came in and bowed. To his amazement, Raj addressed him in Italian, and before he knew it, they were both engrossed in conversation.

'How did this happen?' the barber asked, sounding genuinely interested.

'A mistake on my part,' replied Raj. He was happy he was able to practise the Italian he had learned from the locals earlier that year.

'Not a mistake, signor,' replied the barber. 'Your ear is now permanently a part of the Italian landscape. Maybe they will make it a tourist attraction.' He stopped shaving around Raj's ear for a moment to wave his arms. 'Here, somewhere, is an Indian major's ear. To look for it, you have to find a red rose, and there it will be!'

Raj shook his head but let out a slight laugh and the Italian shrugged. Norah, who was changing the bandages on a lieutenant's arm a few beds down, was watching from afar. She couldn't help but be impressed. She knew the barber only spoke Italian, which she had found out when he'd arrived and blankly stared at her as she instructed him in English. Luckily, an Italian orderly stood nearby and rescued her from the awkward encounter.

The barber continued to carefully shave the hair around Raj's wound in silence. When he finished, he wiped the blade clean on the white towel he had laid earlier on Raj's chest, and pronounced, 'You're a lucky man.'

'Yes,' Raj admitted, 'I suppose so.'

Norah took notice that the barber had finished, and returned to remove the bloodstained bandage around Raj's wound. He took a deep breath. He could smell the perfume she was wearing. Sweet, warm and flowery. The feeling of delightful light-headedness returned. He wondered if the after-effects of the pill had not worn off yet.

Norah, determined to remain professional, decided that it would be best to work in silence and as quickly as she could. She took off the old bandage and saw that what was once a ear was now just a red and swollen hole. Some cartilage remained, but looked jagged from being torn off.

From the basin of warm water she had brought over, she pulled out a new bandage and dabbed around the site to clean it gently. She felt her heart soften.

As she worked, Raj's heart was beating faster than normal. He felt the urge to start a conversation, but wasn't sure what he could say without possibly offending her. He finally sensed an opportunity when she smiled at him.

'What's your name, sister?' Raj thought his heart might pound out of his chest.

'Eggleton,' she replied, not stopping for a moment.

Determined to keep up the momentum, he continued, 'Do you have a first name, Sister Eggleton?'

'Yes,' she bit her lip, debating whether to tell him or not. She finally relented, 'Norah, Norah Eggleton.'

'Norah Eggleton.' Raj liked the way her name felt on his lips.

Upon seeing the grin that grew on Raj's face, Norah regretted surrendering any information to him. She began her internal mantra again: Nothing more, nothing less. She quickly added, 'But I am "sister" to you, so let's leave it at that, shall we?'

His face fell. He blinked, and the door which he saw open was now closed and bolted.

Serves me right, I suppose. I was too forward, he said to himself.

Norah couldn't help but feel a sharp stab of guilt as she saw his discouraged face. She was trying to find the fine line between being professional and personable, but it seemed she was failing miserably.

This poor man probably went through hell fighting and here I am dishing him up more unpleasantness, she thought. She wanted to say something to let him know she meant no harm, but felt the moment had passed. I'm really rotten, aren't I?

'Right, here we are.' Norah fastened the new bandage. 'Good as new.'

She packed up the used cloths into a basin and marked his chart to note when the last bandage was changed. Professional.

She started her walk back to the nurses' station when she heard a meek, defeated and worn voice pipe up: 'Thank you, Sister Eggleton.'

Norah's heart sank. She turned to reply, and as she did, their eyes locked once again. His brilliant grey eyes held her there and a tidal wave of apprehension overcame her. The thoughts of war were suddenly miles away, and frankly, didn't matter anymore. Her stomach jumped, and an immediate flutter moved through her body. She couldn't seem to find her breath or a coherent train of thought, and she forgot why she had created her silly rule in the first place. As she stood there, looking into his eyes, she madly craved to learn more about him. Out of nowhere, she felt the urgent need to have all the attention he ever had to give, and she desired to give him all of hers. Nothing less.

'Sister, sister!' Norah's trance was broken by a nearby patient yelling for assistance.

Coming out of her daze, she looked around. At the end of the hall was Sister Beth attending to another soldier. She turned her attention back to Raj, her feet carrying her to the foot of his bed. She picked up his chart.

Raj watched, a little confused. Hadn't she already written her notes on his chart? He lay in bed with the blankets pulled up under his chin, his head the only part of him visible.

Norah searched her brain for something to say, anything. Without lifting her eyes from the chart, she began in a quiet voice. 'In the ward you *must* call me sister.' She paused for a second and continued, as her eyes lifted to meet his once more. 'Outside the ward, you *may* call me Norah.'

***

The next few days in the hospital were a mixture of dread and delight for Raj. Dread was whenever Norah wasn't working, because the other attending nurse, Sister Edith Pruth, was a dragon in disguise. Her demeanour towards Raj must have been honed in one of His Majesty's prisons. He never saw her smile and she wouldn't tolerate questions. You did what you were told and that was that. Without a doubt, she could scare the sunshine out of the sky. But when Norah arrived, the sun would shine even on a cloudy day.

Raj couldn't wait for Norah to come on duty. It seemed she spent most of her time with him. Others in the ward had noticed and would joke with him, but he didn't care. Raj was in heaven.

'Do you like poetry?' Norah asked Raj.

'I do,' Raj replied emphatically, but maybe it would have been better had he said no. As soon as he had replied, he cringed. The only poetry he had learnt was in boarding school, and that was a long time ago. Since then, he hadn't read a single poem.

'And who is your favourite poet?'

'Oh, I don't have any one particular favourite.' Raj was hoping to end the conversation, but it wasn't to be.

'Do you know John Keats?' Norah asked as she took a seat on his bed.

'Yes,' he replied, having no idea who he was, but distracted by his excitement over her proximity to him.

'How about Rupert Brooke?'

'Yes, very much so,' Raj again replied, not knowing who Rupert Brooke was.

'And do you fancy classical music?'

Raj was fondly reminded of Ronald Roach. 'Why, yes. Yes, I do, especially opera.'

'How wonderful!' Norah stood up with excitement, and Raj longed for her to sit next to him again. 'I love to play the piano. In fact, most of my days off are filled with playing.'

'Is that so?' Raj sat up. Could Norah be any more of a dream? 'And what do you like to play?'

'Well…' Norah sat back down and Raj silently thanked God. 'I am an avid fan of Rachmaninoff, Chopin and Tchaikovsky. Do you like them as well?'

'Yes.' Raj had no idea who Rachmaninoff was, but her perfume smelled so sweet.

'Marvellous.' Norah's smile spread across her face. 'I understand people find Rachmaninoff to be quite radical and too contemporary, but I just adore his music, especially the second piano concerto.'

Raj noticed Norah's eyes light up and sparkle. 'Me too! Those people don't understand a brilliant composer when they hear one, now do they?'

'May I tell you something, Raj – err … I mean, Major?'

Raj nodded. 'Tell me anything.'

Norah blushed. 'My father believes I could have been a great pianist if I hadn't chosen nursing.'

'It seems that your father is a very smart man.' Selfishly, Raj was glad she had chosen nursing.

'Where in India are you from?' she asked, longing to hear more about him.

'The north,' replied Raj and then decided to get a little more specific. 'The Punjab,' he added.

'The captain in the bed next to yours tells me that you chaps are fierce fighters.'

Raj smiled, 'My men were the best a commander could ask for.'

When Norah was around, he wouldn't take notice of anyone else. He was fixated on her. A bomb could drop right on his bed and he wouldn't even blink, so long as Norah was there. Nothing and nobody else mattered, as far as he was concerned.

'I say, old chap,' said the English captain as he leaned over towards Raj once Norah had left, 'you really have it badly, don't you?'

Raj looked at him quizzically. 'Have it badly for who, Captain?'

'Nurse Eggleton, who else? Old Medusa, Sister Pruth?' He let out a single, loud laugh.

Raj smiled and his cheeks ached. He had been smiling a lot these days. 'Do you think so?'

'Oh, good heavens! Everyone thinks so. Even the staff knows. I would say even the Germans know!'

'She is beautiful, isn't she?'

'Cracker, old chap, cracker.'

The rest of Norah's shift was spent attending to the other patients as quickly, and professionally, as she could in order to spend the maximum amount of time with Raj. The captain was quite right – everyone in the ward had taken notice of Raj and Norah.

As Norah walked away from a sleeping Raj and towards the nurses' station, she looked up and saw Sister Pruth with a frown spreading across her face.

'What?' asked Norah, becoming self-conscious of her smile.

'Be careful, dear,' she said, eyeing Norah.

'Oh, there's nothing to be careful about,' replied Norah, unconvincingly.

'I would hope not. You're English and he's Indian.'

'What's that supposed to mean?' Norah asked quietly.

Sister Pruth set down the chart she was holding. 'You are from two very different parts of the world, dear. Some might find it' – she searched for the right word – 'uncomfortable … for an Englishwoman and an Indian man to be romantically involved.'

Norah blinked, finding it hard to come up with a response. She felt as if the wind had been knocked out of her.

'He's probably already married anyhow. An arranged marriage. They all do that, you know,' she continued. 'You would do best to leave him alone.'

***

Sister Pruth's warning echoed in Norah's mind the rest of the day. She had dismissed her remarks as purely prejudiced. However, she couldn't stop thinking that maybe there was something to possibly fear on the being-already-married front. That particular part of the warning kept creeping into her mind as Raj smiled at her from afar. She wanted to believe that he was different. The more they talked, the more Norah felt an overwhelming sense that rang deep in her soul that they were not there together by mere coincidence. Yes, it was scary to think that Raj might have someone back at home, waiting for him, but perhaps an even scarier thought was that Norah and him were meant to be together.

Norah decided it would be best to ask Raj about him being married. She liked him, but if it would only cause heartache, she had the right to know and stop it before it started. She would need to ask subtly, so as to not offend or assume anything, and as she walked to his bed, she thought of a plan on how to achieve that. Her stomach buzzed with nerves, causing her to shy away from making eye contact with him.

'May I ask of your religion, Major?' Norah said, as she changed his bandage again. She knew she didn't need to, and Raj knew she didn't need to – yet, neither of them said anything about that.

'I was born a Sikh.'

Norah was reminded of Captain Grewal Singh. 'I had a patient who was a Sikh. He had made it seem that every man of his religion has to have long hair and a beard, no?'

'Yes, that is quite right,' Raj began. 'I am the exception simply because when I was young, my mum had quite a hard time taking care of my long hair, so she chopped it all off. I've always had short hair since.' Raj's thoughts drifted to memories of his mother. He missed her dearly.

'I'd love to hear more about your family,' replied Norah, bringing his attention back to the present.

Raj smiled. 'I would love that. You could tell me about your family as well.'

His eyes finally caught Norah's. His grey eyes and boyish smile looked up at her, making her lose her train of thought. He had a great talent for doing so. Raj's hand softly brushed Norah's.

Suddenly, Norah jumped up as Sister Pruth's admonishment crept into her mind. 'Are you married?' Norah blurted out.

Caught off guard, he wasn't sure of how to answer. He was about to reply that he wasn't, but then he remembered Esther. To be fair, he wasn't sure whether their marriage was fully legal, and therefore, if it was properly annulled. His mind whirled for a split second, debating whether he should tell her.

'No, I'm not.'

'You haven't had an arranged marriage?' Norah felt ashamed for asking so bluntly, but she needed to be sure.

Raj hesitated. He had, on occasion, thought about Sita. He often found himself filled with anxiety at the thought of marrying someone he barely knew. He thought his life would be different from his parents'– he would love whom he married.

'Well, my mother has someone picked out for me.'

'I see.' Norah abruptly began to gather all her supplies.

I should have known. Norah's thoughts swirled with jealousy and betrayal. Sister Pruth was right.

Raj knew his words had upset her. Anxious to not see her leave, he sat up. 'But just because my mother has picked out someone for me doesn't mean I'm going to go along with it…' His last few words tailed off as he watched Norah walk briskly back to her station.

'I think you've upset her, Major,' the English captain whispered.

'I think you're right.' Raj sighed deeply and hit his head against his pillow. 'It's funny. Try as we might, a man's intentions and his words are sometimes incompatible.'

The captain let out a short laugh. 'I believe my wife has said the same thing.' His eyes glazed over, his mind returning to memories of home. 'I've been married twenty years to the most beautiful lady in the world.'

'Tell me, Captain,' Raj said as he lifted his head again. 'Does it ever get easier?'

The captain screwed up his face, breathed out heavily and then said, 'Well … no.'

Raj rested his head back down on his pillow. The bottom of the world had opened up and he had fallen in.

***

Even though the Allies had gained the upper hand, with the Soviets pushing towards Germany from the east and the British and American forces fighting in France, no one really knew how long the war would last. Raj didn't know if, after his wound had healed, he would have to go back to fighting.

The future was a bigger unknown than it usually was. So, Raj decided to take it one day at a time. Norah didn't work the next few days, which kept Raj feeling anxious and even more guilty for how their last conversation went. Eager to make their next encounter a positive one, he was determined to impress her with poetry and talks of classical music.

'Orderly,' Raj called. He had fervently waited for an orderly to walk by for what felt like hours.

The orderly nodded and approached Raj's bed.

'May I ask you for a favour, please?'

The orderly nodded again.

'Is there a library of some sort around here?'

'Yes. At the other end of the hospital, near the chapel.' He gestured in its general direction.

'Very well.' Raj waved him over closer. 'Would it be possible for you to bring me some books?'

'Of course, sir. Anything particular you might like?'

'Anything on poetry. John Keats if they have it. And classical music. Rachmaninoff and the like.'

'Right away, sir.' The orderly bowed and off he went to the library.

Every waking moment for Raj was filled with studying every John Keats poem and composition by Rachmaninoff he could get his hands on. He had fully memorized 'An Ode on a Grecian Urn' and was impatiently waiting for Norah's shift to begin so he could recite it to her.

However, to add to his despair, Sister Pruth showed up instead of Norah, and with the gentleness of a bull, began to change his bandage.

'Sister?' Raj winced as she haphazardly pulled at the bandage, causing his head to thud heavily on to the pillow.

'Yes, what do you want, Major?' she asked, her concentration not wavering from the bandage removal.

'I was wondering' – another thud on to the pillow – 'where Sister Eggleton is?'

Sister Pruth didn't acknowledge his question and Raj thought maybe she hadn't heard him over the thudding of his head.

'See, usually Sister Eggleton—'

'Yes, yes. This is usually Sister Eggleton's shift, I am aware, but she has gone and got herself ill—'

'Ill!' shouted Raj, as he lifted his head against the weight of Sister Pruth's hand which, by the sour look on her face, was not a good thing to do. She pushed Raj's head back down and continued unravelling the bandage.

'Little thing has worked too much.' Her roughness was getting worse. 'Don't we all.'

Raj couldn't help but think that maybe he was the real reason Norah hadn't shown up for her shift.

'Is she all right?' Raj asked.

'Hmm,' Sister Pruth said. 'Not sure it's your place to worry about, Major.'

'I see. Well, hopefully she'll feel better soon.' Raj wondered if the news of his and Norah's conversation had gotten out.

Sister Pruth roughly cut the bandage and pasted it against his head before she threw her supplies carelessly on to her cart, and without another word, left huffing and puffing down the ward.

'I think you need to pay a visit to a certain young lady.' The English captain leaned over.

Raj scoffed. 'That seems impossible as I don't know where she is. If she's sick, I'd assume she's in a ward somewhere.'

'Oh, good heavens, Major. You don't know anything about love, do you?' he said as his eyebrows rose. 'Have Sister Gibbard come over here and ask her where Sister Eggleton is. I bet you a pound she will tell you.'

Raj wasn't convinced. He'd be too nervous to do such a bold thing.

'You know something, Major, love is wasted on chaps like you.' The captain smiled and saluted Raj.

Raj, for his part, wasn't sure what he should do next. The captain noticed him hesitating and decided to take things into his own hands.

'Sister Gibbard,' he shouted loudly. 'The Major would like to know where he can find Sister Eggleton.'

'Shh!' whispered Raj, who was appalled by the English captain's boldness.

'She's off today, Captain,' replied Ruth, as she walked closer to their beds.

'We are aware. However, the Major would like to make sure she is all right, that's all.'

'Oh, I see,' she replied.

Raj was certain Sister Gibbard had heard about their conversation from Norah. He knew the two of them were exceptionally close. She would not be easily persuaded.

Ruth thought for a few seconds before answering. 'I'm not sure you're supposed to know, Captain. Against orders and all that.'

'You're probably right.' The captain nodded. 'I don't want to get you into trouble. But thanks ever so much.' He turned to Raj, and making sure Sister Gibbard could overhear, continued, 'Sorry, old chap. I know she had asked you to return her book of poems as they mean the world to her, and I know her being sick and all it would've cheered her up to have it back in her possession.'

Unsure what the captain was doing, Raj's forehead puckered. The captain shook his head slightly and winked at him.

Sister Gibbard crossed her arms. 'Well, I can return the book to her.'

The captain's smile faded. Raj could tell that the sister had caught on to their little charade.

'Sister,' Raj began quietly, 'please, I need to speak with her. Please?'

Ruth nibbled on her bottom lip and then gingerly walked over to Raj's bed. 'I'll tell you what I can do. Why don't you give me about ten minutes or so, and then you can follow me discreetly to where Sister Eggleton is.'

'Damn good show, sister,' said the English captain. 'You deserve a medal. By Jove, old chap, Sister Gibbard here is your saviour.'

'If anybody finds out, I'll throw you both out of here.' Ruth gritted her teeth as she pointed at both of them.

Raj smiled. 'Yes, Sister Gibbard, thank you.'

The captain watched the sister walk away before turning to Raj. 'You owe me a pound.'

***

After grooming himself as well as he could, Raj followed Sister Gibbard as arranged. Ruth tilted her head slightly towards a door down a short hallway before disappearing down the next. No one was around as Raj mustered up the courage and opened the door to a private ward. He wasn't quite sure if he was permitted in there, as he had been told that the ward was just for staff. Raj scanned the beds quickly. Each bed was filled with either a resting nurse, doctor or other staff member. As he took in the sights of the ward, he realized just how inappropriate it was for him to be there. However, when he spotted Norah sitting up in a bed about halfway down the room, he no longer cared about the rules. He needed to see her. The attending nurse spotted Raj and walked over to him.

'Major,' she said rather strictly, 'can I help you with something? Patients aren't permitted in here.'

'Excuse me,' he said in reply, as he slipped past the nurse and walked towards Norah's bed.

Norah had noticed him and looked around to see who else had seen him walking in. Raj had made sure that the pyjamas he had been issued were as presentable as possible. He had grabbed the dressing gown belonging to another officer while he was asleep.

'Hello, Norah,' said Raj in a quiet and calm voice. 'Are you all right?' He searched her face for any evidence of illness. She looked perfectly beautiful to him.

'How did you know I was here?' asked Norah, not addressing his question.

'I asked,' he replied with a smile.

She pulled her blanket up to her neck. 'I really don't think it's appropriate for you to be here.'

Caught off guard by Norah's detached response, he paused before continuing. 'But I believe I owe you an explanation that cannot wait any longer.'

Norah raised here eyebrows, curious.

'But first, tell me, are you very ill?'

Norah laughed. 'No, just overextended myself. We are very short-staffed, and so I haven't slept enough over the last few days. That's all.'

'That's not quite true,' said a man's voice from behind Raj. It was an orderly holding a meal tray. Raj turned and faced him.

'Really?' Raj asked him.

'Sister Eggleton has come down with a bout of the flu. She's been given an extended period of rehabilitation before she's ready to go back to work.' The orderly paused for a second before continuing, 'Major, you're really not supposed to be here—'

Norah cut him off as she cocked her head to the side and lifted her eyebrows. Getting the message, the orderly sharply nodded.

'Right. Good day, Major.' He clicked his heels together and went off to deliver the prepared meal to a patient at the end of the hall.

'The flu?'

Norah shook her head. 'Nothing to worry about, really. Now, I don't think it's such a good idea for you to be here.' She whispered as she looked around, hoping no one was paying attention to them.

'I will leave, if you want me to. But please ... I wanted to explain further regarding our conversation the other day.' Raj cleared his throat and lowered his voice. 'I told you that I am not married and that's true. It's also true that my mother has chosen a woman for me to marry after the war...'

Norah let out a sigh.

Raj continued, 'But whom I marry and when is ultimately my decision. I'm afraid I didn't get the chance to explain my side thoroughly to you before, but I hope you now see that I don't care about the woman my mother picked out because...'

Hesitant to believe him, Norah looked away.

Feeling her disbelief, Raj began to succumb to disappointment. His heart ached. He stared at his hands before looking into Norah's eyes. 'I really do care for you, Norah.'

Norah's heart leaped at the sound of her name as it fell from his lips. But her mind immediately corrected her thoughts. She needed to protect herself, nothing more, nothing less. She continued to repeat her mantra in her mind until it was broken by Raj's soft words.

Meekly, he began to recite the first lines of 'Ode on a Grecian Urn'. Norah felt compelled to sit back and listen intently to every word until he was finished.

'My favourite.' She settled deeper into her blanket.

'I know.' Raj walked closer to her side. 'I memorized it for you.'

Norah's cheeks turned pink and he saw the sparkle return to her blue eyes.

'It was beautiful, Raj – err … Major.'

Raj sat down and whispered, 'In the ward you *must* call me Major. Outside the ward, you *may* call me Raj.'

Norah burst into laughter, causing others in the ward to turn to see what the fuss was about. She quickly covered her mouth with her hand to stifle the sound.

'Oh, Raj.' Norah's eyes welled up. 'I'm so confused. If what you are saying is true—'

'It is.' Raj emphatically nodded.

'But…' She shook her head and closed her eyes. 'I hardly know you.'

'My dear, yes, it's true. You've only known me for a short while. However, at the same time…' Raj leaned closer. 'I feel like we've known each other forever.'

Norah bit her lip. 'I know it's rather forward of me to say, but I feel drawn to you. And it seems you feel the same.' She searched his face for any sign of reassurance.

'Yes, Norah. That is the only thing I can be certain of.'

'But it shouldn't be,' she replied as she looked away.

'And why is that?'

Sister Pruth's words started to come alive as Norah spoke. 'We are from two very different countries. How can we ever be together? The odds are against us.'

'They might be. And maybe we are being foolish.'

Norah nodded as she hung her head and quietly wiped away her tears with the blanket.

Raj lifted her head with his finger. 'But if it is foolish, call me a fool. In all my life, I have searched for happiness, true happiness in all sorts of ways, and every time I think I've found it, it's been brutally taken away from me only to leave me devastated. When I think back on if it was worth it, all I hear is a resounding *no*.' He locked his eyes with hers. She needed to know. 'But if you and I were to spend every possible moment that we have left together before we are, God forbid, snatched away from one another and it leaves me devastated, and I go to ask myself the same question … I will only ever hear a resounding and joyful *yes*. I am willing to risk it if you are.'

Out of the corner of his eye, Raj saw the attending nurse walk quietly over to them. He sat back in his chair. He knew he had overstayed his welcome.

'Major,' she said quietly and far more emphatically than before. 'Major, I don't want to break this little tête-à-tête, but I have to. Sister Eggleton needs to get some rest.'

Raj nodded and got up from his chair. 'Of course. I'll just say my goodbye.'

The sister shared a look with Norah before turning and leaving.

'We aren't afforded a free moment at all, are we?' Raj sighed.

Norah smiled softly. 'I'm afraid not.'

'If only we could be alone, just for one day.'

Norah perked up, her mouth open, an idea stirring. 'Raj, what if we, just the two of us, took a holiday to the Amalfi Coast? Would you like that?'

Raj sat back down. 'With me? You'd like *me* to go?' His mouth curved into a smile.

'Only if you'd like that. I've been longing to see the coast. We'd be able to spend a lot of time with one another without being interrupted.'

'You'd want me to go?' he asked again, convinced that he must have blacked out and dreamed up the last bit. 'I'd be absolutely delighted to take such a holiday with you.' A goofy grin was plastered on his face.

Norah smiled. 'Only if you really mean it.'

He bowed his head. 'Forever and always.'

Norah blushed.

'But would it even be possible?'

Norah's face screwed up as she thought out the details. 'I'd have to get permission, but I believe I have a very good chance at getting approval. I'll ask the matron today. Why don't you come back and visit me tomorrow? I'll let you know if she agrees.'

Raj stood up. 'You've got a deal. I'll be back tomorrow.' He bowed. 'I do hope you feel better soon.'

'Thank you, Raj.' Norah lightly touched his hand. 'I have a feeling I will.'

Raj's stomach fluttered at her touch. He so wished he could kiss her on the cheek, but instead settled for one of her warm smiles and the twinkle in her eyes. 'See you tomorrow, Norah,' he whispered.

He smiled at her one last time and then slipped out of the ward.

Overflowing with excitement and adrenaline, Raj decided to pay the library a visit. He had a lot of reading to do on the Amalfi Coast.

***

On his return the next day, Raj brought along a copy of a book on Capri. He had stayed up through most of the night, turning page after page and learning all there was to know about the Amalfi Coast and the surrounding towns. Eager to share what he had learned and his thoughts on their schedule while they were there, he practically burst into the ward, making the attending nurse narrow her eyes at him.

The aura surrounding Norah had changed, however, and Raj sensed something was wrong.

'Norah, is everything all right?' he whispered as he dropped the book on the bedside table and dragged over a chair to sit close to her. He was worried that she had changed her mind about going on a holiday with him.

It was her sickness talking and she was delusional, he thought. Why would she want to spend a whole holiday with me anyhow? He prepared himself for the worst.

'I talked to the matron,' she said, her eyes dewy.

Raj was now convinced that the matron must have heard about him visiting her in the private ward. She was to be put on probation and they would be forbidden from going near one another ever again. He held his breath in anticipation.

'They are sending me to a convalescent home in Rome.' Norah covered her face, no longer able to hold back her tears.

Raj slowly stood up. 'But why?'

'They believe I've exhausted myself here. They think that the slower pace there will treat me better,' she mumbled, burrowing her face in her hands. 'And it's not of much use having me here.'

'Rubbish.' Raj's volume increased. 'Absolute rubbish. How could they do such a thing? Rome won't do you any good.'

Raj, filled with confusion and rage, began to pace back and forth by the side of her bed. He stopped and sat back down when he saw Norah waving for him to be quiet.

'You can't go. Please don't go.' He leaned forward and clutched her hand under the cover of her blanket.

'I'll try.'

'Please,' he implored, his voice cracking.

A monstrous wave of hopelessness washed over him. Never in his whole life had he felt as powerless as he did now. Neither of them had the strength to say anything. They both began to feel again the weight of the responsibility they had towards their posts.

Deep down, they knew it was not in their power to question orders. They had an obligation to go where they were told and to do what they were told.

Norah picked up the book about Capri from her bedside table and defeatedly opened it, turning a page.

'I don't know what I would do if you left…' Raj was about to add the word 'me' but managed to catch himself. He pinched the bridge of his nose and closed his eyes. He felt his eyes getting wet, and to save himself embarrassment he removed himself from the ward without another word.

That night was awful, not because of any physical pain Raj was experiencing, but because the very thought of Norah going away consumed him. They hadn't known each other for very long, he knew that, but he also knew she was special. They were special.

He didn't sleep, or if he did, he slept very little. His mind was working overtime, planning ways for them to actually be together after the war. She was from England, no doubt she'd want to return to be with her family and friends. He was from India and longed to be close to his mother and his friends. He was silly to think this could be anything more after the war. And if he knew that, why did he allow himself to fall in love?

Norah hoped to see Raj the next day. She couldn't bear letting the matron's orders be the last thing they dwelled on before the day ended. Determined, she called for the matron before bed.

***

'I have good news.' Norah was too excited to wait to see if Raj would come and visit the ward, and instead greeted him at his bedside.

'Norah.' Raj looked around to see if anyone had accompanied her. 'You're ill, you shouldn't be out of bed.'

'I'm fine.' She shook her head, eager to tell him her news. 'Aren't you curious about what I've come to tell you?'

Raj nodded hesitantly.

Her voice lowered. 'I have convinced the doctors and the matron that a trip to the Amalfi Coast would do me a world of good.'

Raj's jaw dropped. 'Really?'

Norah emphatically nodded and giggled.

'Did you tell them I would take great care of you?'

Norah shook her head and looked behind her, hoping no one could hear. 'I'm not sure what they would say if I told them I was going away with you. So, I told them I was going with some friends.'

'And they believed you?'

'Why not? You're a friend, aren't you?'

'Of course,' he replied, even though he had hoped Norah saw them as more than friends.

'I hope you still want to go, Raj?'

'Still want to go? There's nothing I would like more.'

Hidden by the blanket on his bed, the two held hands tighter than ever before. This is going to work, they both thought separately and silently.

Later that evening, when Norah had retired to her ward, Sister Gibbard walked by Raj's bed and winked.

'Have fun, love,' she whispered, and a crooked grin spread over Raj's tired face as he fell into a deep slumber.

# CHAPTER TWENTY-FOUR

## *Naples, 1945*

Raj and Norah knew that they needed to come up with an excuse for why Raj was leaving the hospital for the same days Norah was. After brainstorming what seemed like eccentric ideas, they finally came up with what they deemed a solid plan.

Raj had convinced his doctor, along with the matron, that he had some relatives in Rome, and that he had promised them in a letter that he would visit them while he was in Naples. After a few back-and-forth discussions, he was granted leave.

Raj and Norah discretely cheered upon hearing the news. It was all going according to plan – nothing was going to stop them from having a holiday all to themselves.

Norah squeezed Raj's hand. 'I guess I need time to pack. I'll leave you to do so as well,' she whispered. 'I will see you bright and early.' It took much discipline on her part to keep from jumping up and down as she walked to her quarters.

Raj laughed to himself – packing would take him possibly a minute, or less. Unlike Norah, he didn't need to mull over what to wear for all he had was his uniform. There were no private living quarters equipped with assigned drawers for wounded soldiers to place their belongings, so all of Raj's possessions camped out under his bed in his military bag. Motivated by the thought of their trip, Raj pulled his bag from under the bed. His clothes were already folded and placed within as if they were eager to leave with Norah too.

'You must pack your blue dress,' Ruth said as she peeled it off the hanger and handed it to Norah.

Norah folded it and placed it neatly on the growing pile on top of her bed.

'Where are you going again?'

'Sorrento, Capri and Positano,' Norah said as she debated which one of the two floppy hats she owned deserved to accompany her on their trip.

'Oh, what a dream, Norah.' Ruth sat in the chair, dramatically placing her hand over her forehead. 'You must tell me everything when you get back, even the drab bits.'

Norah smiled. 'Of course. Who else would I tell?'

'Do you think you'll get married?' Ruth uncrossed her legs as she leaned forward towards Norah, who sat on the ground folding her clothes.

'Don't be silly, Ruth.' Norah waved away the thought with her hand, even though she had found herself often thinking of it. She couldn't help but fantasize about being married to Raj. They would have a small wedding in a church in Kidlington. All her brothers and sisters would be there. Her father would walk her down the aisle, with Raj waiting for her in his immaculate uniform. They would settle in a cottage near her father's, Normanhurst. They would have two children, one boy and one girl.

'I suppose it is silly. A little difficult to be married to someone of a different culture, isn't it?' Ruth's words seeped into Norah's fantasy and then she watched it dissolve.

'I … I guess you are right,' Norah said. 'That's why Raj and I will take one day at a time, to prevent any disappointment.' She repeated her statement to herself in her head. She was trying to convince Ruth, but she really needed to convince herself most of all.

***

Raj was too excited to sleep. His mind drifted in and out of sleep, interrupted by his constant need to peek at his wristwatch and count the hours as they went by.

As soon as the first rays of dawn squeezed through the windows above, he jumped out of bed and began to get ready. After a few minutes, he was fully dressed and ready to go. But it was still an hour until they were to meet, so he decided to eat breakfast in the dining hall. Though he loaded his plate with sausages, eggs, toast and fruit, his nerves kept him from enjoying his meal. He barely ate a thing. To help pass the time, he drank three cups of piping hot tea. The warmth of the liquid eased his nerves as each sip made its way down his throat into his stomach.

He checked his watch. Fifteen minutes until he was supposed to meet Norah. He drained the last bit of tea from his cup, uncovering a hidden heap of sugar at the bottom.

He scurried back to his bed to grab his bag and situated himself near a window by the front entrance of the hospital to watch for her signal. Norah would leave, making sure to pass by the window on her way to the bus station down the road. To make sure no one caught on to their plan and saw them together, Raj was to leave ten minutes later.

Out of the corner of his eye, he saw Norah in a bright yellow frock dotted with tiny red and blue flowers and topped with a floppy straw hat, stroll by the window holding on to her very obviously overpacked tweed-print suitcase.

Raj watched as she subtly sent a smile his way before continuing down the path to the road, disappearing behind the hedges that outlined the front entrance. Raj's eyes fixed on to the hands of his watch as they ticked by.

Ten minutes.

Nine minutes.

Eight minutes.

He watched a man on his bike struggle up the hill only to eventually give up and walk his bike past the hospital.

Seven minutes.

Six minutes.

Five minutes.

Raj wondered if those around him could hear his heart beating.

Four minutes.

'And where, pray tell, are we off to so early this morning?'

Raj turned to see Sister Pruth frowning down at him, her eyes scrutinizing the bag he was clutching.

'Morning, Sister Pruth.' He bowed his head ever so slightly. 'Just off to visit some relatives of mine.'

She pursed her lips. 'Hmm.' Her eyes narrowed with scepticism. 'They live nearby, do they?'

Raj nodded as he moved his sleeve to check his watch. Two minutes.

'Funny. Sister Eggleton also received leave for this exact day.'

'Really? I guess the spring is a busy time to travel.'

One minute.

'Indeed.' Sister Pruth crossed her arms. 'And where did you say these relatives of yours live?'

Thirty seconds.

'In Rome.' Raj stood up. 'I would love to stay and continue our conversation. However, I do need to catch my bus. Farewell, sister.' He quickly shuffled out the door. He could feel Sister Pruth's watchful eyes on the back of his neck, examining his every move. He scurried down the path and turned right, anxious for the protection of the hedges. Raj picked up pace after reaching the street to see Norah standing on the corner a few yards away and waving at him.

'Home free,' Norah whispered as she hugged Raj.

He smiled as he breathed in her perfume and thought: Yes, home.

They took notice of the sun's rays spreading out in the cloudless sky, bringing a welcoming warmth to the otherwise chilly air. Raj watched Norah as she closed her eyes, turning her face to the sky and soaking up every bit of heat there was to offer. He followed suit, and as they stood there basking in the sun, careful about who could see, she slid her hand into his. Their mood defrosting and thawing, they were ready for what was to come.

Suddenly, their little moment was interrupted by the sound of a decrepit bus sputtering and shrieking, sending plumes of smoke into the air as it stopped in front of them and creaked open its door.

'Where are you going?' the driver asked in English with a strong Italian accent.

'Wherever you end up,' Raj replied in Italian and the driver beamed.

'Si, si, si.' He waved them in.

'How much?' asked Raj, digging into his pocket for some Italian money. The driver shrugged.

'You don't know where you are going, so how can I charge you!'

'Sorrento, we want to go to Sorrento,' Raj said finally. 'So, how much?'

'What happened to your ear?' asked the driver, pulling on his.

'It got blown off,' Raj replied and the driver and the passengers within earshot winced.

The bus driver nodded slowly. 'In that case, I think you have paid enough.'

Raj bowed his head slightly. The door shut and Raj carried his and Norah's bags to the back of the bus, to the only unoccupied bench. The other travellers smiled as they walked past. The two of them sat down and Norah clutched on to his hand tightly, out of view of those around them.

As was evident from first sight, the bus was not in road-worthy condition. The driver had to stop numerous times to perform some maintenance miracle, which helped the bus negotiate another few miles before it coughed, spluttered, belched thick black smoke, and stopped again with a whimper and a hiss. Every time it stopped, everyone jumped out to stretch their legs. Raj and Norah found amusement in how the other travellers would take the allotted break to argue with one another in a more demonstrative fashion, which the confines of the bus did not allow. Once the engine roared back to life, everyone jumped back on board and they inched closer to their destination.

Finally, the bus found its way to the coast, opening to a scene like nothing Raj had seen before. His heart fluttered as he looked upon the lush green-covered stone cliffs that commanded attention from high above the dotted cities, and the turquoise sea that lazily lapped upon their sandy feet.

Unlike Raj, Norah, who sat close to the window, found it hard to admire the landscape when the bus started to chug along in fits and starts on a thin road that rose vertiginously high above the sea. She closed her eyes and held on tighter to Raj's hand. Raj put an arm around Norah to further allay her fear of running off the cliff.

To Norah's relief, there were no mishaps, and they were finally deposited, intact, in front of a hotel that stood across from a sandy beach and an endless sea. Raj thanked the driver and again offered to pay him, but to no avail.

'Here, this is the best hotel in Sorrento.' The driver spoke in Italian as he pointed towards the ocean. 'You must have the best view for your honeymoon.'

'Oh, we're not…' Raj started to interject, then thought better of it. 'Thank you. Now, please do me the honour of letting me pay for our fare,' he said as he reached into his pocket and pulled out his wallet.

The driver shook his head emphatically. 'No, you must not pay. It is not allowed.'

Raj looked to Norah, who stood there wondering what they were discussing.

'Fine.' Raj put his wallet back into his pocket. 'We thank you so ever much.'

'Prego, Prego.' The driver nodded. 'Now, get on with your honeymoon!' He winked.

Raj blushed. 'Ciao.' He picked up his and Norah's suitcases.

'Ciao, ciao!'

'Ciao.' Norah waved, before turning to Raj. 'Don't I look so silly. I felt like a bumbling infant as I looked back and forth between the two of you as you conversed, not understanding what was being said. What was he saying to you?' Norah inquired. She put a hand on top of her hat to keep it from flying off in the breeze.

Raj hesitated. He thought about mentioning the honeymoon talk but decided against it. 'Just that this is the finest hotel in Sorrento.' He led them into the lobby.

Norah took off her hat as she surveyed the hotel's décor – highly polished red-and-yellow tiled floors, lined with various Renaissance statues made from stone, which led them to a small wooden desk where they were greeted by a joyful attendant.

'Ciao, signor e signora. How may I assist you?' The man's already thin moustache elongated as he smiled.

'Good morning.' After Norah's comment, Raj felt the need to speak in English. 'We just arrived and are in need of lodging.'

'Si, let me see…' The man opened and scanned the hotel register for availability. 'Ah, bene. We have a room with beautiful scene of the sea. You will love it. What is names?' He picked up a pen, readying to write the appropriate details into the book.

'Thank you. However, we will be needing two rooms,' Raj clarified.

'Oh, you are not married?' the man asked, perplexed, as he pointed to the both of them.

Raj noticed Norah cover her mouth, holding back a giggle, and he cleared his throat. 'No, afraid not.'

'Allora, we get you two rooms.' He winked.

Both Norah and Raj secretly could not help the desire they each felt separately of wanting to stay in the same room together. However, they did not want to assume that the other shared the same sentiments.

Raj signed the register and a bellboy appeared.

'Buongiorno. Let me guide you to your rooms.' The bellboy grabbed their suitcases, and before they could blink, was already halfway up the stairs.

He continued up to the top floor, down a narrow hallway to the end, before opening Norah's room and then Raj's, which, to their pleasant surprise, were next to one another. Norah's stomach buzzed at the thought of sleeping in a room next to Raj's.

'Your rooms, signor e signora.' He bowed.

'Thank you.' Raj tipped him.

The bellboy bowed again. 'These rooms have the best view we offer. They also,' he smirked, 'have door that connect one to the other.'

Raj and Norah peeked into their rooms to find, standing in the middle of the walls in each, a wooden door. One turn of the doorknob and their desire for a shared room would come true.

The bellboy, who not-so-discreetly counted the tip Raj had handed him, clapped his hands as he added, 'May I get you anything else? Coffee, something to eat?'

Norah, unsure if tea would be available, settled for the next best thing: 'I would love some coffee, please.'

The bellboy bowed. 'Si. And you, signor? Coffee for you as well?'

Raj didn't particularly enjoy coffee – he would much sooner drink a cup of mud. However, he didn't want Norah to be alone. 'Yes, coffee would be good.'

The bellboy bowed again. 'I will have them delivered to your rooms. Enjoy your stay.' He disappeared quickly down the hall, leaving Raj and Norah outside their respective rooms.

'I think I'm going to freshen up a bit,' Norah said as she squeezed Raj's hand, before picking up her bag and entering her room, closing the door behind her.

Norah stared at the connecting door. She bit her lip, debating whether she should unlock it. Raj was just on the other side. This was their chance to finally be alone and not have to worry about hiding their affection. They could hold hands and not worry about others seeing. They could kiss.

Raj entered his room, set down his bag and opened the balcony door. An immediate cool breeze flew in, causing the sheer white drapes to gently sway.

'Signor.' There was a knock on the door.

Raj opened it to find the same bellboy as before, wheeling a cart with two cups of coffee and a basket filled with an assortment of breads.

He was about to ask him why he had delivered both to his room as one order was Norah's, when the bellboy interrupted him. 'Maybe signora will join you.' He winked at Raj, accepted the tip offered and left.

Raj cleared his throat before knocking on the connecting door. 'Norah?'

'Have you received your coffee yet? They haven't delivered mine,' he heard Norah say through the door.

'Yes, they have,' he replied. 'Just to the wrong address.'

'Oh.'

'Go to your balcony.' He picked up the two hot porcelain cups.

'My balcony?'

'Yes, I'll meet you there.' He started to carry them outside.

'With the coffee?'

Raj turned to speak towards the connecting door. 'Yes, with the coffee *and* some bread.'

'Some what?' Norah replied.

'Bread. Some bread, they brought an assortment,' Raj said, balancing the cups.

'Oh, they delivered bread, did they?'

'Norah.'

'Right. I'll meet you on the balcony.'

Raj carried the two cups. 'Here we are,' he said as he handed one to Norah.

'That's very hot, isn't it?' Norah said, blowing on her coffee.

Raj ducked back into his room to return with the basket of bread. He held it out for Norah as she mulled over which to choose. She decided on a crusty one that felt warm to the touch, possibly pulled from the oven moments before.

Setting down the basket, Raj and Norah sipped on their coffees on their separate balconies as they took in the view in front of them. Besides the common seagulls that cawed incessantly, the beach was quiet. The sea was a hue of blue that Raj had never seen before, and it seemed to go on forever into the horizon.

His attention turned to Norah, who was intermittently soaking her piece of bread into her coffee before taking bites. The wind caused her dark brown hair to blow softly against her fair complexion. Raj agreed – this was the best view offered.

They stood there watching the fishermen out in their tiny boats with hungry, noisy seagulls hovering above them. Raj could have stayed there all day.

After finishing what he could of the strong cup of coffee, Raj reached out and pressed Norah's hand gently. She smiled, though her eyes stayed transfixed on the seagulls.

For a fleeting moment, the thought of the future flitted into their minds. However, they made sure it encountered no obstacles on its way out, and it vanished as quickly as its unwelcomed entrance.

Norah took a deep breath. 'Lovely, isn't it?'

Raj agreed.

'Shall we take a walk by the sea, then?

'I don't see why we shouldn't.'

Raj took her cup, along with his, and placed them back on the tray, ready to be picked up later by the hotel service.

They crossed the street to the sand, and Norah noticed Raj watching her as she balanced on one leg, taking off one shoe at a time.

'Well, aren't you curious about how the water will feel?'

Raj smiled. It was spring, though a slight chill remained. 'I'll take your word for it.'

Norah smiled as she carried her shoes in one hand and walked gingerly over to the water, hopping over rocks and sticks. As she reached the sea, she looked back and waved at Raj. He watched as her slender frame delicately dipped a pointed toe into the water, only to quickly remove it and run back to him, laughing.

'Cold, is it?' he asked as a wide smile spread across his face.

'Very.' She shivered.

He wanted to hold her in his arms to warm her up. 'Glad I didn't do it then.'

'Yes, you're very smart.' She laughed and slipped her shoes back on, this time using Raj as support to lean on. 'I saw a piazza not far from our hotel when we drove in. Shall we go take a look?'

'As long as you don't want to dip your toes into any fountains,' Raj teased.

'No promises.' Norah beamed and led the way, giving Raj a look before she turned that sent chills up his spine. He let out a breath, helping him to focus once more, before following her on the cobblestone path.

It was around 2 p.m. as they strolled in Piazza Tasso. The piazza was magical, with its medieval buildings, all in the same yellow ochre with red tile roofs, and small cafés with gaudy umbrellas, and statues and fountains of numerous saints stationed throughout. The flowers were in bloom, yellow marigolds and red roses amongst others, filling the air with their exotic fragrance. And while they were conscious of not displaying affection out in public, they did so in subtle ways: Norah felt light-headed every time Raj lightly brushed his fingers against the back of her hand as he walked past her.

They dawdled in and out of little shops as they sampled loads of sweets and breads, and sipped limoncello, which quickly became a favourite of Norah's. Raj conversed with the owners. He was happy to practise his Italian, and with every conversation, Norah found herself more impressed and proud to be walking the streets by his side.

The sun was starting to make its descent, and they were subtly reminded by their stomachs that they hadn't partaken of a meal since arriving in Sorrento. They went back to the hotel, where the front-desk attendant directed them to the restaurant.

They were guided to a table by a large window that overlooked lush grapevines, which were already showing the smallest of red grapes. Raj scanned the menu and suddenly remembered that, even though he was quickly growing to love the coast of Italy, he was never too fond of pasta or seafood. He liked to believe that one shouldn't have to work for their food, so unless the shrimp were peeled, they better stay clear of his plate. Norah, on the other hand, liked pasta very much and seafood even more, so for her a menu containing both those items in abundance was absolutely divine. Raj settled for ravioli, and much to Norah's excitement, she was served a pasta dish of some sort that was piled high with unpeeled shrimp, all shining in a pool of dark green olive oil. Upon seeing Norah's plate, which appeared far more appealing than his, Raj thought maybe he ought to be more adventurous at the next meal.

A few other couples filled the dining room as Raj poured the last of the white wine from the bottle into Norah's glass.

'Do you miss your home?' Norah asked as she sipped on her wine.

Raj thought of the last time he had seen his mother. 'Very much.'

'Do you have plans of returning after the war?'

He looked down at his glass. He wasn't sure what the future held for him and answered the only way he knew how: 'If I am blessed to do so.'

Norah nodded solemnly as she took another sip. 'You know, I promised the Indian captain that I would visit India one day.'

'I hope you keep your promise.' Raj stroked the back of her hand ever so lightly with his thumb.

Norah, whose face was feeling hot, wondered if the wine was to blame. 'Do you think I'd like it there?'

Raj smiled. 'Of course. India is such a wonderful place.'

'Would India like me?'

Raj laughed. 'I believe so – you're wonderful as well.'

'Would your parents like me?' Norah was sure the wine was to blame for that one.

'They would be crazy not to,' he replied and wondered why anyone wouldn't.

Norah blushed. 'Oh, I'm sorry. I'm being too forward, aren't I?' She leaned back in her chair, her leg brushing against Raj's.

'Not at all, my dear.'

'I told myself, and I think you would agree, that we take moment by moment, day by day, and not jump ahead and ruin the paradise we have right in front of us.' Norah emphasized her comment with a majestic sweep of her hands. 'I just want to live in this tiny snippet of time and soak in every moment we have left together. Do you feel the same?' Norah bit her lip, awaiting his reply.

'As far as I'm concerned, there is no life outside of where we are now,' Raj replied and sat back, knowing it was frowned upon to show any form of affection when in uniform. He so badly wanted to hold her hand in his. He scolded himself for not having other clothes.

They talked for another hour and stared out the window at the starry sky, until their glasses were empty. When they had reached their rooms, they both hesitated as they said goodnight.

Norah twisted her hands behind her back. 'Well, a successful first day, don't you agree?'

Raj pulled at his jacket. 'Yes. One to remember forever.'

He bit the inside of his cheek. He wondered if she too was plagued with the thought of pressing her lips on his.

'And tomorrow…'

Norah's words drifted away in Raj's mind as his focus gravitated towards her smooth lips, a natural pink in colour. Her perfume teased him with its inviting warmth. His breathing and pulse quickened. A tingling sensation in his stomach bubbled and soon spread to every nook and cranny in his body. His fingers and toes prickled and suddenly his mouth became dry.

'Raj?'

Raj blinked. 'Yes?'

'Are you feeling all right? Your face looks a little flushed.'

He swallowed. 'Yes, very well, thank you. And you?'

Norah laughed at his formality. 'Yes. Quite well.' She paused to examine his nervous demeanour.

Suddenly, Raj's lips were upon hers. His arms brought her in closer and held her tight against him. Her eyes closed and the tingling sensation that overtook Raj's body moved to hers. His kiss was delicate, and somehow, familiar. She didn't want the moment to end.

His lips softly pulled away. 'I've been wanting to do that for some time now.'

Norah smiled and fit her palm into his. 'Next time, don't wait.'

'Never again,' Raj responded, kissing her forehead.

'Goodnight, Raj,' she whispered.

'Goodnight, Norah,' he said as he watched her walk into her room and wave slowly before closing the door.

Raj walked into his room and stood outside the connecting door. He was going to unlock it. He needed to. He let out a quick breath as he put his hand on the doorknob and turned it halfway. He heard it click. Closing his eyes, he released his grip on the handle and stepped away.

***

The next morning, Raj and Norah decided to enjoy their coffee outside at the hotel's restaurant. Another cloudless, sunny sky greeted them, promising another unforgettable day. As they sat down, a sharply dressed waiter started to address them when the bellboy from before interrupted by yelling at him in Italian. They yelled back and forth, speaking with great speed and using many colloquial terms, so Raj was only able to catch bits and pieces. It seemed the bellboy was determined that Raj and Norah were his responsibility, and his alone. Finally, the waiter made one last gesture and stormed off, at which the bellboy turned to them with a giant smile and bowed.

'Buongiorno. What will you be having today? Coffee?'

Norah held back her laughter. 'Yes, coffee, please.'

'Of course.' He left only to turn around and walk back to them. 'My name is Giuseppe. If you ever need anything, you call Giuseppe and Giuseppe will deliver.'

'In that case, how about a pot of tea?' Raj replied.

'Of course!' he answered animatedly. 'Instead of coffee, then?'

'Yes, please,' both answered in unison, but soon regretted their decision as the tea was not up to the same standard as tea in India or in England. Raj smiled as sweet memories of his men drinking doodh waali chai filled his mind. Half a cup was all they could stand, and they reverted to coffee in earnest.

The day was spent just as the one before: strolling along the beach and into the piazzas, sipping on limoncello, and conversing with each other and the locals.

The sun was beginning to descend once again behind the hilltops, casting dark shadows over the piazza. And with those shadows, came the romantic strumming of a guitar.

Raj and Norah looked behind them and saw a man dressed in a medieval costume, playing a guitar and singing a song they didn't recognize. He walked slowly towards the tables where they were sitting, and when he spotted the two of them, he began to play a very familiar song, 'Return to Sorrento'. Raj found himself wishing he were a poet so he could conjure up the right words to aptly describe how he was feeling. But alas, he would have to leave that to those who were better equipped, and instead savoured the moment.

Soon after the guitarist finished his rendition, the crowd, which by then was rather large, applauded him and a waiter came out with two overflowing plates of pasta with shrimp and clams, and placed them in front of them.

'On the house,' he said in Italian. 'Thank you for liberating us from Mussolini and the Nazis.' He left and returned with a bottle of red wine, Lacryma Christi.

Raj felt good to be alive, and even better to be in the company of the woman he knew he was falling in love with – and who, he prayed, was feeling the same. The evening wore on, and soon the last rays of the sun had left the sky and the stars came out to look down upon them. Neither of them was in any hurry to leave that most romantic of piazzas. They just wished it would never end.

They walked out of the piazza, taking turns to lightly brush the other's hand with their own. The music lingered in the air and accompanied them all the way back to the hotel, all the way up the stairs to their rooms, where they said goodnight to each other once again.

They quickly looked around to make sure no one was within sight, and when they figured the coast was clear, Norah stood on her tiptoes as they kissed, bringing goosebumps to the back of Raj's neck.

'Goodnight, Raj,' she said breathlessly.

'Goodnight, Norah.' Raj lightly kissed her hands.

Norah found herself staring at the connecting door as she brushed her teeth. What is it about a closed door that makes it so tempting to open, she wondered. She shook her head, shaking away the thought, and finished getting ready for bed. Her hand grazed the doorknob as she passed by.

# CHAPTER TWENTY-FIVE

## *Capri, 1945*

The next day was better than the day before. In the morning, Giuseppe brought their faithful cups of coffee to Raj's room. He was all smiles and he bowed appreciatively when Raj tipped him well again, but frowned when he heard that they would be leaving later that day. However, his joyful demeanour returned when Raj informed him that they were heading to the island of Capri.

'Capri? Bene! One moment, please,' he said as he hurried down the hall and the stairs.

Raj carried the coffees to the balcony for them to enjoy one last time. As he handed Norah hers, he heard a knock on his door.

'This is a hotel owned by my brother in Piazza Umberto. He will look after you very well,' Giuseppe said excitedly as he handed Raj a scrap of paper. 'I will call and tell him to expect you, signor colonel.'

'Thank you, Giuseppe. But I'm a major not a colonel.'

He waved off Raj's response with a flurry of his hands. 'I see the future – you will be a colonel soon.' He shrugged. 'Maybe a general.' He winked before he left again, no doubt to attend to other hotel guests who tipped well.

'A general, eh?' Norah raised her eyebrows as she sipped on her coffee.

Raj shook his head in response.

'What? You don't see it?'

Raj hesitated. 'Who's to say?'

Norah lowered her cup. 'Do you think you will stay in the military after the war? Is that your dream?'

Again, Raj didn't know what the future held for him, but he knew that there wasn't a good answer to her question. He didn't like to talk about the future as an absolute, finding it foolish to do so.

'I'm not sure how to answer that, Norah,' he said. 'What would you like me to say? That maybe I don't, and that I return to England with you?' He knew his tone came off harsher than he meant and immediately regretted it when Norah responded by silently drinking her coffee. 'I'm sorry,' he continued. 'Let's go back to our vow to only live the life we have right in front of us, in the present.'

There wasn't a rush to get to the ferry. They were told that it ran every hour, and when they were finally ready and the bags were packed, they took the lift downstairs and walked into the lobby to a congregation of staff.

'Don't forget to stay at my brother Mario's hotel,' Giuseppe said with a nod of his head.

'Of course, that's where we're off to. Thank you again for everything. Ciao,' Raj responded, and after paying the bill, they walked out into another bright, sunny day.

It was a very quick walk – the harbour wasn't very far from the hotel. Once they arrived, Raj paid for two tickets, and even though the timetable said that the ferries left the harbour on the hour sharp, he was warned that that was always open to interpretation. When the ferry showed up, the ferry showed up. Never a minute before nor a minute later. And that day wasn't going to be an exception.

Eventually, the annoying shrill sound of a boat's horn could be heard in competition with the ever-present screaming of the seagulls. The horn also served two purposes: first, to wake anyone asleep on the boat, and second, to wake those asleep on the shore. It excelled at both.

Raj picked up the bags and they walked down to where the ferry would dock. No one was in a hurry, neither those disembarking nor those embarking. They had both been in Italy long enough to know that this was the pace at which business was transacted, and the sooner one learned it the sooner life became stress-free.

After one final blast of its shrill horn, the boat began its slow, meandering journey across the calm waters. Under normal conditions, the journey wouldn't have taken very long, but the captain, perhaps wanting to limit the number of crossings he had to do in one shift, was in no hurry. Raj and Norah weren't in any hurry either. They sat on deck, watching the receding Italian coastline and the passengers on board.

As the journey continued, the collective smell of humans and animals combined with the rocking motion of the boat started to make Norah feel woozy. She closed her eyes and prayed the journey wouldn't take too much longer. Raj noticed Norah close her eyes, he wanted very badly to wrap his arms around her as she laid her head on him to rest, but instead he settled for laying his little finger on her hand as it rested on the bench. Finally, the ferry's horn sounded, announcing their imminent arrival in Capri.

As they approached the pier, instructions were shouted from both the bridge and the dock. The volume of the instructions, together with the number of epithets, grew as the boat got closer, before it reached a final crescendo. When the boat bounced against the tyres lining the floating jetty, it caused one sailor to fall into the water with a loud splash, to the absolute delight of everyone. A plank was lowered once the boat had been secured, and everyone on the boat tried to make their way in unison to the shore.

Norah and Raj just watched the throng of people from the rear and waited for the traffic jam to clear. They had no schedule, so whether they got off the boat in an hour or in five minutes was of no consequence to them.

Once off, they were approached by a taxi driver in his somewhat dilapidated vehicle. 'Where do you want to go?' he asked them in Italian.

'Piazza Umberto, to Hotel Andiamo,' replied Raj, much to the amazement of the driver.

'Come, I will take you,' he replied, jumping out of the driver's side and opening the rear door as an invitation. 'The hotel is owned by my brother.'

'Your brother owns the hotel?' Raj asked, sounding a little surprised as he looked at a confused Norah.

'Si,' replied the grinning taxi driver.

Raj couldn't tell if the driver was telling the truth or not. However, they jumped into the taxi, and after much crunching of gears, they reached their destination.

'How much?' asked Raj.

The driver took a moment to look them both over. 'No money. It's my pleasure, and thank you for liberating my country.'

Raj nodded in acknowledgement. 'Thank you, but I insist I pay.'

The taxi driver shrugged. 'If you insist then that's different.'

Raj paid him, and with another round of crunching gears, the taxi went off, no doubt ready to pick up another fare.

'Ciao! Ciao!'

Raj and Norah turned to see a tall man, dressed in nicer clothes than most, walk up to them with a smile as wide as he was.

'I am Giuseppe's brother, Mario!' he said in a booming voice. 'He called and told me you were coming.'

'How about the taxi driver, is he your brother as well?' asked Raj jokingly.

He laughed. 'Who? Claudio?' His eyes squinted as he tilted his head from side to side and explained: 'We are all brothers, but not from the same family. Giuseppe and I are real brothers. Now come, follow me. I will get you your room.' He clapped and started to waddle back towards the hotel.

They followed him into the unpretentious lobby of his little hotel. He walked around to the other side of an old wooden reception desk.

'I will fill in your names,' he said, picking up a pen.

Raj was about to tell him their names, but he finished writing and turned the book around for them to see: *Major and Mrs Raj Kohli*.

'Thank you, however, we are not married.'

Mario's face contorted with confusion. 'Not married? I was told you were on your honeymoon.'

Raj smiled, picturing a winking Giuseppe.

Norah pursed her lips tightly, hiding her smile.

'Not to my knowledge,' Raj answered.

'I see.' Mario turned the book around and hesitantly scribbled out what he wrote to rewrite it correctly on a different line. 'I will get you two rooms then.'

After Norah had spelled her name for him, he picked up their bags and lugged them upstairs. Mario dropped their bags outside their rooms, as he held out their keys and said, 'Thank you for choosing the island of Capri and Hotel Andiamo.' He took out a handkerchief and dabbed his forehead, ending with a bow, then turned and made his trek back down the hall, clutching his side as he did.

Unlike at the other hotel, Raj unlocked Norah's room for her and carried her bag inside, where he set it on top of the luggage rack.

Norah walked over to the large window and stood there, watching the comings and goings of the sleepy world. Raj, fully aware that they were finally alone, walked up behind her and slid his arms around her waist. He could sense her smile as she closed her eyes.

'This is so beautiful, Raj.' Norah turned around to face him. 'Can we pretend we are on our honeymoon?'

'Of course,' whispered Raj, his mouth going dry. Guilt started to creep in. He hadn't revealed his marriage with Esther to Norah. Never in his wildest dreams had he thought he'd be able to have a real relationship with her, but now as they stood holding one another, he knew she needed to know. He didn't know when the right time would be, but he knew it wasn't right now – or at least, he didn't want it to be. He just wanted to hold her and not ruin the moment by talking about his regrettable past.

They stood there holding on to one another. Norah bit her lip. She wanted to ask a question but was feeling nervous to do it alone without the presence of wine encouraging her. She took a deep breath and closed her eyes, readying herself in anticipation.

'Do you think there's a chance we can get married?' she asked.

Raj closed his eyes as well. If that wasn't a sign to tell her about Esther, he didn't know what was. He thought for a moment. He could either tell her everything he'd been wanting to or choose to delve into fantasy with her. 'Of course, there's a chance. As long as we are alive, there's a chance.' He opened his eyes. 'Being at war, I have seen things I never deemed imaginable and somehow I have prevailed, leading me to believe in the existence of God.' He lifted her chin, their eyes meeting. 'If there's a future for us together, then He will make sure it will happen.' Another time would have to do.

Norah nodded sombrely and leaned her head against his chest. She had believed in God, she was raised to believe in God. However, after witnessing what humans were capable of and seeing no intervention from Him, she concluded that a good and real God would not allow such things to exist, therefore, He did not exist.

'I hope so, Raj. I hope your God knows how much I care for you.'

Raj lifted her chin once more, gazing into her eyes before kissing her gently on the lips. 'Yes, he is a good God. He knows how much I love you, and He knows that my life would be incomplete without you.'

Norah, caught off guard, pulled away slightly and searched his eyes, her heart pounding. 'Love? You love me?'

Raj realized that it was the first time he had uttered those words to her. And even though they had slipped off his tongue, he meant them. 'It would be a lie to say otherwise.'

Norah's mouth curved into a smile as she kissed him. 'I love you too, Raj,' she whispered in his ear.

Raj let out a breath of relief and grinned. 'No matter where our lives take us, I will love you. Forever and always, Norah.' He lifted her hands to his lips and kissed them.

The next hour or so, they only looked away from the sea to kiss and hold on to one another tightly. Norah's belief in God's existence started to grow again.

***

After a while, they decided to make their way downstairs into the piazza, where they found a table in the sun near the entrance of the hotel, and sat down.

Mario came out and handed them menus. 'You can make your selection from here, but I must tell you that the best food cannot be found on the menu because it's on its way up from a boat.'

'Lovely!' exclaimed Norah.

'What is it?' Raj asked, concerned that it might be some mollusc or squid.

'Flounder,' he replied, putting his fingers to his lips and making a kissing sound. 'It will be baked with tomatoes, garlic, olives and capers. I can serve you with either pasta or rice.'

'Pasta,' said Norah.

'Rice,' said Raj at the same time, and Mario left, laughing, to give the cook instructions.

He returned a few minutes later with a bottle of cold, crisp white wine and three glasses. For a moment, they thought he was going to join them for lunch, but were relieved when they found it was only for a toast, in which he thanked Raj for helping liberate his country. He pointed to his missing ear and added, 'And a souvenir from the war, yes?'

'Yes,' Raj replied, at which he took a large swig and left with his glass.

Norah sipped her wine, but Raj noticed her excited demeanour had disappeared and she was looking irritated.

'Something wrong?' he inquired as he quickly scanned the last few moments in his mind, wondering what he had done to cause her mood to shift.

She pursed her lips. 'It's silly.' She waved away the thought and consequent discussion.

'No, please. I'm sure it's not,' Raj said, preparing for the worst.

Norah rolled her eyes, 'I'm not trying to diminish the importance of your – or any Allied soldier's – effort in the war,' she began. 'However, I don't feel nurses or women receive the same respect when one is expressing gratitude for their service.'

Raj hadn't taken notice, nor had the thought crossed his mind. 'I'm sorry, Norah.'

Norah took another sip. 'I do realize you are, in fact, dressed in uniform and I am not. I would like to believe that is the reason.'

Raj smiled. 'Whether others decide to thank you or not wouldn't matter anyhow.' He took a sip.

Norah's eyebrows lifted.

'I say that only because, even if they did, their mild-mannered thank yous would dull in comparison to how truly thankful I am. Your service to the war changed my life.'

Norah giggled. 'As yours did mine.'

Raj bowed. 'Thank you for your service, sister.'

Norah returned the bow. 'Thank you for your—'

Raj held up a finger. 'No, I do not deserve your praise, or anyone's for that matter. You saved lives. Countless lives. Mine included. I am the luckiest man alive.'

Norah tried to hide the tears that began to well in her eyes. There better be a God, she thought. It would be cruel to bring such a wonderful man in my life only to snatch him away from me – don't you dare do it.

After they managed to drink half the bottle of wine, which left them feeling tipsy, Mario returned with their lunch. Pasta for Norah and rice for Raj. A filet of flounder swimming in a sea of olive oil, topped with green olives, morsels of capers, cloves of garlic, and diced tomatoes. As they took their first bites, they agreed it was by far the best meal either of them had had in Italy.

When Raj asked for the bill, he told him it would be added to the room charge, which reminded Raj that he hadn't asked them how long they would be staying in his establishment.

He didn't care. 'Whenever you leave, you leave,' was his answer.

After the last sip of wine, Norah and Raj set off to explore the island, and in particular, the Villa San Michele. The sun was still high above them in a cloudless, deep-blue sky, though a refreshingly mild breeze blew in from the sea as they made their way through the narrow streets. Norah stopped now and then to admire the rose bushes of all colours, which decorated their path.

'Lovely, aren't they?' she rubbed the velvet petal of a pink rose between her fingers. 'I hope to have my very own garden overflowing with roses one day.'

After about the tenth time she stopped, Raj plucked an orange rose from a bush. 'Here.' He held it out to her. 'Now you can stop taking breaks at every flower and look at this one. You can also use it to remember our time together. Press it between the pages of a book for safekeeping.'

Norah breathed in its fragrance. 'It's perfect. Better than any souvenir a shop could offer. Thank you.'

Raj bowed. 'My pleasure.'

They reached the front gate that led up to the villa. Raj pushed it open and they walked in and up the short driveway, to the grand and spacious open veranda scattered with Greek and Roman statues, and looked out over the deep blue sea. The home itself was locked, but they believed the best part of the villa were the grounds and gardens, and the magnificent views that surrounded it. A sight that took one's breath away.

Raj looked at his watch – it was 4.30 p.m. After taking in one final view, they headed back to the piazza. The journey back was all downhill and much less strenuous, taking them not nearly as long, especially since Norah chose not to stop to look at the roses this time, and chose instead to admire the one in her hand. They went back to wandering through the narrow streets, which opened up into the piazza and the hotel. It had been a tiring afternoon, and so they both plonked themselves in a couple of chairs to rest their weary feet. Soon, Mario appeared as if from nowhere with some glasses and a bottle of water.

'So, the dancing will start soon, and eating and drinking,' he told them with pride.

'Dancing?' Raj and Norah recited in unison. Norah with delight, and Raj with reluctance.

'Si, si! Major, do you not have other clothes?' Mario's eyes widened.

Raj shook his head.

'But this will not do,' he replied, and left only to reappear a couple of minutes later carrying a shirt and a pair of slacks. 'For you to dance in,' he said, thrusting them towards Raj.

'Oh, that's very kind of you. However, I will have to politely decline. I'm not much of a dancer.'

'But I insist!' Mario sharply threw his hands up, accentuating his plea.

'Yes, Raj. You must!' Norah egged him on.

'Yes, Raj. Must!' Mario's mouth curved into a frown. 'Please, you are in Capri. When you are here, you must do as we do.'

Norah nodded. 'A good argument, I must agree.' She did her best to hide her smile.

Raj looked at the clothes Mario held out to him and then to Norah. 'If I must…'

Norah giggled and Mario hugged Raj. 'Si! It will be a night you will not forget.'

Norah giggled again. 'I guess I should change my outfit as well then.'

'Si, now go.' Mario concluded the conversation with a wave of his hands, and dutifully, they both got up and left to change.

In his room, Raj slipped off his uniform and pulled on the button-up shirt and slacks that looked as if they were Mario's hand-me-downs. In hers, Norah stood over the clothes she had now strewn about, sifting through the pile, deciding which one would do the job of taking Raj's breath away.

Soon, Norah knocked on Raj's door. 'Are you ready?'

Raj opened the door to showcase his outfit – the shirt which ballooned on him and which he did his best to tuck into the trousers that were held up by a very tight belt. Raj felt silly, but his self-consciousness evaporated as soon as he laid eyes on Norah. She had changed into a royal blue dress that matched her sparkling eyes.

'Shall we?' Norah asked as she noticed Raj's expression. She hooked her arm in his.

They made their way down and into the piazza, where already a small crowd had gathered in anticipation of the night's revelry.

Mario applauded when he saw Raj in his clothes and asked the two of them to follow him. When he got to the centre of the crowd, he clapped his hands to silence everyone and informed them of his guests of honour.

Each line was greeted with applause, and Raj didn't know whether Mario knew he spoke Italian, for the stories he was feeding them were wildly untrue and made Raj out to be much more than what he really was – like tales of Raj single-handedly shooting down a German aircraft that was headed to bomb an orphanage.

'I speak Italian,' Raj said when he finished.

'Yes, I know. Giuseppe told me.'

'But what you told them isn't true.'

Mario's reply was a shrug and one word: 'And?' He grinned from ear to ear, adding, 'They need something to be excited about tonight. And you are the first British army officer they have met. A little story here and there doesn't hurt.'

Raj was going to correct him, and felt even more guilty when the talk he and Norah had at lunch sprang into his memory. However, he thought twice about it. Maybe it didn't matter. They were looking for an escape from the horrors the war had brought. Weren't he and Norah doing the same?

Soon, the music and dancing began. The next few hours grew blurrier with each drink, and people and places became one. Everyone, including the two of them, were having the night of their lives. Norah danced the entire night with most of the men, but try as she might, Raj politely declined. He maintained that he had two left feet.

'Ah, Major, why aren't you dancing with the beautiful lady?' Mario gestured towards Norah, who was giggling, clearly enjoying herself.

'I'm afraid I was not blessed with such talent.'

Mario patted Raj on the back. 'But everyone can dance in Italy.'

Raj nodded in acknowledgement as he turned his attention back to Norah. Her smile and laugh were contagious. How that dress flitted and fluttered up as she twirled. And before he knew it, Raj found himself floating towards her.

'May I?' Raj tapped on her shoulder.

Norah's eyes twinkled. 'I thought you didn't dance.'

'Apparently' – he clasped her hand in his and slid another hand to her waist – 'everyone can dance in Italy.'

The music suddenly slowed, and Raj saw Mario wink as he stood next to the band. Norah inched her body closer to Raj as they swayed. He hoped that Norah hadn't noticed how his heart picked up pace.

Norah marvelled at how the inhabitants of the country could carry on like that each and every night without dying young. And they didn't, they lived long, productive and stress-free lives.

'Maybe we in the rest of the world are doing things wrong,' Norah wondered out loud.

'I would say so,' Raj replied as he lifted her head, their eyes meeting.

A faint glint of sunrise had made its appearance by the time they successfully navigated the stairs up to their rooms. Norah's feet ached and she resorted to holding her shoes in her hand as she hummed and twirled back up to her room.

'What a wonderful night,' she said.

'The best night of my life,' Raj agreed.

Norah's hair had fallen out from its pins, and Raj brushed a lock from her face as he kissed her softly.

'Good night, Norah. I love you. Forever and always.'

'Night, Raj, and I love you,' said Norah.

He watched as she disappeared behind her door. Upon entering his room, he fell upon his bed. Could this day have been any better, he wondered as his eyes closed.

A soft knock came upon his door. Raj snapped open his eyes. Mario must want to make sure we got to our rooms all right, he thought. With much effort, he pulled himself out of bed and turned the door handle.

Norah stood there in her blue dress. Without a word, she slowly walked in, closing the door behind her.

# CHAPTER TWENTY-SIX

## *Capri, 1945*

The sun came blazing through the large window, waking Raj, who covered his eyes as a sharp pain pierced his forehead. He turned his head to a sleeping Norah, whose head rested on his chest. His arm was around her, and even though it was tingling he didn't move it. He lay there, watching her breathe lightly.

And for the first time in his life, Raj realized he had found his happiness.

Her eyes began to flutter open and she stretched her arms out, almost hitting Raj on the head.

'Buongiorno,' Raj whispered.

'My, what time is it?' Norah yawned.

'1 p.m., I believe,' Raj replied, looking at his watch.

She nestled her head back on his chest. 'Oh good, plenty of time to sleep more.'

Raj let out a slight laugh. 'Maybe for you' – he kissed her forehead – 'but I need a shower.'

Norah groaned.

'You sleep, I'll be right back.' He gently moved her off him. Norah smiled, remembering last night's events as she closed her eyes once more.

As Raj showered, he tried to summon the courage to tell Norah about his past marriage. He prayed she would understand why he hadn't told her until now. He was a coward, and unsure of how to explain it in a proper manner without upsetting her. He was ashamed of his failed marriage and hated how it blemished his past.

'Now, what is on the schedule for today? More walks in the piazza, or have we both ruined our feet?' Norah asked as he walked out of the bathroom with only pants on, drying his hair with a towel.

'Norah…' he began. It was now or never.

'Yes, Raj.' She smiled.

Raj instinctively grinned upon seeing her, her hair all messed up and knotted from sleeping and her eyes sparkling with excitement. She loved him, he could tell. This would not be easy.

'I have something rather important that I need to tell you. Something I've been wanting to tell you and had every intention of doing so. However, I have delayed it on account of choosing to stay in the perfect little world we've created, and to not let real life matters and issues interrupt. But I can't be selfish, I need to tell you.'

Norah's eyes narrowed as she tried to discern what he was about to confess. She sat up in bed. 'Go on, then.'

Raj took a deep breath and readied himself. 'You asked me in the hospital in Naples if I was married.'

Norah's stomach dropped.

'I am.'

Norah's head raced with thoughts. She blinked trying to comprehend what he had said.

He continued, 'Or was. I must tell you that I believe it to not be a legal marriage—'

'Don't,' she interrupted. The noise all around her was becoming too loud to bear.

Raj unexpectedly felt nauseated, unsure if it was his hangover or his ever-growing anxiety.

'You're ... you're married?' she asked as she stood up and reached for her dress.

His heart stopped. He wrestled with what to say.

'Why didn't you tell me sooner?' Norah closed her eyes. She was right. Sister Pruth was right. She never should have started something. She should have stuck to her rule.

'Norah—'

'I asked you!' She quickly covered her mouth, caught off guard by her own volume. 'Remember?' she continued quietly as a tear rolled down her face. 'You could have told me. You *should have* told me.' She shook her head as the gates around her heart began to lock once more.

'And I ... It's complicated...'

She would never be so stupid again. 'I need to get out of here,' she said as she pushed past him, out the room and into hers.

Raj followed her. 'Please, let me explain.'

Norah threw her belongings haphazardly into her suitcase.

Raj continued trying to plead with her, detailing the facts as fast as he could. 'We did get married. However, I found out she wasn't telling me the whole truth and then I was called to war. I don't even know if our marriage is really legal considering she was married to another man at the same time. I have every intention of making sure the marriage has been annulled once I am back in London.'

'She's English?' Norah turned to face him, her eyes wide.

'Ye—Yes, I met her while I was at university.' Raj's mouth and throat went dry.

Norah shook her head as her mind raced with thoughts of Raj meeting another woman and falling in love. Her make-up streaked down her face. 'Even if it's true that you want the marriage to be over—'

'I do,' Raj interrupted.

'How can I believe it? And not choose to think that you were just interested in a little war romance. And that upon returning, you'll go back to her. Back to how your life was.'

'Because my life did not begin until I met you, Norah.'

'Don't.' Norah's eyes closed once more. Him saying such things was just causing her heart more distress. 'Why didn't you tell me?' she asked, almost inaudible. 'Why?'

'You're right. I'm a fool. An utter fool. I should have told you.'

'Yes, you should have. That way, I would have never gone on this stupid holiday with you, where you could just smash my heart into tiny pieces.' She closed her suitcase. 'Stupid, stupid girl,' Norah mumbled as she shook her head.

'No, you're not stupid. I am. I'm the stupid one, Norah—' Raj begged as he grabbed her hand.

'Please!' She pulled her hand away and shut her eyes. 'Please, leave me be.'

Raj watched as she walked past him. He followed her to the hall, then went to his room to pack as quickly as he could.

'Are you ready for another night of dancing?' asked Mario from behind the wooden desk.

Raj sombrely shook his head as Norah walked out. Mario noticed this and shook his head in reply. 'It's hard to keep women happy. I know.'

Raj took a deep breath. 'How much do we owe you?'

'Please, no. You are family. Family does not pay.'

Raj tried again and took out his wallet.

'You tipped Giuseppe very well,' Mario said. 'That was payment.'

***

On the ferry back to Sorrento, Norah sat on the opposite side of the boat, as far from Raj as possible. Raj watched her as she stared off into the distance, taking moments to hide her face in her sleeve.

She wanted to throw a fit, she wanted to scream, but instead looked off into the distance, wanting to be far from him.

Raj wished he could end his misery. Maybe I should dive into the cold waters and sink to the bottom – it's the least I could do, he thought.

After the ferry, they caught a bus that would take them back through the winding roads to Naples. Still not exchanging words, Norah sat on a bench next to an elderly woman, forcing Raj to sit somewhere else. The entire journey, Raj watched the back of Norah's head, wondering so very much what she was thinking. They made it to Naples and were greeted by cloudy skies and large drops of rain.

Norah walked briskly in front of Raj, up the hill and into the hospital. He watched her turn down the hallway to her room, while he was left standing as people moved past him. He dragged his feet back to his bed, but was surprised to see it was occupied by someone else. Someone whose entire face was bandaged. Raj stood at the end of the bed, staring, lost.

'Major,' an orderly disrupted his train of thought. 'We moved you to another ward. I'll show you the way. I'll have the doctor come and see you.'

Raj followed him into a ward that was far from the surgical one. Raj climbed into bed and stared at the ceiling. He was numb.

'Major Kohli, you have recovered quite nicely here. However, you are still in need of further treatment. Treatment we are not equipped for. A request for you to be transferred to London has been accepted, and you will be leaving in a few days,' the chief surgeon reported as Raj lay quietly.

The night passed slowly, and Raj found himself praying for sleep to ease the pain.

***

The next day, he decided that he should tell Norah about the news. She'll be relieved to hear it, he thought.

'Norah,' he called out meekly.

He knew she was in her quarters – he had heard rustling coming from within before he knocked. But then it stopped, and no one answered the door.

'Figures. Why would she want to speak with me?' he said under his breath, and made his way back to bed.

'I think he's gone now,' Ruth whispered to a crying Norah. She had her head in Ruth's lap as Ruth gently stroked her hair.

'Good.' Norah wiped her nose with a handkerchief.

'Oh, love, I'm so sorry you had to experience this.'

Norah shut her eyes, hoping that if she were to close them tight enough, she'd be able to erase all the memories and subsequent pain.

'That bastard.'

'Ruth!' Norah said.

'What? I can't call him that?' Ruth's eyebrows lifted. 'He deserves to be called something worse, he does.'

'I hate that Sister Pruth was right. I dismissed her comments, but she was right.' Norah pulled up her sheets, the blanket covering her face, catching her tears.

'It is mad how these soldiers think. Wanting some attention from a lady during war. We're just pawns to them, really. Not realizing the repercussions.' Ruth shook her head with disappointment.

Norah sniffled and nestled further into the blanket.

'Now, now,' Ruth whispered. 'It's going to be all right.'

Norah drew her knees closer to her chest. For her, it would never be all right again. She wholeheartedly felt as if she and Raj belonged together. How could her heart betray her so? She had made rules for herself for a reason – to shield her from the very feelings she was enduring at this moment. How could she be so stupid, she wondered. She'd let her heart get the best of her. There were so many things she wished she could take back. And as her tears stopped briefly, she vowed that she'd never find herself heartbroken again, ever. She had to protect herself.

***

Raj spent most of his day in bed, only getting up once or twice for the bathroom. His face was unshaven, he had large dark circles under his eyes, and it wasn't until he heard Ruth's familiar voice that his stare, which had not once wavered from the same spot on the ceiling, broke.

He looked up to see her sauntering down the hall, carrying towels. They made eye contact. She quickly forced herself to look away from him. Without thinking, Raj shot out of bed and blocked her path.

'Sister Gibbard,' Raj's voice cracked.

'Major, I'm going to have to ask you to move.' Her eyes were fixed at a point past him.

'I just wanted to ask you to send a message to Sister Eggleton for me, please,' he whispered, making sure no one could hear. 'Please, just tell her that she'll never have to worry about me ever again. I'm leaving for London in a few days.'

Ruth's eyes lifted, her silence continuing. She corrected her posture before speaking. 'I don't think that's any of her concern. Anyhow, she and the rest of the staff are being posted to Rome shortly. So … there.' She cleared her throat.

'Rome?' Raj's face fell.

'Yes, Rome. It's another city in Italy, if you didn't know,' Ruth said.

Raj nodded as he slunk out of her way. 'I'm sorry for bothering you, sister.'

He slipped back under his covers, praying that time would pass quickly as he fought contradictory feelings of wanting to see Norah walk by and then praying she wouldn't.

***

Norah was glad to hear they were all transferring to the hospital in Rome. She needed a change and that would be sufficient. She did her best to avoid Raj and walked the long way around corridors and wards to avoid seeing him.

The day arrived, and Raj was awoken by an orderly.

'Sir, a jeep will be here shortly to transport you to an airfield.'

Raj nodded in acknowledgement and struggled for a few minutes to get out of bed. Finally, his legs swung over the side and he found himself standing and getting ready to leave.

'The jeep is here, sir,' the orderly reported.

'Yes, one moment please. Do you mind carrying my bag out? I'll be there soon.'

The orderly nodded and left. Raj slowly turned and walked to the surgical ward. He didn't know what he was hoping to do there, but if he could see Norah just one last time…

She was attending to a patient with a wound to the abdomen when she happened to look up and see Raj standing at the end of the ward, half hidden by the wall. Their eyes locked for a moment. He opened his mouth as if to say something, and Norah looked away, continuing her work with her patient. Raj let out a sigh. It was time for him to go.

Goodbye, Norah, he thought as he climbed aboard the jeep. You shall be in my heart. Forever and always.

# *Part Four*

# CHAPTER TWENTY-SEVEN

## *London, 1945*

The flight back to London was lonely. The Douglas DC-3 was filled with other passengers, all of whom were servicemen and women. Many were conversing with one another, but Raj was in no mood to engage with anyone. The perpetual hum of the propellers' whizzing and whirling forced his mind into a spellbound state where all he could think about was his time at war. As he looked out the window, he pleaded with himself to think of something, anything, else.

His mind dug up memories he had long tried to forget – about Egypt, Palestine, Faenza. Memories that were now all too painful to dwell on. Try as he might, his wayward thoughts always found themselves coming back to Norah. He knew that, for him, life did not exist before he met her, and was coming to the conclusion that it wouldn't afterwards either.

Raj tried desperately to work out scenarios where they could be together, where she would forgive him. But the hurdle he couldn't get over was how they were to ever meet again.

He had no idea how long the war would last, even though it was winding down, or even for how long he would remain in London, and if she would return during that time or be posted somewhere else entirely.

However, he knew that even if he were, by some miracle, to ever see Norah again, she probably wouldn't want to have anything to do with him. He was a liar in her mind. He decided she deserved a full explanation from him. He promised himself, as soon as he could, he would write her. He could detail everything in a letter, and it would be up to her if she wanted to read it and believe him or not. He owed her the truth. They would never be together, but at least she wouldn't go on blaming herself for falling in love or believing that his love wasn't real.

The future was a great unknown, but there was a little light at the end of the tunnel. Raj realized that once he had returned to India and been demobbed, he could return to London to complete his education. But before anything else, he was certain of one thing: he needed to find Esther and officially end the marriage once and for all. Esther had ruined their marriage, and somehow, the relationship he had with Norah too. He needed to see an end to it.

The plane landed in Paris to refuel and was quickly airborne again. The propellers' buzzing returned. It wouldn't be long before the familiar coastline of England came into view. Entering England this time around would be so different from his first visit. He was equal parts jealous and ashamed of the naive boy he had been back then. Little did he know then, how much his life would change shortly after docking. He'd attend the school he thought would set him up for the best future, only to transfer to a London college a year later where he would first encounter death: the suicide of a colleague. He would meet a beautiful lady whom he'd marry on a youthful whim, only to then learn that she had been deceitful. He would ship off to war to witness his friends being killed one by one and narrowly escape death himself. And all of that would lead him to the love of his life – only to be ripped apart from her in the end.

He had arrived in England years ago, hopeful of the future. Now he returned jaded and sure that all life brings is disappointment and death.

He anxiously peered out of the window. However, the view was constantly obstructed by heavy clouds, causing the plane to drop and bounce around in the sky. What he did manage to see of the English countryside looked the same as what he had left behind four years ago. That was until they began to descend and broke through the clouds. It became apparent that London had also seen her fair share of devastation. It looked, from up high, as if there were only a few buildings left standing. But when on the ground and driving into London proper, Raj was relieved to discover that a number of her famous landmarks still remained.

'Welcome home, Major,' he was greeted by an attendant who directed those on the plane to a bus that would take them to the barracks. Once he was deposited in what would be his quarters, he put his bag down and sat on the bed. It was a small room, with minimal furniture, but it did come equipped with a desk and chair. A good spot to write letters.

Airmail paper on the desk and fountain pen in hand, he prepared himself to write, even though it wouldn't be easy. Every time he sat down to write, he got up and walked outside to try and relieve himself of the stress. But it only prolonged the agony. Finally, he made up his mind and forced the pen down on to the paper.

It was a difficult letter, but a cathartic one. He was closing a chapter in hopes she would find a new one. A better one.

He slowly put the cap back on the pen, laid it down gently on the desk and pushed his chair back. He closed his eyes for a moment to take in all that he had written. A large part of Raj had been ripped out. There was no more looking at a rose and thinking of it as only a rose. He might never be able to pick up the book, *The Story of San Michele*, without thinking of them walking along the verandas and marvelling at the sights and sounds of the island. But there was nothing more to be done. He folded the aerogramme.

He got up from his chair and walked the letter over to the censor's office. Raj was glad he wasn't there when he put the letter in his box and left. He needed a double Scotch and soda to help wash away his sadness, and the mess hall was just the place for that.

It was now six in the evening, and the hall was filled with other men who, Raj figured, were there hoping to be washed clean of the leftover hurt and desolation of war.

'Are you happy to be back, old chap?' a lieutenant, who had his nose deep in a glass of whisky, slurred as he slapped Raj on the back.

Raj raised his glass, hoping it would be answer enough.

'Aye, me too.' He reciprocated by raising his own glass. 'It's a horrible thing, isn't it though?' He shook his head as he took a sip. His neck worked overtime to keep his head upright. 'Coming home that is.'

Raj, not feeling up to engaging, sipped at his glass.

'Coming back from the trenches of war, I've realized' – hiccup – 'I've got not a thing to wear.' Another hiccup. 'Not a thing, Major.' He turned his glassy gaze upon Raj. 'Only got what's sitting on my body now.' He grabbed at his uniform. Hiccup. 'Shame.' Another sip. 'I got to buy new clothes and I'd rather be in the trenches than buy new bloody fashionable clothes.' Hiccup. He downed the last of his drink and set it down with a thud. 'Ah, that ought to do it.' He patted Raj on the back. 'See you, old chap, but you might not recognize me next time. New trousers and all that.' He winked and stumbled out of the mess hall.

The man had left Raj confused, but he made a good point. All Raj had besides his uniform were the clothes Mario had gifted him which he would never wear again. Raj finished his drink and ordered another. As the night wore on, Raj decided that he would walk to Savile Row the next day to be fitted for civilian clothing.

Raj reckoned the Scotch and soda had done its work when he lay his head down on his pillow and swiftly fell fast asleep.

***

The next day, before he visited Savile Row and the Burlington Arcade, Raj decided he would take a walk around the streets and try to reconnect with the London he once knew so well. He left the barracks and walked out into the bustling street, the old familiar sights and sounds of double-decker buses and black taxis, and most of all, civilization. Italy was civilized, of course, as were Egypt and Palestine, but for Raj, the definition of being civilized was London with its people. However, it became glaringly apparent that so much had changed in the time he was away. Debris from bombed buildings was spread everywhere, and the pub he used to frequent on the Strand was gone, reduced to rubble. He was happy to find that Trafalgar Square, with its lions, was untouched, as was Nelson's Column with Vice-Admiral Nelson himself still looking out to sea.

Raj felt the urge to visit the embankment, to see if his most favourite of structures was still there. Slightly damaged, but still passable, Westminster Bridge stood faithful. Much to Raj's relief, the feeling of awe had not dulled since the first time he had visited it in 1937. However, now he had brought with him memories of friends lost and buried in Italy and North Africa, of Ronald Roach and the men killed at Faenza and other far-off places. A feeling of moroseness threatened to rear its ugly head, but Raj quickly shook it away, determined to not blemish the holy ground he stood on.

He walked back to Trafalgar Square, and then to a shop he had visited in Savile Row before the war, where he was well received. At first, as he stood in front of the mirror, Raj felt odd and out of sorts to be wearing something that did not bear the royal insignia

– as if he were a traitor – but after a few moments of reluctantly allowing the world outside of the war to seep back in, he was measured and fitted for two suits, one a grey houndstooth and the other a blue charcoal stripe.

From there, he went to Burlington Arcade, where he bought a few pairs of slacks, shirts and jackets off the rack. With those securely fastened under his arm, he walked back to the barracks and to his room. He set his new purchases down on the floor and sat on his bed. He lay down and kicked his feet up; they ached from his travels around London. The room was dark, his lamp casting only a bit of light upon the desk on which it stood. And suddenly, as if from nowhere, an awareness of him being the only one in the room made him panic. He felt his heart and breathing pick up in speed, his thoughts racing. He hadn't been alone since he could remember. He swung his legs over, his feet touching the floor as he worked to catch his breath. Nothing another Scotch and soda can't fix, he finally decided.

The officers' mess was full, with several officers singing and swaying at their tables. He was waved over by another major. Raj felt relief as the anxiety retreated with each sip. Eager to keep it at bay, he ordered another one ahead of time.

'Joining in on the celebrations, are we?' The major lifted his glass.

Raj's eyebrows drew together in confusion.

'What? Haven't you heard the news?'

'I don't believe so,' Raj responded.

'My, where have you been all day?' He laughed. 'Our allies advanced into Germany!'

A collective cheer rang out around the hall, and from Raj as well.

'Won't be too long now. The war will end.' The major smiled.

Raj nodded. 'It's about time.'

'You're right! It's about bloody damn time!' shouted a rowdy captain from the far end of the table.

The conversation exploded into talks of what everyone was going to do after the war.

'I'm going to finally marry my lady!' a lieutenant exclaimed, and the clinking of glasses followed in approval.

'I'm going home!'

'I'm finally going teach my boy how to play cricket!'

'I'm eating all the food I can, and no one can stop me!' A roar of laughter erupted throughout.

The jubilation continued, but the end of the war, for Raj, was bittersweet. It meant a journey back to India, but in doing so he would be leaving Norah behind on a different continent.

***

The days went by, and it had been about a week or so since Raj had written his letter to Norah. He wondered if she had received it, and if she did, whether she had actually read it or not. His thoughts were interrupted one day when he received a knock on his door.

'Sir.' A private saluted and handed him a note before saluting again and leaving.

Raj opened the note to read a detailed order for him to receive reconstructive surgery for his ear at the Queen Victoria Hospital in East Grinstead, West Sussex.

Raj arrived at the hospital and was directed to a small waiting area. Upon reaching the room, he immediately felt like a fraud. Others around him had suffered worse. Some had eyes missing, arms missing, legs missing, and all he had was a missing left ear. As he sat down in a metal chair, he noticed all the stares he was receiving. No doubt wondering why I'm here, he thought bitterly.

He shifted in his seat as each minute ticked by and prayed that time would move faster. Finally, his name was called, and he was taken back to see the surgeon.

'Well, well. This might be a first,' the surgeon said as he lifted his glasses to look at where Raj's left ear used to be, scrunching up his nose and scratching his head as he did. 'I suppose there are two avenues we could go to help you, Major Kohli.'

'Yes, doctor.' Raj hoped that one would be getting him out of the office as soon as possible.

'We could try to grow you another ear, but I'm afraid there is no real guarantee that it would look like, well … an ear.'

'And the other option?' Raj wanted to laugh but thought better of it.

'Well.' The doctor sat back in his chair and clasped his hands. 'We could make you a prosthetic ear.'

'Yes, I think that would do.'

'You would need to get a mould of your other ear.' He pulled at his own. 'From that, we can shape your new ear. You would have to get the mould done at a dentist's office and then come back here, and we'll fasten it for you. How does that sound?'

'Quite all right, I suppose,' Raj said as he shook his hand.

A few days later, Raj found himself sitting in a dentist's chair as a mould of his right ear was created. However, once the mould was done, they had two issues to deal with: the first being the colour and getting that right, and the second being how they were going to attach it to his head. He went through several attempts, but after a day or so the ear inevitably turned either yellow or green. Finally, the colour issue was resolved, and it was fixed to his head. He was handed a mirror to examine it and was pleased. Up close, it didn't look completely like a real ear, but it wasn't as noticeable as having only one.

It was now the middle of April and Raj, now complete with two ears, decided it was time to pay Esther a visit to finalize the annulment. He navigated his way to her flat in Middlesex.

He caught a bus, and after he paid, he walked back to a seat. The other travellers were looking at him. Not just looking at him but gawking at his left ear. He even saw one child point at him and lean into her mother to whisper something. Unable to go through with a journey that made him so self-conscious about everyone's stares, without thinking, Raj reached up and pulled the ear off. He found it had deformed and turned black. He put it in his pocket. To his surprise, the bus cleared out at the next stop, with the exception of the driver and himself.

As he reached his stop and exited the bus, he worked to come up with a plan of what he would say when he saw Esther. As he rang the doorbell, a big part of him wanted her to not answer.

'My! What are you doing here?' A slightly older version of the Esther he once knew stood at the door.

'Hello, Esther.'

'What happened to your ear?'

'Oh, it's a dreadful thing really – war, that is.'

Her eyes narrowed. 'Ah, well, you haven't changed a bit. Except now you look a little … worn.'

'Esther, look, I've only come to follow the procedure to make sure our … the marriage … is properly annulled.'

'Oh, is that it, dear? Come all the way from God-knows-where to make sure I'm no longer your problem?' she hissed.

'Esther, please.'

'Well, don't you worry your pretty little head. I've gone and made sure of it while you were gone.' She crossed her arms.

'What do you mean?'

'Well, after you left and didn't have the decency to write me any letters, I figured you'd either gotten yourself blown up or' – her jaw tightened – 'you didn't want to be with me anymore. So, as I said, don't you worry. It's been taken care of.'

'You're sure?' Raj's eyebrow lifted.

'Yes, dear,' she mimicked his tone. 'You've had your way. It's as if it was never real. If you don't believe me, check at Somerset House yourself. See if I care.' She spat out the last few words.

From within the house came a man's voice 'Who's that, dear?' A few seconds later, the door was being pulled open a smidge to reveal a pudgy, balding, middle-aged man with a silly smile plastered on his face. 'Oh, well, hello there.' He looked at Raj and then at Esther.

'Dear, this is an old acquaintance of mine,' Esther finally said. 'How do you do?'

'Very well, thank you.' Raj nodded his head ever so slightly. 'Didn't mean to bother you, just returned from war and—'

'Oh! Returned from war, have you?' The man's large smile grew even bigger. 'How wonderful! I myself almost joined, but then met this beauty.' He wagged his nose in Esther's direction. 'Can't stand to be away from her for one moment.' He finished with a giggle as he put his arm around her.

'Ah, well then, happy to hear it. I better be going. Farewell now.' Raj nodded and quickly left.

He was thankful that the marriage had been officially annulled. He could put her, and it, in the past. But unfortunately, he couldn't put Norah there.

***

The end of April came and went, and as each day passed, the feeling of relief that the war was finally coming to an end increased.

On 8 May 1945 – the day that victory was announced – all the bells of all the churches and cathedrals in all of London rang out in unison. Crowds gathered wherever they could to celebrate. Parties broke out in the streets, with food and drink in abundance. The king and queen appeared on the balcony of Buckingham Palace to acknowledge the growing crowd gathered in front of the gates. But with the exuberance and collective sense of relief, also arrived the fear of what was to come.

Raj had to start thinking about returning to normal life. He kept up to date with news from India by reading the newspapers as often as he could. Independence talks were going on between

British viceroy, Lord Mountbatten, on the one hand and Mahatma Gandhi and the Congress party on the other. He found himself in a quandary. Yes, he was Indian, and India was his home, yet he had been brought up with a very British education, both in India and England, so any independence from Britain would be bittersweet for him.

The months passed. Raj spent most of his days walking around London or conversing with the others in the barracks. It had been four months since he'd arrived back in England, and he still hadn't received any information regarding his repatriation to India. Every day, he woke up to the thought that he was going to be informed that day, only to be disappointed as he turned out the lights each night. He was eventually told that his return to India would be delayed, as all the transportation was first being used to bring the hundreds of thousands of soldiers back to England.

***

One morning, Raj received a phone call informing him that Subedar Ali Khan, who had carried him back to the lines from Colombara Ridge, was in England and would like to meet with him.

A few days later, they met at the entrance of a transit camp outside London. Both of them were in their uniforms.

The subedar saluted Raj, and after he returned his salute, Raj extended his hand. Ali Khan shook it firmly, then took a step back looking confused.

'We had been told you were awarded a Military Cross. Where is it?'

Raj let out a laugh. 'Nobody told me I got a Military Cross.'

'No, no,' Ali Khan replied animatedly, 'the whole battalion knows you got a Military Cross. Where is it?'

Bemused by this line of questioning, Raj wasn't sure how to respond.

'Military medals aren't plucked from trees, you have to earn them—' Raj began.

'Yes,' Ali Khan interrupted him, 'and with the action you planned, we reached our objective. If that doesn't deserve a Military Cross, what does?' He reached up to his own chest, took off his gallantry award and threw it on the ground.

Raj had to think for a moment. Here were two servicemen outside a military camp, and in the middle of them, on the ground, lay a military medal. It was obvious to him that the subedar didn't intend to put the medal back on his chest. 'How many medals have been awarded in this war?'

'Thousands,' Ali Khan replied.

Raj continued, 'Who puts the medals on the uniforms of the receivers?'

Ali Khan raised an eyebrow and replied, 'The king, the generals, the viceroy.'

Raj nodded. 'Did any of them receive a medal from the men they commanded?'

The subedar's eyes narrowed. 'What do you mean?'

'You amongst other soldiers put your life in my hands with the confidence that I would do what is right. It maybe not be a traditional medal, but you and the other men have given me the greatest honour I will ever know. It doesn't matter if I never received an actual medal, because in my mind, you awarded me something far greater than a Military Cross.' Raj paused for a second. 'How many people can say that the men they commanded gave them a decoration?'

'None.' Ali Khan's face was relaxing from its stern composure.

'I feel terribly lucky that you, even though you're under my command, gave me a decoration.'

The subedar's eyes fell to the ground, eyeing the medal. 'I understand.'

'So, pick up the bloody medal,' Raj directed him, which he did, and Raj pinned it back on his chest. Raj then saluted him, his eyes glistening.

***

The summer wore on and Raj made a list of what he would do with the time he had left in England. He had written to visit Ronald Roach's parents to pay his respects. However, the emotions triggered by just thinking about it overwhelmed him. He decided that, if he could muster up the courage, he would go. Until then, he would conquer the rest of his list. As Raj wrote, he found himself adding 'visit Kidlington'. He wasn't sure if he meant it, but writing it down felt cathartic enough.

At the beginning of September, Raj was sent to a convalescent home in Canterbury, Kent, to await further orders. As he was in the Indian army, he could not be demobbed in England and would have to return to the regimental centre in Jhelum. There was nothing more for him left in England except the love of his life – who he was sure had returned home – and the memories of his friends and men whom he had lost during the war.

He had resigned himself to living a life without Norah. He had also resigned himself to the probability that he would return home to his family in Mussoorie and prepare for his marriage to Sita. His mother would be very anxious to see him, as would his father – though he tended not to show it. The last time they had seen him, he was a second lieutenant with two ears. Now, he was a major with one.

He spent many hours sitting in a lounge chair in the beautiful gardens of the convalescent home, or going for walks in the afternoons of a late British summer, engaging passers-by in idle conversation, counting down the days to when he would say goodbye to England.

The nights began to get chilly as winter approached.

Maybe they will wait until after Christmas to ship me home, Raj thought.

On the morning of 5 October, the sun came glaring through the front window right into Raj's room, accompanied by a stiff breeze. He opened his eyes and pulled up a blanket to cover his shoulders. He lay there for a few minutes after checking the time. It was 6 a.m. of another boring day. But just as he was about to jump out of bed and make his way into the bathroom, there was a sharp knock on the door. Raj answered and his doctor entered the room. Raj thought of reasons why the doctor would pay him a visit this early in the morning but couldn't come up with any good one.

'How are you feeling today, Major?' the doctor asked as he took a seat on the chair closest to Raj.

'Tired, bored and hungry,' replied Raj. 'May I ask why you're here, doctor?'

'Want to go home, do you?'

'Very much so,' replied Raj, still half asleep.

'Then I have good news for you.'

Raj immediately sat up. 'What do you mean?'

'You will be catching a train to Southampton in a few hours, and then a ship bound for India,' he said as he slapped his knees.

Raj began to panic. The doctor noticed the change on his face.

'Is that not what you want, Major?' the doctor asked, perplexed.

'No, no, that's exactly what I want. I am just very surprised. I thought I would be here at least past Christmas. Every time I asked, I was told my repatriation wasn't a priority,' replied Raj, still in shock.

'Well, Major, it wasn't. But it is now.' With that, he got up and shook Raj's hand. 'Better leave you so you can get ready, then.' The doctor smiled and with a bow of the head, left the room.

Raj's mind was left swirling with so many emotions. What he knew for certain was that he would not have an opportunity to visit Kidlington. He instantly became annoyed that he had left it to the last moment. He gradually resigned himself to the thought that he may never return to England again. Even his ideas of going back to university seemed far-fetched. He had waited for this moment for so long, but now that it had arrived, he was asking for it to slow down. But he had no choice. He had to return to India to be demobbed before he could even think of his next step.

He went into the bathroom and readied himself. However, when he came back into his bedroom, there was an orderly there, awaiting his instructions.

'I'm here to help you pack, Major,' he said with a nod.

Raj didn't know what to say. 'What time is my train?'

'I believe it's at ten. First to London and then to Southampton.'

Raj nodded. 'Thank you. However, I can pack myself, Corporal. It's not as if I have much.' He smiled.

'Orders are orders, sir. Maybe they want to make sure you leave,' the corporal replied with a wink.

Raj let out a laugh and shrugged. He picked up his change of clothes and returned to the bathroom.

When he finally came out, his bag had been packed, and his cap lay next to it on the bed. At 9 a.m., a car came by and Raj climbed into the back.

The train pulled out of Canterbury West station at 10.05 a.m. on the dot. Raj sat back in an empty compartment and gathered his thoughts. He was very disappointed he hadn't taken the time to visit Kidlington. But fate obviously had other things in store for him. He resolved to rid his mind of everything Norah.

It was a short journey to London, and in approximately an hour and a half, the familiar outline of its towers and bridges filled the horizon. Raj began to look forward to boarding the troopship later that evening, and to his new life back in India. The train began to slow down, and soon it pulled into Victoria Station. He needed to switch stations in London, and as it was midday, Raj jumped out of the carriage carrying his bag, walked out into the misty, cool London air, and jumped into the first taxi he could summon. At 3 p.m., Raj entered his compartment on the Southampton-bound train with mixed emotions. He sat down in the compartment and placed his duffel bag next to him. What a different feeling from the last time I was on board this train, he thought solemnly as he watched the scenery fly past him. The train began to slow down. Southampton was now only minutes away.

Raj wasn't in any rush to get off. He allowed everyone to rush for the exits as he sat back in his seat and breathed in every last bit of English air his lungs would allow. Then, he picked up his duffel bag and caught a taxi to the dock where the *Winchester Castle* was anchored.

# CHAPTER TWENTY-EIGHT

## *Rome, 1945*

Norah had received Raj's letter a few weeks ago. She did not open it – she knew what it said. She wasn't sure how, she just knew. She thought there was no need for her to confirm her suspicions, at least not immediately, and certainly not after returning time and time again from long, gruelling days in the operating room. She would read it when she was emotionally prepared.

The day had been exhausting. They had lost four soldiers during operation. They had been very badly wounded and lost copious amounts of blood. The medical staff had done all they could for them; unfortunately, it wasn't enough. Everyone always took it personally when a soldier didn't make it. Norah knew they weren't supposed to, but it was very difficult not to, especially when they knew they had loved ones at home, waiting for them to return. The war was ending, but not fast enough.

The staff of the military hospital had left Naples a couple of weeks earlier, about a day or so after Raj had flown back to London. She tried her best not to think about him, but somehow her mind always wandered, finding its way back to Raj. She was heartbroken and begged herself to think of something, anything, else.

Her heart felt betrayed. But, she figured, it was all her fault. She had let herself fall in love. How could she have been so silly? How could she think that a wartime romance could be real? They were from two different continents – how did she think it would last? Or that he didn't have a life back home? But that was the problem – she knew it, yet she had let herself get caught up. It was foolish and she was sure to never let it happen again. If she were to allow herself to love someone again, it would be on her terms. No more mistakes.

However, when her mind did drift back to Raj, only sweet memories remained. She was tricked, she knew that, but somehow the trick didn't hold up next to the memories of how she felt when she was with him. It certainly felt like real love. She shuddered at the idea. But even if she were to forgive him, there was an insurmountable obstacle – there was simply no possible way they could ever meet again.

Norah picked up Raj's letter and held it to her face. She could swear it smelled of him. She put it down on the bedside table and lay on the bed, covering her eyes with her forearm. It was late in a spring evening, and although the sun was still up, she was exhausted and needed sleep. Norah turned to face the wall and fell asleep the only way she knew how, in those days – she began to sob into the palms of her hands, becoming so numb that sleep took over.

Norah awoke the next day, right before sunrise. She eyed Raj's letter, which stared up at her from the nightstand. Norah thought that the longer she delayed reading it, the longer she could delay reality. But she knew it couldn't be delayed forever. So finally, after an internal tussle with herself, she sat up and slowly opened the letter. Upon reading the first words – *Dear Norah* – she closed it again.

She could hear his voice say her name, could feel his hand caress hers, could see his grey eyes stare into hers … A lump rose in her throat. She took a deep breath and exhaled slowly, opening the letter once again.

*Dear Norah,*

*It has only been a few hours since I left Naples, but to me it seems like an eternity. I know, perhaps, that to read a letter from me is the last thing you would want to do, but I believe it is the proper thing for me to do. To explain everything in detail, not to persuade you to stop disliking me – I deserve it – but so that you may cease to question true happiness, as I have.*

*With that, I will explain that I met Esther before I left for war. I had two very rotten years in school, and after a fellow student committed suicide, I went to drink away my sorrows at a pub. That's when I met her. I was lonely, stupid, and eager for any semblance of affection. After forcefully convincing myself it was the solution to finding happiness, I quickly married her. That is when I found out that happiness cannot simply be forced. Shortly after we married, I learned of her marriage to another man, one whom she had never divorced. She never disclosed any information of it to me and showed no remorse for doing so. Finally, seeing who she truly was, I left her. Before I was able to see that our marriage was properly annulled, I was called to war. I was under the impression our marriage was never truly legal, that is why I neglected to mention it to you sooner. I now know that I was a fool to do so. It has been brought to my attention that I have an apparent skill of tricking myself into believing I have found my source of joy time and time again, only to have it revealed for what it truly was:*

*a mirage. Fleeting. A hoax. But once I met you, I finally felt my unrelenting search was complete.*

*My heart aches for you, my mind is devoid of any other thoughts than of you. I see you in everything I do and say. I do not know how I existed before I met you, and I don't know how I will after. I wish, above all, that you were here, right now, beside me, or even better still, you and I were together in the warm sunshine of Capri.*

*I often think of the holiday we had, and the fun that was life with you. Even the excessive drinking is now a fond memory, as are the awful headaches we suffered subsequently. Yes, that was by far the best holiday, and I am forever grateful to have experienced true joy, even if it was only for a sliver of time. What I wouldn't give to relive that experience once again!*

*I will forever be upset with myself for being the cause of pain in your life. I am truly sorry. I pray that God may forgive me, and that He may put your heart, that I have broken, back together even stronger than before. Thereby enabling it to receive the unfailing love you so much deserve, even if it's not with me.*

*I meant it when I first told you, and I still do – I love you, Norah Eggleton.*

*Forever and always,*
*Raj*

Her heart pounded faster with each sentence, opening once again a deep wound. Somehow though, she cried not because she felt hurt by him, but because she believed him. He loved her. Undeniably. She felt it when she was with him, and she could feel it now. She loved him too. Had she made a mistake? She should have stayed and listened to him back in Capri. But what did it matter now? They could never be together. Norah closed her eyes. They were never destined to be together. How cruel love is. It doesn't care who you are or where you're from, it will sneak up on you and be relentless. Love knew they couldn't be together, yet it dug its claws deep into both of them, leaving marks that would last forever.

It was impossible that they would ever be together. They were separated by different lives. By different cultures. Different religions. By thousands of miles. By the time Norah got back to England, he would be back in India. She would have to accept that and move on.

But why was it so difficult?

Norah immediately wanted to sit down and write him back, to confess her love. But the more she thought about it, the more she knew it would just prolong the inevitable. What would it matter? He didn't need to receive a letter from her. Raj was obviously suffering as well, and all that a letter from her would do was intensify their pain. They both must heal, and to do so, they needed time. A letter to him would be inconsiderate and selfish. She would always love him, but now it was time to put away those feelings and get on with life. No more dwelling on the past or what could have been. As Raj had said, if it's meant to be, it will be. But most likely not.

Her eyes threatened to unleash a flood of tears. She took deep breaths. No tears, not now.

Hoping to ease the overwhelming desire of writing a letter to Raj, she decided she would write to her sister Muriel instead.

Norah wiped the rogue tears which fell upon her cheeks. She walked over to the desk and picked up her beautiful Parker pen, a gift from her father upon graduating from the Radcliffe. Whenever Norah picked it up, she felt an immediate connection with her family in Kidlington. She began to write.

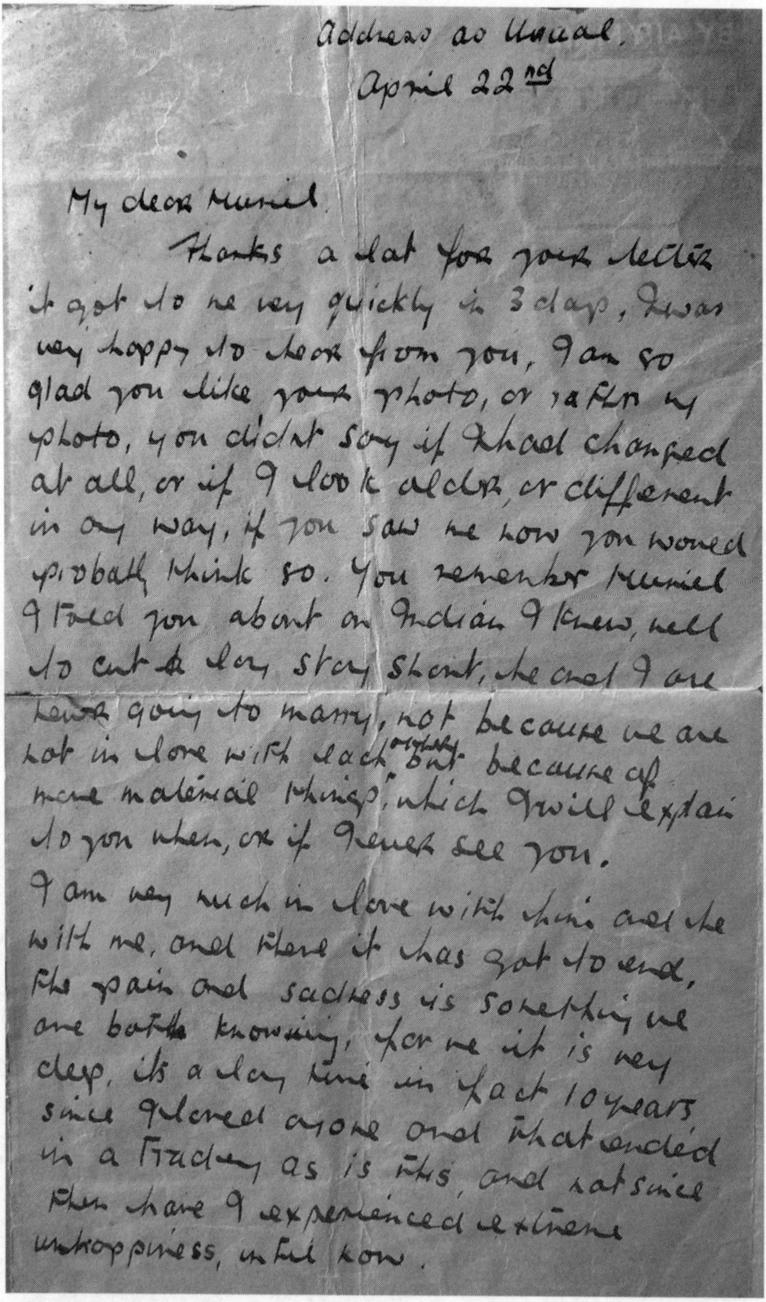

Address as Usual.
April 22nd

My dear Muriel
Thanks a lot for your letter it got to me very quickly in 3 days, I was very happy to hear from you, I am so glad you like your photo, or rather my photo, you didnt say if I had changed at all, or if I look older, or different in any way, if you saw me now you would probably think so. You remember Muriel I told you about an Indian I knew, well to cut a long story short, he and I are never going to marry, not because we are not in love with each other but because of more material things, which I will explain to you when, or if I ever see you.
I am very much in love with him and he with me, and there it has got to end, the pain and sadness is something we are both knowing, for me it is very deep, its a long time in fact 10 years since I loved anyone and that ended in a tragedy as is this, and not since then have I experienced extreme unhappiness, until now.

*Address as usual,*
*April 22nd*

*My dear Muriel,*
*Thanks a lot for your letter. It got to me very quickly, in three days. I was very happy to hear from you, I am also glad you like your photo, or rather my photo, you didn't say if I had changed at all, or if I looked older, or different in any way. If you saw me now, you would probably think so. You remember, Muriel, I told you about an Indian I knew? Well, to cut a long story short, he and I are never going to marry, not because we are not in love with each other, but because of material things, which I will explain to you when or if I ever see you.*

*I am very much in love with him and he with me, and there it has got to end. The pain and sadness is something we both know, for me it is very deep, it's a long time, in fact, 10 years since I loved anyone and that ended in a tragedy as has this, or not since then have I experienced such extreme unhappiness, until now.*

*You would think probably, or even say to me – you'll get over it – but one doesn't get over these things. They leave a scar and change one's whole life. The things that go to make up a person's personality and character are the things you love about them, and it's just not a case of forgetting, it's a case of trying to do without the things that mean happiness to you, therefore it's bound to cause misery. I have travelled about a good deal, as you know, and I've met lots of people, and I know only too well the things life can offer, and I know myself very well. I have learned to appreciate, and learned to value things in other people, but there comes a time when one person holds everything you value, and everything that is lovely, as I have said – that has happened to me on two occasions – and what happens now? These last few mornings, I have asked myself that question when I first wake up, and it's something to which there is no answer.*

*I've got to go on living. Though I have no desire to live. I wonder why I am writing all this to you, it would be much better for me if I could lock myself away miles from anywhere, and anybody, but again that's an impossibility – so there we are. Do write soon. If you don't hear from me for ages, don't worry – just go on writing.*

*I will write again when I feel less sick at heart and soul. At the moment, I am faced with something very hard to bear so I won't write to anyone –*

*Keep well, and God bless you*
*Love*
*Norah*

She felt decidedly better after writing to her sister. However, she felt the need to re-read it a few times so as to convince herself it didn't sound pathetic. Norah finally folded the aerogramme and set it upon her desk.

She could have gone to the officer's lounge and had a drink, maybe a gin and tonic or a shandy would help her alleviate the symptoms of her misery, but that would only be temporary. Once the effects wore off, Norah would be left alone to deal with the pain once again.

She turned to the only healer she knew, poetry, and decided to read some of Keats's. Norah picked up the book she travelled with, removed the Star of David necklace that she used as a bookmark, and lost herself for an hour or so in its pages. The book was the only friend that could provide solace, and for that she was grateful. She closed the book, staring at its worn, red cover. She rubbed her fingers over the edges of the tattered spine, strings from the stitching popped up from its binding. She opened to the beginning and blinked rapidly. Looking up at her was a handwritten note she had never noticed before. Etched in black ink were the words:

*May these poems bring you comfort when you need it most. May it bring you home safely. Safely to wander back into my heart. – Norman*

Norah brought her hand to her mouth. How had she never noticed this before? Had it waited for a moment such as this to reveal itself? She closed her eyes and pictured sensible Norman. He was brilliant, kind, established and warm. But why had he never said anything to her on their many tea outings? She wondered if he still thought about her. Norah, however, had put a stop to fantasizing a future with Norman years ago, only to protect the future she had envisioned for herself. But now, what good was that? She had intervened to take control of her destiny. But that was of no use. She realized that she never really had any sort of control and never would. She had meddled with fate for too long, creating curves and alternative paths that perhaps never existed and ultimately led to dead ends. Maybe it was time to give in to the inevitable and live the life she was allotted, not the one she wanted.

Norah wondered many times what she would do upon her return to England. The only choices that seemed available were to either go back to St Mary's or stay in the army. But as she sat there, she realized, this time, she would need to let life happen. It was fate's turn to take over.

***

It was now May, and the war had finally ended. All the people of Rome broke out into the streets to celebrate. Amongst the jubilant crowds was dancing and large amounts of wine and champagne. Members of staff, and the patients who could, gathered among the crowds.

'Come on, Norah! Let's go!' shouted an elated Ruth, who was jumping up and down in the doorway of Norah's room, eager to join the celebration.

'I'm not sure if I'm up to celebrating, at least, not in that fashion.' Norah pointed towards the window, beyond which strangers clumped together in the streets. Singing and clapping erupted amongst them.

'Rubbish. The war is over, and the evil Nazis have been defeated.' Ruth's eyes widened with excitement. 'If that doesn't make you go mad in celebration, I'm not sure what will.'

Norah cracked a smile. 'Fine. But only for a little while. I don't think we want to get caught up in the rowdiness of it all.'

Ruth rolled her eyes. 'Yes, how absolutely awful to be caught up in contagious joy.'

Norah playfully elbowed Ruth's side and they walked out. They soon realized that the walls of the hospital had muted much of the noise. Now, standing at the entrance, the sound was almost deafening. Norah and Ruth exchanged looks. Huge smiles formed on their faces and they broke out into joyous laughter.

A war that never needed to be fought, a war that had brought so much devastation and destruction to the world, was finally over.

After a few glasses of free-flowing wine, Norah and Ruth broke from the crowd and wandered into the innermost streets of Rome, where it was quiet. Norah wondered if she would ever visit these towns again, and if she happened to, would she expect to see Raj around the next corner. She closed her eyes, hoping to prevent her mind from thinking about him again.

'You think you'll go home or stay in the army?' Ruth asked as she sat on the ledge of a fountain.

'I'm not really sure. I guess wherever my services are needed the most,' Norah answered as a wave of homesickness washed over her. She missed her family greatly. 'How about you, dear? Going home, I expect?'

Ruth shook her head. 'There's no point now, is there? Mikey is gone. Won't really feel like home, I suppose. Being in war, I knew I wouldn't see him. But if I were to go home, I'd expect him to be there and I'm not really sure what I'd do when he isn't.' Her eyes glistened.

Norah put an arm around her and hugged her tightly.

Ruth sniffled and wiped her nose with her sleeve. 'War really hasn't been good to either of us, has it, Norah?'

Norah smiled sadly. 'I'm not sure it has to anyone.' Her words echoed in the empty piazza, with only the statues and fountains and the occasional pigeon to listen to them.

***

The next few weeks were spent patching up the wounded and working in the infectious diseases ward, but as the days went by, the beds in the wards emptied with no new patients arriving. Now there was active talk about going home. In fact, such rumours abounded, and each one had a different date or a slightly different twist. They were all welcome distractions for Norah as she debated where life was going to take her.

'I think I'm going to request to remain in the military.' Ruth informed Norah while they walked to the mess hall for dinner.

'Really? Are you certain?' Norah asked with apprehension.

'Yes, quite. It only makes sense. There's nothing back at home for me.' Ruth nodded.

As the day went by and Norah tended to her patients, she thought she might also put in a request to stay in the army. As she passed by the matron's office, the thought became overwhelming, making her turn around and walk into the office.

'I'd like to put in my request to stay with the military,' Norah informed the matron, who was sitting at her desk.

The matron peered up over her glasses. 'Sister Eggleton,' she said, her gaze falling to the paperwork in front of her. 'Very well, then. I will inform you if your request has been granted in no less than two weeks from now.' She gave a nod and Norah left.

The days went by at a gradual pace, and with the usual workload. It was so slow that the hospital staff were told that, at the beginning of June, they would be heading back to the old hospital in Naples where their services would be of better use. Norah felt apprehensive – those halls were haunted by too many memories. But she was elated that she would get to see the Teatro di San Carlo and its manager once again – she hadn't been able to say a proper goodbye before.

***

The end of May arrived, and the staff began the task of packing up the trunks and having them loaded on to lorries. Just before they were to leave, Norah was summoned to the matron's office.

'Ah, Sister Eggleton. Please have a seat,' the matron said as she welcomed Norah into the room.

Norah was sure she was about to hear whether she was to stay in the army or not. Ruth had just received her news and was granted stay. Norah's palms were warm and sweaty, she was equal parts ready and not ready to hear the news.

'Sister,' the matron began, 'you had submitted your request to remain in the army nursing corps and that has been willingly accepted.'

Norah nodded. So, fate did want her to stay in the military. 'Thank you, matron,' Norah responded as she got up to leave.

'My dear, sit.' The matron let out a laugh. 'Don't you want to hear where the army is sending you?'

'My apologies. I thought I'd receive the news of my posting at a later date.'

'Yes, well, not this time. The army has made up their mind, I suppose.' The matron nodded slightly as Norah slowly sat back down and leaned in, her hands fidgeting with her uniform. 'You will be returning to England in August, where you will go on leave for a month...'

Norah felt her body relax. She would get to see her home, her family once again – and soon.

'And then,' the matron continued, 'head to India.'

Along with her heart, Norah's face fell. 'India?' she asked, blinking fast.

'Yes. India,' the matron confirmed. Noticing Norah's flushed face, she asked, 'Are you all right, sister?'

Norah summoned the strength to nod. 'And where would I be stationed in India, matron?'

'Bombay,' came the reply.

Norah got up from her chair cautiously, afraid she might fall over. 'India?' she asked again, maybe she had misheard.

The matron's eyebrows drew together. 'Did you not hear me? Yes, India. Bombay, India.'

Norah shook her head and her eyes widened, letting out a laugh.

The matron, perplexed by Norah's reaction and getting agitated, asked, 'Something funny, dear?'

'No, no. Sorry, er ... my apologies ... I ... thank you. Matron. Thank you.' Norah stood up, and in a state of utter disbelief and confusion, left.

Norah needed fresh air, so she made a beeline for the closest bench in the garden and closed her eyes. So many thoughts raced through her mind, but the one thought that dominated them was whether she would ever find Raj.

'Of all the places,' Norah said out loud, 'I am going to India.' She laughed. If it wasn't fate, she didn't know what was. But she knew that India was a very large country, and that Raj came from somewhere in the north, possibly hundreds, if not thousands of miles from Bombay.

'What's so funny?'

Norah turned to see Ruth walking towards her. And as she told her the news, Ruth's eyes and mouth rounded with shock.

'What a fickle friend fate is, isn't she?' Ruth said as she clasped Norah's hand. 'Do you think you could find him?'

Norah sighed. 'I don't know. It's a very large country, with a large population, and who's to say that he'll be in India at all? He could very well be stationed somewhere else. He did say he wanted to return to London to complete his education. It would be just my luck that he'd be in England while I'm in India.' She chuckled.

'Rubbish. Put that out of your mind, Norah,' Ruth said as she gripped her hand tighter.

Norah took a deep breath. 'I will. I guess nothing to do now except … lunchtime?'

'No.' Ruth smiled. 'Leave time.'

Norah hugged Ruth, tears in her eyes. 'Thank you, Ruthie. You've always been there for me.'

'Oh, don't go blubbering on me now. We still have time left together in Naples. Come on,' Ruth said as they left the bench and headed to the lorries.

***

Until her mind had settled, which took more than a week, Norah was obsessed with dreaming up scenarios in which she could end up finding Raj. She wondered, with much giddiness, if he thought about finding her as well.

The conversation at the hospital had now turned to going home, and of course, as it always was, rumours regarding the date they would be shipped back to England spread like wildfire. Unfortunately, none of the rumours proved to be true – the end of June came and went. However, at the beginning of July, they officially heard of their departure date, which would be at the end of the month.

Norah made a point of saying goodbye to the manager of the Teatro di San Carlo after a week or so of being back in Naples. As expected, he pleaded with her to follow her dreams of playing the piano professionally, especially after she had told him that she had planned on staying in the army.

'Madam,' he said quietly to match his mood, 'Madam, please, for the sake of the musical world, please go to the Royal College and finish your studies.'

'You were always too kind,' said Norah with a smile. 'I'm not sure if I will have time after my posting in India.'

'India!' interrupted the slightly despondent manager. 'You never said you were going to India. How long will you be there?'

'I haven't the slightest idea. I guess whenever they think we've done a thorough enough job of training their nurses.'

The manager shook his head animatedly. 'What a shame. Our world will never know a great musical talent.'

'Ah, but you know.' She winked. 'I promise to play and think of you as often as I can.'

He lay a hand on his chest. 'Signora, it has been an honour knowing you.'

'Thank you for everything you have done for me,' Norah said as she went to shake his hand goodbye. But in the most Italian of traditions, he pulled her closer and kissed her on both cheeks.

'Buon viaggio, signora, buon viaggio.'

He escorted her out of the theatre, and with one last look around the foyer, Norah nodded and left.

# CHAPTER TWENTY-NINE

## *London, 1945*

The next two weeks were frantic, filled with goodbyes and shopping and eating in Naples's many outdoor cafés, and numerous group photographs. The excitement now grew by the day, but at the back of everyone's minds were the memories of those who had died during the war. At the suggestion of the matron, the staff held a prayer service the day before they left.

There had been those on board the hospital ship, the *St David*, who had lost their lives – Ruth's husband among them – and there had been the hundreds, if not thousands, of servicemen, both Allies and Germans, who had died on board the *Leinster* and were buried at sea. Norah couldn't forget the soldier who had died on the deck of the *Leinster* – his blank stare stayed with her, his Star of David necklace kept her company.

Not a word was spoken amongst the staff while all the nurses, doctors and hospital orderlies, regardless of rank, stood in a circle holding hands, listening to the words spoken by the chaplain. There was not one dry eye amongst the lot of them when he concluded his prayer, each one of them lost in personal pain and memories. The matron started tightly hugging those around her, and eventually everyone followed suit, saying goodbye to the members of their makeshift family.

The next day arrived, and in the midst of tears and smiles and waves goodbye, the hospital staff piled into lorries that took them to the airfield. Waiting for them were a few transport aircrafts, and everyone let out a shout of joy when they saw the RAF insignia painted boldly on their tails. They were nearly home.

Norah and Ruth took seats next to one another. Ruth had shared the news of her posting to Ireland earlier with Norah. Both knew that these might very well be the last moments they had together, and they aimed to make them count.

As soon as they were airborne, all the non-stop chattering among the passengers gave way to silence, until hours later someone spotted the white cliffs of Dover. Everyone made a mad dash to one side to have a look, and as soon as they flew over the cliffs, a mix of joy and solace overcame the group. Norah's eyes misted at the thought of hugging her father once again, and her hand grasped Ruth's. Slowly, a spontaneous rendition of 'God save the King' broke out, until the entire aircraft joined in harmoniously. Norah's heart raced in excitement when the familiar skyline of London came into view. She gasped as she surveyed the extensive damage that could be seen from up high.

Soon, the plane began to descend, and Norah's heart thumped against her chest when she heard the lowering of the wheels. And then, with a series of small bumps, the plane landed at Hendon and taxied on the tarmac. They waited for the stairs to be brought up to the plane, and as the door opened, Norah heard someone shout, 'Breathe in the English air!' And as if on cue, they all did.

They ran down the stairs and into the arms of those waiting below. It didn't matter if they did or didn't know them – they were English, and that's what mattered. Some of the staff had relatives waiting, others were going to get rides home as they lived close by, Ruth among them.

Norah was introduced to Ruth's mother and father as they held tightly on to Ruth and covered her in kisses. Ruth finally managed to pull away to say goodbye to Norah.

'Ruthie, you're my best friend, and I am forever grateful for who you are. You have shown me great strength in the most devastating of times. I am going to miss you so much.' Norah could no longer hold back her tears as she hugged Ruth.

'You have no idea how bloody brilliant you are.' Ruth laughed. 'I am so proud to call you my friend. And know that this is not goodbye forever.' They hugged once more, their eyes puffy from crying. As Ruth walked away with her parents, she turned around to wave and mouthed, 'See you later!' to Norah.

Norah dried her tears and caught transportation into Central London. As the lorry drove through the streets, the devastation caused by the German bombing became painfully clear, and when they turned on to Praed Street, she breathed a sigh of relief to see that St Mary's was still standing, untouched by bombs. When they parked, Norah jumped out and thought for a second about whether she should pay St Mary's a visit, but the yearning to be home with her father, her brothers and sisters overcame that desire.

She entered Paddington Station. 'A first-class ticket to Oxford,' she told the man in the booth.

'Welcome home,' he said with a smile as he handed her the ticket.

Norah found an empty compartment and sat and watched with a great smile as the familiar English countryside flew by. With each level crossing and tiny station they passed, she knew Oxford was getting closer and that she would soon be reunited with her family.

Set on surprising them, Norah hadn't shared the news of her arrival date, so she wasn't sure who would be home. The spires of Oxford came into view, and as the train pulled into the station, Norah stood up, eager to get off. She caught a bus to Kidlington, which passed by the Radcliffe, and all the lanes and roads that were still very familiar to her. The bus drove into the countryside and down High Street to the bus stop, not far from The Moors. A couple of lads helped her down with her trunk and carried it home for her. Mere teenagers, they still wouldn't accept a tip when they dropped it off at the front door of Norah's childhood home.

The door was just the same, chipped navy blue as always. Norah closed her eyes, taking in the moment. She opened her eyes, straightened her uniform and knocked.

'My, Norah—' Her father froze, and his pipe nearly fell out of his mouth. And then, without warning, he took a step forward and hugged her for dear life.

'Daddy,' Norah said with a smile as she rested in his embrace.

It was then Norah heard a scream. 'Norah's home!'

Her sister Betty came flying out and joined them in the hug. Norah looked over her father's shoulder to see her two brothers, Peter and John, standing in their naval uniforms. She broke away from her father and Betty and ran over to them. Each picked her up and hugged her tightly. Their hugs felt noticeably different than the rest of her family's – a little bit tighter, a little bit more hesitant. But she knew why: they all had a common bond now. They had witnessed the evil of war and now lived with memories of it.

By then, her stepmother came out of the kitchen hearing the commotion, as did Norah's stepsister Vera. They took turns tightly embracing Norah.

'I bet Norah would love a cuppa,' Norah's stepmother said as she tied her apron around her waist.

'I think we all would,' her father's booming voice responded. 'And after, why don't we go down to The Railway Hotel to see Frances and Cyril and have a celebration?'

The teacups clanked against their saucers as Norah and her family talked endlessly. Peter, John and Norah took turns sharing stories, all pausing apprehensively at certain parts – some stories would never be shared.

And although Norah was very glad to be home, she missed her sisters who couldn't be there: Muriel, who lived in Sutton

Coldfield, and Beatrice in Rottingdean. Norah remarked that she would have to visit them at some point in the very near future. After several cups of strong tea, they all walked together down the street to The Railway Hotel.

Upon entering, Cyril's voice shouted, 'She's here!'

Frances came rushing out. 'Norah!'

As they hugged, Norah asked, 'Did you know I was coming?'

Frances's eyes welled. 'No. Cyril came up with that signal and told me he'd shout to high heavens when you walked in again.'

'It worked, didn't it?' Cyril said as he raised an eyebrow. 'Now, how about a pint, Norah?'

'Oh yes. A shandy, please,' Norah said as she took a seat next to the rest of her family at a table near the entrance.

Suddenly, the pub became crowded with locals who had heard of Norah's arrival. Each came up to her to give her a handshake, welcoming her back home. Beer and food flowed freely, and she lost herself in all the good wishes and laughter that surrounded her as the night went on.

***

Before she left Kidlington, Norah knew there was one stop she must make.

Sir Athelstane and Lady Baines were sitting in their favourite chairs near the large bay window in their home, overlooking the luscious green lawn and rosebushes. Norah hesitated for a moment before she gathered the courage and walked over to the two of them.

'Norah!' Sir Athelstane exclaimed as she entered the room.

Norah curtsied before moving forward. 'It's so good to see you,' she said, coming to a halt. They looked the same – polished and poised – however, more worn. Their hair, which had been grey the last time she saw them, was now fading into white.

Lady Baines slowly rose from her chair and bowed at her neck. 'My, Norah, my how long it's been.'

Norah kissed her cheeks. Her stomach fluttered with nerves as an uncomfortable silence lingered. 'Yes, I'm ever so sorry for not visiting sooner.'

'Nonsense,' Sir Athelstane responded with a scrunch of his nose. 'We are so delighted to be in your presence now.'

Norah smiled slightly. She knew Lady Baines thought differently. Yes, she was happy to see Norah visit, of course, but ever since Norah discontinued her lessons, she was a little more reserved around her.

'Shall we hear you play something, for old times' sake?' Sir Athelstane prompted.

Norah looked towards Lady Baines, as if waiting for approval. 'I'd be happy to. It's been a long time since I played on the grand piano.' She gestured to the piano basking in the sunlight in the next room.

'Have you played at all, Norah, since you left us?' asked Lady Baines.

Norah disregarded the slight tone of disappointment in her voice. 'Actually, I think you'd be pleased to know that I played a few times at the Teatro di San Carlo – the opera house in Naples. Just for the manager, not a whole audience, but exciting just the same.' She grinned.

'Oh, how marvellous!' Sir Athelstane said as he clapped his hands.

Lady Baines's expression softened. 'We have sorely missed your playing, Norah. Please, if you wouldn't mind.' She nodded toward the piano.

'Of course, I'd be honoured.' Norah walked over, remembering her etiquette lessons, and curtsied before sitting down on the bench.

'Rachmaninoff?' asked Lady Baines.

Norah smiled. 'If you'd like.'

Sir Athelstane nodded emphatically and then sat down in great anticipation. Norah took a deep breath and began to play. It was as if she'd been transported back in time, to when she had first played for them.

'Just like I remembered,' Sir Athelstane said quietly after Norah stood.

'Thank you, Norah.' Lady Baines smiled sadly. 'I hope you're going to stay in Kidlington, now that the war is over.'

'Well…' Norah shifted. 'I've been accepted to stay in the army. I've been posted to India.'

'India!' they both exclaimed.

Norah's eyes widened at their response.

'It's not very safe there right now, I've been told.' Sir Athelstane looked at Lady Baines.

'I'm not sure if you know this or not, but Sir Athelstane was in India for many years,' Lady Baines said.

'No, I did not,' replied Norah, who looked to him to further explain.

'Yes.' He leaned forward in his chair. 'I was in the Indian Civil Services, posted to Calcutta at first and then Delhi. I love India. It's so vibrant. So many different cultures and religions, and the food … Oh, yes, the food is simply magnificent.' He paused for a second and smiled at his wife. 'Lady Baines, on the other hand, didn't care much for the country.'

Lady Baines let out a slight laugh. 'I hope you won't be there very long.'

Unsure of how to respond, Norah just smiled, grateful for the interruption when the tea arrived, together with a plate piled high with warm buttered scones. They enjoyed cup after cup, as Norah stayed at the Baines's for quite a while, discussing more of Sir Athelstane's experience in India and laughing at Lady Baines's intermittent interjections to remind them how awful of a time she'd had.

All of it made her even more excited for her new adventure.

'Thank you both so very much for the tea and the amusing stories,' Norah said at last.

Lady Baines rose from her chair and took Norah's hands in hers. 'My dear, please don't forget to play as often as you can.'

'I promise.' Norah hugged her tightly.

Sir Athelstane cleared his throat as he shook Norah's hand. 'As always, Norah, it's been a great pleasure. Now, enjoy India. I hope it does not disappoint,' he said with a wink.

***

Norah busied herself over the next few weeks, visiting Muriel and then making a separate trip to see Beatrice and her family. There was so much to catch up on.

Norah, of course, had members of her family, her father being the most vocal, who wanted her to demob and stay with them in England. Maybe get married, settle down and have children. But she couldn't very well do that, as she had committed herself to going to India.

At the end of September, Norah said goodbye to her family once again and headed to London before going down to Southampton. Norah was in London for a few days, and after debating with herself, she decided to call and meet Norman at their old tea shop. She was curious to know how fate felt about Norman now.

Norah arrived early and ordered a cup of tea. As she waited, she found herself jumping every time the door opened. She sipped on her hot tea and bit her lip.

'My, you haven't changed a bit.'

Norah looked up over her teacup to see Norman smiling down at her.

'Norman.' She stood, engaging him in a warm embrace. 'Only in my extensive knowledge of Keats,' she said and smiled.

Norman took a seat and placed his hat in front of him on the table.

'Would you like a cup of tea?' Norah asked.

'No, not right now,' Norman replied with a hint of apprehension.

Norah noticed his hesitation and shifted in her seat. 'Thank you so much for meeting me. I was so pleased you agreed.'

'Of course, Norah. I'm—I'm glad you made it back safely.'

'Yes, I did.' Norah couldn't shake the awkwardness between them. 'As your note said.'

Norman swallowed and sat back in his seat. 'So, you saw it?' A sadness enveloped his eyes.

'I picked up that book so many times never noticing it. It revealed itself to me at my darkest hour.' Norah smiled.

He sighed and looked away. 'Norah,' he began, 'I've married.'

Norah watched as fate closed the door. 'I see.'

He shifted forward, his voice quieter. 'You left. I didn't know when you'd be back. I didn't even know if you shared the same feelings.' His eyes searched Norah's.

'It's quite all right, Norman. I didn't know if I felt the same about you either. And even if I did, I couldn't expect you to wait.' Her hands fell into her lap.

'You've always had a place in my heart, Norah,' he said, and Norah could tell he wanted to say more but held himself back from doing so.

'And you in mine.' She smiled sadly. 'I called for you only to say hello and then goodbye again.'

'Goodbye?' His face fell.

'Yes, I've accepted a position to stay in the army. I'm being posted to India. I leave in a few days,' she said and sat up straight.

'India?'

'Yes.'

'Where?'

'Bombay.'

'For how long?'

'I don't know.'

'God, Norah.'

'I beg your pardon?' Norah asked, confused.

He shook his head and turned to look out the window before turning back to her. 'You are hard to hold on to, aren't you?'

Norah wasn't quite sure what to say, even though she was sure there was no need to reply.

She reached into her bag, 'I've brought back the book you gave me. To return it to its rightful owner.' She set *The Poetical Works of John Keats* in front of him.

He eyed it and then slid it back to her. 'It never really belonged to me, did it?' His eyes told her that he wasn't talking about the book.

Norah sat there, her mind refusing to come up with a response.

Norman stood. 'It was good to see you, Norah. I wish you the best of luck in India.' He smiled.

Norah hugged him one last time, 'Goodbye, Norman.'

He put on his hat and nodded. Norah watched as he walked out the door and back on to the streets. She sat and finished the rest of her tea before picking up the book to put back in her bag. However, it slipped and fell to the floor. A small object fell from its pages. She reached down and picked up the book. Lying nonchalantly on top was a single, dried, orange rose petal, a remnant of the past. And although it was dehydrated, it did not lack in colour. Her mouth curved into a smile as she heard the faintest memory of Raj's voice say, 'My pleasure.'

***

After a few days of shopping for personal items Norah knew she would need in India, she decided to end that chapter of her life and start anew.

'Ready for a drastic change, are we?' the hairdresser said as she examined Norah's hair.

Norah looked at her reflection in the mirror. 'Yes, I think it's about time.'

Norah sat in the chair for half an hour as the hairdresser snipped away the split ends.

'Too short for you, love?' the hairdresser asked as she put away her scissors.

Norah brushed her fingers through her hair and stared into the mirror at the new Norah who stared back at her. 'No, it's absolutely perfect.' She beamed.

The day came and she, along with the other nurses who had also been posted to India, caught a train to Southampton from Waterloo Station. October in the south of England was always very pleasant, and even though a few trees here and there had decided to turn colour, the majority remained ever so green.

The journey, however, turned into a stressful one as they took a taxi from the station. Even after Norah's and the rest of the nurses' constant pleading, the taxi driver lazily manoeuvred through the streets of Southampton to the dock.

'Sir, is there any way you could drive a little faster, please?' Norah sighed. 'Our ship leaves in thirty-five minutes.'

As he did every time they asked, he nodded politely and kept at the speed he was going. Norah, who was leaning forward, leaned back, let out a deep breath and crossed her arms. She was coming to the conclusion that, at that rate, they'd miss the ship entirely. But as she sat there fuming, she remembered her resolve to give up control. If she were to miss the ship, and as awful a headache it would cause, it was up to fate.

Things happened for a reason.

# CHAPTER THIRTY

## *Southampton, 5 October 1945*

She wasn't a very big ship, the *Winchester Castle* – probably somewhere around 20,000 tons. Men and women in uniform streamed steadily up from the dock and on to the deck of the ship.

The departure time was set for 6 p.m., which was about an hour-and-a-half from when Raj had arrived. Being an officer had its privileges – a porter greeted him to carry his luggage on board.

'Sir, if you follow me please, I can show you to your cabin,' the porter said as he lifted Raj's military bag over his shoulder.

'Yes, all right,' Raj replied. He paused for a moment before he climbed on to the gangway, hesitating to take his last step on English soil. He lifted his foot, already longing for the moment when he could set it back upon her shores – if he ever got the opportunity. He looked towards the bustling dock and then to the skyline in the distance.

'Farewell, old friend,' Raj said under his breath as he turned and finished the journey on to the ship. His mood immediately transformed into a sour one.

Raj followed his luggage on to the deck, where a naval officer checked his name off the accommodation list. The porter lifted the bag above his head as he guided Raj into the passageway to his cabin.

'Here you are, sir,' the porter said, depositing the bag on to the floor of the small room.

Raj tipped the porter, who left with a quick nod. Raj took a quick look around the cabin and grumbled to himself. It was small and didn't have its own bathroom. There was barely enough room for the bed, but it did have a bedside table and a closet to hang his clothes.

He sat there and read the warnings painted on the door, as there was nothing else to do. At 5.35 p.m., after reading about what to do in case of a fire emergency for the tenth time, Raj decided he needed to get out of the room, or he'd go mad. He walked upstairs to the deck. It was a cloudless October evening. He wished the weather could have had the decency to reflect his mood – by being grey, cold, rainy, and absolutely dreadful. Seagulls drifted noisily above, hovering over the mass of passengers and hoping for a morsel of something thrown their way. If only they would take their incessant squawking elsewhere, he thought.

He looked down at the water and his reflection stared back at him as he clung to the railing of the ship. Suddenly, he realized just how lucky he was. So many of his friends and men under his command didn't have the luxury of returning to their homes – men who were now buried in foreign lands. And there he was, pouting over the fact that he had to return home to India. How ungrateful he was, he thought, feeling even worse.

The ship blared its horn, alerting all who could hear that it was 6 p.m. and time to leave. Tugboats surrounded the ship, pulling her away from the dock. She pushed down the Solent and into the English Channel, depositing plumes of black smoke into the cloudless sky, forcing the seagulls to fly away.

Raj made his way to the officer's lounge on a mission to drown his sorrows in several glasses of Scotch, hoping there was some on board. If not, any liquor would do.

'Any single malt?' asked Raj of the formally dressed bartender, who was surprised to see a patron that early.

'We have Glenfiddich sixteen years, sir,' the bartender replied in a cultured accent. 'However, most officers find they can get more for their money with beer.'

'I'll take the Glenfiddich, please,' Raj replied without skipping a beat as he plonked himself down at the bar, waiting for it to appear in his hand. 'Make that a double, please.'

The bartender dutifully poured. 'Drowning our sorrows are we, sir?' He set the glass down in front of Raj.

'How did you guess?' Raj asked sarcastically, taking a large swig.

'Easy, sir,' the bartender replied with a raised brow, 'you ordered a double.'

'Hmm.' Raj took another sip. 'Start a tab, please.'

Raj turned to find a chair, preferably in a corner that lacked light or any human activity. He spotted one directly in line with the stairs that led up to the deck above, and slouched in it.

The Scotch had already begun to leave its mark as he hadn't eaten all day. He was too anxious for the passage to begin and the day to be over to allow himself to eat.

Raj finished his double, and before he had a chance to attract the bartender's attention, he was already on his way over with another glass. The room was half full with other officers, but he was the only one who had a drink in front of him, and the only one sitting alone.

'Thank you,' said Raj in a slightly less intelligible fashion, which elicited a smile from the bartender.

He took another sip. A smaller sip than the one before. The warm bite of the Scotch dragged its way down his throat into his empty stomach. He felt his mind beginning to cloud up, a feeling he disliked intensely. The last time he'd felt that way was when he went to the pub after Alan had committed suicide. He shook his mind of that memory.

He set the glass back down on the table, sat back and closed his eyes for a second, only reopening them when he decided it was time for another sip. The combination of alcohol and the gentle rolling of the ship as it made its way out of the Solent and into the English Channel made Raj succumb to his emotions at last. His throat burned and ached as he did his best to hold back sobs. His thoughts tormented him with painful memories. He thought about Ronald Roach, and how he would give anything to hear his infectious laugh once more. But most of all, he thought about Norah and how he could have prevented their parting. Or perhaps there was no way to prevent it, but damn it he could have tried, couldn't he?

Raj opened his eyes again and saw the bartender keeping a watchful eye on him. Eager to be left alone, he pretended that everything was just fine, and to prove it he leaned forward to take another sip.

As he lifted his glass to his lips for the umpteenth time, a group of women descended the stairway – the shape of a very familiar figure among them. Raj shook his head and blinked several times, chalking it up to hallucination. He curiously eyed his now nearly empty glass of Glenfiddich, silently cursing how quick the drink was working as it seemed to meld fantasy and reality into one.

He was about to remark on the exceptional medicinal qualities of the drink to the bartender as he went to get another pour, when a familiar voice interrupted.

'Oh my God!'

It was followed by the sound of rapid footsteps as they made their way back upstairs.

Raj spun around, his heart beginning to pound. Was his hearing succumbing to the effects of the alcohol as well?

He kept his sight on the stairs, not daring to blink, believing if he did, the hallucination would evaporate. He only had to wait a few seconds before a foot reappeared on to the first step. The entryway blocked his view, and he swayed back and forth, hoping to get a better glimpse.

The figure hesitantly took another step down. Then another. Raj felt as if he was going to throw up. Another step down, slowly unveiling a hemmed green wool skirt. He held his concentration so hard that his vision began to blur. Unable to keep his eyes from blinking, he quickly rubbed them – making them sting with dryness. He held his breath.

His eyesight began to gradually refocus on a fair complexion and the brightest pair of blue eyes he'd ever known.

'Norah,' Raj breathed. His eyes scanned her, praying that the vision wouldn't desert him. Desperate and scared to find out if it was really her in front of him and not a figment of his imagination, he walked forward. Her brown hair was short, shorter than he remembered, 'Sister, what have you done to your hair?'

Norah slowly lowered the hand that covered her mouth. 'Oh…' She reached up and lightly touched a curl. 'Don't worry, it will grow back.'

She made her way down the rest of the steps and into Raj's life once again. This time, forever.

Raj closed his eyes as the sweet sound of her voice drifted into his ears and the warm flowery fragrance of her perfume engulfed him. He opened his eyes again and stepped, one foot in front of the other, until he stood inches from her. Instinctively, his hands reached for hers. Their fingers entwined.

'I told you, as long as we're alive—'

'There will always be a chance,' Norah interrupted. She silently thanked God as Raj pulled her in, gently pressing his lips against hers.

'Forever and always.'

# EPILOGUE

## *Mussoorie, 2019*

'Sir, sir.'

Suddenly, Raj was back in his ninety-nine-year-old body.

'Sahib, may I take your cup?' Manju asked in Hindi.

'No, no.' He shook his head slowly. 'Please, let me take it.' He lifted his crooked fingers so she could see. 'Gives my hands something to do.'

She smiled and bowed. 'Ji, Sahib.' She left from the forest-green side door, which stayed bolted while Raj slept, and was unlocked during work hours.

Raj took in a slow, deep breath as he sat across from the large glass windows on the veranda. He looked outside. Some children made their way to school down the winding road, and waved. Raj nodded in return. His eyes were cloudy, his hair wispy and white, and his skin wrinkled and spotted with age. He reached up to touch where once, a long time ago, a left ear was.

'My, how lucky I am,' he said out loud as he closed his eyes and smiled faintly. 'Lucky, lucky me.'

He opened them again when Manju came back through the side door, bowing. She carried one single, orange rose. Raj watched as she placed the flower on top of a clay pot, which sat across from him.

'My pleasure,' she said in her broken English as she bowed deeply and then opened the side door, bowing once more before leaving.

Raj's eyes fell back upon the clay pot, reading the sign that lay at its feet.

*Norah Elizabeth Kohli*
*1913-2002*

Raj looked up. 'Forever and always, my darling, forever and always.'

***

After Norah's tour of duty ended, she resigned her commission and married Raj on his birthday, 26 August 1947, in Srinagar, Kashmir. They honeymooned on Dal Lake.

They had two children, a boy and a girl.

Raj stayed in the Indian army, from where he retired as a brigadier in 1967.

As a family, they then moved to Kidlington, England, in 1968, before Raj and Norah returned to India in 1972.

Raj and Norah settled in their modest home they so fondly called Florence Cottage in Barlowganj, Mussoorie, where Norah lined the garden with roses of different colours.

When Norah fell ill in 2002, they went to live with their daughter, son-in-law and grandchildren in Gurgaon. While holding on to Raj's hand in her hospital bed, Norah peacefully passed on.

They were married for fifty-six years.

Besides the sporadic visits from his children and grandchildren, Raj lived alone for many years in Florence Cottage. Although he would often say that he was never truly alone, believing Norah had never left his side.

In the middle of June 2019, at the age of ninety-nine, Raj asked to be taken to the same hospital in Gurgaon where Norah took her last breath. Since the hospital was no longer in service, he rested in his daughter's home in Gurgaon.

Raj – who always had a sweet tooth – sat in his wheelchair while enjoying some burfi and a shandy before lying down on his bed, taking his last breath on 20 June, in the arms of his daughter and granddaughter, just two months shy of his hundredth birthday.

Raj and Norah's ashes were mixed together and sprinkled on the river Jhelum, a place of much importance to their family.

# ACKNOWLEDGEMENTS

*'About the book you and Shaina wrote about Mummy and me. I hope it's more about Mummy than about me. Please do not make me out to be more than I really am.'*

Those were the last words my father said to me in person, as I was leaving his home in the beginning of February 2019.

I have carried the story of my parents in my heart and mind for years, vowing that one day I would put pen to paper. Alas, that never seemed to happen, until one day about ten years ago, I decided that I had procrastinated far too long and finally, devoid of excuses, began.

Over the preceding decades, I have related my parents' story to innumerable people, and the common reply was, 'Just like *The English Patient*'. To which my answer was simply, 'Yes, only better, because it is true.'

In 2011, I visited two cemeteries in Northern Italy. One at Corriano Ridge and the other in Forli. To this day, the Commonwealth Graves Commission keeps those places immaculately manicured. Each gravestone is in pristine condition. The ensuing decades have not degraded them one iota. At

Corriano Ridge is the grave of one of my father's best friends during the war, Major Ronald Roach. His epitaph, with a heartfelt inscription by his mother, still bears the grief she must have felt the day she found out that her son had been killed.

At Forli, the entire cemetery is dedicated to the Hindu, Sikh and Muslim soldiers who fought and died in the nearby campaigns. The most meaningful to me are those of the Muslim soldiers under my father's command, who gave their lives on the night of 8–9 December 1944, while attacking Colombara Ridge. The night my father was severely wounded.

Standing there, surrounded by the gravestones of those men, made it even more important for me to complete the book. Only in recent years has the invaluable role the Indian army played in the defeat of the Nazis received well-deserved recognition.

Writing the book was, at first, incredibly daunting. I spent many months trying to settle on the form. My youngest daughter Shaina provided me with the final decision. And thus, the writing began.

My father refused to talk about his wartime experiences in detail, and his standard reply would be, 'Oh how long ago that was!' Translation: 'I don't care to remember those times.'

However, when it came to talking about how he met my mother, it was difficult to get him to stop. He provided us with all the rich detail we needed. He truly felt that life for him did not begin until 2 January 1945 – the day he first met my mother in Naples.

At the end of January 2019, I visited my father at his home in a small village outside Mussoorie, determined to get him to tell me all he could remember of his wartime experiences.

'Daddy,' I said to him, 'Shaina and I have written a book about you and Mummy, and one of the things I would like to accomplish during this visit is to make sure that we have written about certain accounts correctly.'

His answer: 'If I can remember properly.'

I was delighted. It was the first time he hadn't deflected my questions. Over a period of two weeks, at various times, I asked him some questions, and much to my delight, he answered them. And not only did he answer them, but the answers were better than the fictionalized passages I had written. This meant hours of rewriting by both Shaina and me when I returned home. There is much truth in the old saying, 'Truth is stranger than fiction.'

Unfortunately, my mother, Norah, passed away on 4 December 2002, so I couldn't get her to answer some questions that only she had the answers to…

I would like to mention here, those who encouraged me to complete the project:

First and foremost, my youngest daughter Shaina, who visited India with my wife and me on numerous occasions and recorded sessions with my father. Shaina also wrote many chapters of the book, especially those I had the most difficulty with. Two of my other children, Daniel and Maraina, had very important inputs and acted as sounding boards. While my fourth, Joshua, was always in my mind. Without their help, writing the book would have been twice as hard.

My wife Susan, who first edited the book and made it more coherent, and also had the added distinction of being around me so as to suffer the indignities of my mood swings, regardless of the time of day or night.

To my family in India, who made sure that my parents remained in their home and visited them as often as they could.

I must also mention two books given to me by my parents from which I was able to make sure that the dates, personnel and places I mentioned were accurate: The first is, *The History of the First Punjab Regiment 1759–1956*, by Major Mohammed Ibrahim Quereshi; the second is, *The Ships of Youth: The Experiences of Two Army Nursing Sisters on Board the Hospital Carrier Leinster*, by Geraldine Edge and Mary E. Johnstone.

I would also like to take this opportunity to extend my thanks to three very special people without whom this project would had remained an unpublished work.

First and foremost, to Mr Kevin Jonas Sr, who believed in the project and encouraged my daughter Shaina to complete it, and provided us with the guidance which eventually led us to our second special person, our literary agent, Priya Doraswamy. Both Shaina and I talked with Priya after she had been initially contacted by Kevin Jonas Sr. All three of us immediately felt very comfortable with each other, and it was obvious to both Shaina and I that Priya believed deeply in the story of my parents. Priya demonstrated undying commitment to the project, and her perseverance culminated in a publishing deal with HarperCollins India. And at the publishing house we are deeply indebted to Rahul Soni and Prerna Gill, who not only provided us with the essential guidance we needed, but also the vision required to bring the project to a successful completion. I also have to thank my youngest daughter Shaina, who first saw the project in its very incomplete state and decided to bring the beautiful story of her grandparents to life. Truly, without her this manuscript would still be on my computer, where it had lain dormant for nearly twenty years.

And finally, I dedicate this book to my parents, who endured so much during their lives, but whose love for each other transcends time. Growing up with them was indeed a joy, and they were – and still are – the best parents anyone could ever ask for. God has certainly blessed them, and us.

– PETER R. KOHLI

I grew up listening to my father tell the story of how my grandparents met, time and time again, and every time, I found myself entranced. It was a real-life love story that seemed better than any movie I had seen.

Unfortunately, I was very young when my grandmother passed away, but I was fortunate enough to visit my grandfather on many occasions at his home in India, or when he would visit the States. He never ceased to amaze me. From his impeccable memory, even in old age, and his intelligence and ability to speak several languages fluently, to his love for poetry. He was a very superstitious man, who lived a life ruled by rituals that always made me smile. One of them was his morning and night routine of talking to my grandmother as if she were still with him, even though she had passed. My hope, while writing this book, was to do our best to honour and respect my grandparents' memory and story. As my father and I were not present during the time to witness their experiences unfold as they happened, we relied heavily on the stories from both Raj and Norah, as well as historical accounts told by others, and even Ancestory.co.uk. When we felt stuck, we simply had to ask ourselves: 'What would Raj or Norah do?' and often we'd find their spirit with us.

I hope they can live on through these pages, and that we were able to capture the essence of who they were: two incredible individuals who led incredible lives.

And although I did not know my grandmother well, I felt she was with me as I wrote. This book has been a lot of things for me: both a source of frustration and excitement at times, but most importantly it has been a source in which I found a deeper connection to my Indian heritage, and for that I am blessed.

This book would not be what it is without the incredible team behind it.

It was truly a special experience to be able to write this alongside my dad, who is a fantastic writer and from where I believe I get my passion to tell stories. Thank you, Dad, for trusting me to tell this story with you.

To Kevin Jonas Sr who, from seeing a silly video of a silly girl asking his son to her college dance, saw something special and took a chance. Kevin, I can't tell you how grateful I am to you and how inspired I am by you. I grew up praying that someone, anyone, would give me a shot in this crazy world called the entertainment industry – you are an answer to those prayers. Thank you for your patience, guidance, and all the incredible opportunities you've given me. Even though your son didn't go to the dance with me, I got something even better (thanks, Joe). I am so lucky to have you in my corner.

To our literary agent, Priya Doraswamy, we are forever indebted to you. Thank you for believing in this story. We mean it when we say that there was no better person to represent us in this venture and we are beyond lucky to have found you. You are one incredibly special person, whose love of literature and whose spitfire attitude to fight for your writers is something I greatly admire. You are an amazing agent, and I am so proud to have you as a vital member of the team.

Rahul, Prerna and the whole HarperCollins India team – from the bottom of my heart, thank you. Simply put, you have made our dreams come true. Thank you for your incomparable guidance throughout the editing process to challenge us to be bigger and better. Thank you for the opportunity to tell this too-often untold story of the men and women who gave their lives for the betterment of others. Literally, there would be no book without you. In the words of my grandfather, 'My, how lucky I am.'

To our attorney, Brian Murphy, thank you for your support and advice as we navigated through the scary world of contracts. I met Brian while working as a receptionist at a co-working space, and he was always so easy to talk to and eager to help whenever needed. Thank you for everything you did for us to help bring this project to reality.

I also want to acknowledge and thank my mom, who encouraged me on many occasions and was my guinea pig, reading

the chapters first to give me comments. She also was the first to tell me I should be a writer. Well played, Mom. Well played.

Also, this book would not exist if it weren't for the continual emotional support from my friends, family and above all from my amazing husband, Matt. While I spent many a night and weekend tucked away in a room, clacking away at my laptop, he was taking care of what I neglected around the house.

Most importantly, I want to acknowledge God, who I believe saw to it that my grandparents met, and who listened to my prayers as I asked for the words to write to make sure I honoured Raj and Norah.

– SHAINA KOHLI RUSSO